Trusts of Land and Appoi
Trustees Act 199

C000148919

A Practitioner's Guide to

The Trusts of Land and Appointment of Trustees Act 1996

Hugh Barraclough
LLB, Solicitor,
Consultant with Veale Wasbrough
Visiting Lecturer,
Department of Professional Legal Studies,
University of Bristol

Paul Matthews
BCL, LLD, Solicitor
Consultant with Withers
Visiting Professor,
King's College London

CLT Professional Publishing
A Division of Central Law Training Ltd

© Hugh Barraclough and Paul Matthews 1996

Published by:
CLT Professional Publishing
A division of Central Law Training Ltd
Wrens Court
52-54 Victoria Road
Sutton Coldfield
Birmingham B72 1SX

ISBN 1 85811 115 3

Produced by Palladian
Typeset by Cheryl Zimmerman
Printed in Great Britain by
Redwood Books, Trowbridge, Wiltshire

Contents

Preface   vii

Table of Cases   ix

Table of Statutes   xiii

Table of Abbreviations   ix

1   Introduction   1

2   Prohibition on new Settled Land Act Settlements   20

3   Abolition of the Doctrine of Conversion   32

4   Rapprochement of Express and Implied Trusts of Land   38

5   Powers of Trustees of Land   51

6   Delegation by Trustees of Land   69

7   Consents and Consultation   81

8   Rights of Occupation   89

9   Powers of the Court   97

10 Protection for Purchasers   103

11 Appointment and Retirement of Trustees   123

12 Consolidated Key Provisions and Main Practical
    Consequences of the Act   137

Appendix 1 – Chart: Will giving Right of Residence   149

Appendix 2 – Assents: as affected and unaffected by the
                  1996 Act   150

Appendix 3 – Sale by Survivor of Co-owners   157

Appendix 4 – Outline Checklist   159

Appendix 5 – Appointment of New Trustees   160

Appendix 6 – Trusts of Land and Appointment of Trustees
                  Act 1996   163

Appendix 7 – Law of Property Act 1925 (ss 23-36 as amended) 200
                  Trustee Act 1925 (ss 34-40 as amended)

Appendix 8 –– Precedents   212

Index   227

Preface

"All changed, changed utterly:"
W B Yeats

The harvest of property legislation this year has been heavy. The Trusts of Land and Appointment of Trustees Act 1996 makes fundamental changes – "fundamental" in the sense of transforming the very foundations of our property law. If you thought the 1925 legislation an immutable law of the universe, think again. This Act phases out settled land. It abolishes statutory trusts for sale and diminishes express trusts for sale in importance, both former cornerstones of co-ownership as well as of trusts and settlements. Many of those familiar conveyancing phrases will in future be redundant. There are new requirements to learn and new issues to consider. All our textbooks need to be rewritten.

This however is a practitioner's guide. The changes go much further than textbook principles. The aim of the legislation is to improve the practice of the law. The focus of this book is on how the Act will make changes in practice. We have asked over and over again, and tried to answer, the same questions – what difference will the Act make in practice to the client, to the conveyancer, to the draftsman of wills or settlements and to those negotiating or litigating over co-ownership or other trusts of land? We have tried to explore the provisions of the Act, to set them against current law and practice and to confront problems when they are apparent.

The book itself is a collaboration. We have both contributed to Chapters 1 and 12 and the precedents – they are a sort of joint tenancy. The rest was partitioned. Paul Matthews wrote Chapters 7 to 9 and 11. Hugh Barraclough wrote Chapters 2 to 6, 10 and Appendices 1 to 5. We have both looked over the party fence and offered and accepted advice. We have also been much assisted by our publishers Jane Belford and Andrew Prideaux and are grateful for their help.

We did not finish the quotation from W B Yeats. It goes on: *"A terrible beauty is born"*. In our context, that, of course, could only be a gross over-statement.

Hugh Barraclough and Paul Matthews
October 1996

Table of Cases

Baldwin v CIR [1965] NZLR 1 15
Ball, *Re* [1930] WN 111 40
Bank of Nova Scotia v Yoshikumi Lumber Ltd (1992)
    99 DLR (4th) 289 88
Bannister v Bannister [1948] 2 All ER 133 21
Battle v Saunders [1950] 2 All ER 193 52
Beale's Settlement Trusts [1932] 2 Ch 15 83
Berchtold, *Re* [1923] 1 Ch 192 37
Beverly, *Re* [1901] 1 Ch 681 59
Binions v Evans [1972] Ch 359 21
Bond v Pickford [1983] STC 517 88
Bowes, *Re* [1896] 1 Ch 507 90
Bowman v The Secular Society Limited [1917] AC 406 14
Brockbank, *Re* [1948] Ch 206 ....123, 160
Buchanan-Wollaston's Conveyance [1939] Ch 738 ....90, 92, 99
Bull v Bull [1955] 1 QB 234 ....39, 47, 89
Butlin's Settlement Trusts, *Re* [1976] Ch 251 92

Carmel Exporters (Sales) Ltd v Sea-land Services Inc [1981]
    1 All ER 984 98
City of London Building Society v Flegg [1988]
    AC 54 ....104, 115, 157
Cook, *Re* [1948] Ch 212 33
Crawley Borough Council v Ure [1996] 1 All ER 724 ....15, 84

Davis v Johnson [1979] AC 264 17
Duce and Boots Cash Chemists (Southern) Ltd Contract,
    Re [1937] Ch 642 ....111, 154

Earl of Carnarvon, *In re* [1927] 1 Ch 138 59

Gartside v IRC [1968] AC 553 ....10, 89, 126
General Accident Assurance Corporation, *Re* [1904] 1 Ch 147 ...127
Grant v Southwestern and County Properties Ltd [1975]
    Ch 195 126

Hadmore Productions Limited v Hamilton [1983] 1 AC 191 17

Harvela Investments Ltd v Royal Trust Company of Canada
  (CI) Ltd [1986] 1 AC 207 87

Harwood v Harwood [1991] 2 FLR 274 49

Henry Biggs & Co Ltd v IRC [1961] 1 All ER 220....................84

Hodgson v Marks [1971] Ch 892 116

House, *Re* [1929] 2 Ch 166 ....11, 84, 98

Huntingford v Hobbs [1993] 1 FLR 736 49

Jones v Challenger [1961] 1 QB 176....................42, 90, 92, 99

Kehr, *Re* [1952] 1 Ch 26 125

Kempthorne, *Re* [1931] 1 Ch 268..33

Kings Will Trust [1964] Ch 542 ....155, 162

Kirby v Manpower Services Commission [1980]
  1 WLR 725 87

Lipinski's Will Trusts, *Re* [1976] Ch 235 90

London Borough of Hammersmith & Fulham v Monk
  [1992] 1 AC 478..15, 84

LRT Pension Trust Co Ltd v Hatt [1993] PLR 227....................135

Luke v South Kensington Hotel Company (1879) 11 Ch D 121 92

Lyas v Prowsa Developments Ltd [1982] 1 WLR 1044.............115

Mayo, *Re* [1943] Ch 302 ....42, 92

Midland Bank Trust Co Ltd v Green [1981] AC 513...................13

Nelson, *Re* [1928] 1 Ch 920n 10, 125

Newman, *Re* [1930] 2 Ch 409 33

Oxley, *Re* [1914] 1 Ch 604 129

Pearson v IRC [1981] AC 753, HL; *reversing* [1980]
  Ch 1, CA...11, 95

Peffer v Rigg [1977] 1 WLR 285...115

Perry Almhouses, *Re* [1899] 1 Ch 21 14

Pepper v Hart [1993] AC 593 ....17, 43, 44, 88

Pickworth, *Re* [1899] 1 Ch 642 12

Power's Will Trusts, *Re* [1947] Ch 572 ....52, 58

Pryce-Jones v Williams [1902] 2 Ch 517................................127

Ray's Will Trusts, *In re* [1936] 1 Ch 520..........................12, 59

Rooke, *Re* [1953] Ch 716 40

Roome v Edwards [1982] AC 279 88
Rydon's Settlement, *Re* [1955] Ch 1...16, 87

Saunders v Vautier (1841) Cr & Ph 240 ....10, 125
Skinner's Trusts, *Re* (1860) 1 J&H 102...90
Smith, *Re* [1928] 1 Ch 915 ....10, 125
Speight v Gaunt (1885) 9 App Cas 1..79
Springette v Defoe [1992] 2 FLR 388...49

Thompson, *Re* [1947] VLR 60..12

Wakeman, *Re* [1945] Ch 177..9, 52, 58
Walia v Michael Naughton [1985] 1 WLR 1115 ....53, 117
Waller v Waller [1967] 1 WLR 451..82
Wellstead's Will Trusts *Re* [1949] Ch 296 ....52, 58
Williams & Glyn's Bank Ltd v Boland [1981]
    AC 487 ....33, 89, 104, 116, 157

Table of Statutes

Administration of Estates Act
  1925....................................44
s6(3)...................................150
s9 127
s14 150
s33 45
s36 ....25, 112, 150
s36(1)..................................150
s 36(4).................................151
s36(5), (6)............................153
s36(7).........111, 150, 154-156,
                                   158, 159
Agriculture Act 1970................5

Bodies Corporate (Joint
  Tenancy) Act 1899............135

Charging Orders Act 1979.....99
Charities Act 1993—
ss36, 37................................66
s37(1), (2)............................29
ss38, 39................................66
s39(1), (2)............................29
Children Act 1989................83

Enduring Powers of Attorney
  Act 1985 ..69, 70, 76, 118, 120
s9(6)...................................119
Sched 2...............................119

Family Law Reform Act
  1969....................................86
Finance Act 1991—
s110(5)(b).............................36

Housing Act 1985—
s159 15

Inheritance Tax Act 1984—
s237(3)..................................36
Insolvency Act 1986—
s335A..................................100
s335A(2) 100
s336(5)................................100
s337(6)................................100
Interpretation Act..................60

Land Charges Act 1972—
s17(1)...................................34
Land Registration Act 1925—
s3(viii) 34
s18 53
s20(1)..................................115
s21 53
s23(1)..................................115
s25 53
s49(2)..................................115
s58(1)..............64, 65, 115, 116
s58(3)..................53, 115, 117
s74 ....115, 116
s94 ....114, 116
s94(4)...................................65
s95 115
Law of Property Act 1922....135
Law of Property Act
  1925.................7, 13, 200-204
Part I......................13, 82, 121
s2 ....101, 105, 110-113
s2(1)(ii)................103-105, 114
s2(2)....................103, 105, 114
s19 28
s20 71
s23 ....35, 105, 112
s23(1), (2).............................82

Law of Property Act 1925—
cont.
s24 35
s24(1)..........................132, 162
s25 ....35, 40, 44
s26 ....35, 81, 83, 107
s26(1)........................64, 81, 82
s26(2).............................82, 83
s26(3).......................15, 83–85
s27 ....35, 55, 74, 103, 104,
        110–115, 119, 122, 146
s27(1)..................104, 110, 152
s27(2).....................75, 104, 161
s28 ....17, 35, 51, 53, 55, 217
s28(3)..61
s29 ....35, 69, 78, 80
s29(3)...78
s30 ....35, 42, 43, 83, 97–99,
        101, 102, 143
s31 ....35, 45
s32, 33 35
s34 ....35, 39, 45, 47
s34(2)...............................47, 49
s35 ....35, 44
s36 ....35, 45
s36(1)...............................47, 49
s58(1)..................................64
s205(1)(ii)..............................15
s205(ix), (x)............................34
s205(1)(xxi) 13, 82, 101
s205(1)(xxix) 85
Law of Property (Joint Tenants)
    Act 1964............112, 155, 157
s1(1)....................................157
Law of Property (Miscellaneous
    Provisions) Act 1994..112, 157

Mental Health Act
    1983............................136, 145
Part VII 131
s96(1)(k)..................................83
s99 83

Mental Health Act 1983—*cont.*
s99(2)......................................83

Pensions Act 1995.................65
s35(4)......................................65
Powers of Attorney Act
    1971............80, 117, 120–122
s5 118
s5(2)......................................118
s5(4)......................................147
s5(4)(a), (b) 118, 121
s9 117

Reverter of Sites Act
    1987................................44, 45

Settled Land Act 1925 20–24,
    46, 51, 53, 54, 56, 57, 65, 70,
        72, 101, 224
s1 46
s1(1)..................................22, 31
s1(1)(v)...................................29
s5(1)......................................159
s10 ....26, 27
s17 ...24, 25, 111, 138, 149, 159
s17(1)..............24, 31, 138, 144
s19(1)......................................72
s27 ....28, 29
s29 ....14, 29
s36(4)..................................39, 47
s51 52
s67(1)......................................25
s110 ....25, 104
s110(2)....................................26
s117(1)(ix)...............................34

Taxation of Chargeable Gains
    Act 1992—
Sched 5, para 9(4) 16
Trustee Act 1893—
s10(2)(c)..............129, 134–135

Trustee Act 1893—*cont.*
s11 ....129, 134–135
Trustee Act 1925...................14
s17 ....52, 106
s25 ....69, 70, 74, 117, 118
s25(4)................................118
s30(2)................................129
Part III....................35, 205–211
s34 ....14, 160
s35(1)........................132, 162
s36 ....131, 160
s36(1)...123, 130, 131, 160, 161
s36(6)..........123, 130, 160, 161
s36(7)................................130
s37(1)(c)..............129, 135, 161
s37(1)(d)............................129
s38 160
s39 ....123, 129, 135
s39(2)................................129
s40 ....149, 152, 153, 155,
                          156, 162
s41 ....123, 125, 127, 128, 160
s44 128
s51 128
s57 64
s68(6)..................................34
Trustee Investments Act
  1961...................................56
Trusts of Land and Appointment
  of Trustees Act 1996 ..163–199
Part I..............................4, 7, 48
s1 .....4, 7, 38, 39, 138, 140, 141
s1(1)................................8, 67
s1(1)(a)................................56
s1(2)..............................8, 146
s1(3)......................................8
s2 .....4, 20, 26–28, 34, 138, 141
s2(1)....................22, 114, 138
s2(2)................................23, 24
s2(3)................23, 24, 138, 144
s2(4)................25, 52, 144
s2(5)..............66, 114, 141, 147

Trusts of Land and Appointment
  of Trustees Act 1996—*cont.*
s3 ....3, 4, 32, 33, 104, 138,
                          140, 150
s3(2)....................34, 114, 140
s3(3)............................33, 114
s4 ....4, 38, 48, 49, 50, 138,
                          140, 141
s4(1)..............15, 40, 41, 42, 44
s4(2), (3) 41, 114
s5 ....4, 38, 45, 48–50, 141
s5(1)......................................45
s5(2)......................................46
s6 ....4, 9, 17, 27, 39, 40, 44,
     45, 48, 51, 54, 55, 62–68, 71,
      73, 85, 106, 107, 108, 109,
      139, 140, 146, 213, 217, 218
s6(1).14, 54, 108, 139, 141, 146
s6(2)......12, 58–62, 85, 99, 107,
                          125, 142
s6(2)(a), (b) 61
s6(3)................57, 58, 107, 139,
                          141, 146
s6(4)..........55, 57, 58, 141, 146
s6(5)..........44, 57, 60, 63, 104,
                          107, 142
s6(6), (7) 27, 65, 66
s6(8)..................27, 65, 66, 107
s7 ....4, 27, 44, 45, 48, 51, 54,
     57–59, 61–64, 67, 68, 85, 107,
      108, 109, 139, 140, 142, 146
s7(1)...........................12, 61, 62
s7(2)...........................12, 59, 62
s7(3)......................................101
s7(5)......................................62
s8 ..4, 45, 48, 51, 54, 65, 67, 68,
     107–109, 116, 139, 140, 146
s8(1)....15, 44, 63, 65, 108, 109,
                          139, 140
s8(2)....15, 44, 64, 65, 108, 109,
                          139, 140, 214
s8(3)............................27, 63, 65

Trusts of Land and Appointment
of Trustees Act 1996—*cont.*
s8(4)......................................65
s9........4, 12, 51, 55, 69–72, 74,
    75, 77–80, 103, 119–122, 139,
        140, 143, 147, 224
s9(1)..........11, 14, 71, 74–77, 90
s9(2)..14, 75, 79, 109, 120–122,
        147
s9(3)..............................76, 120
s9(4)..............11, 14, 71, 77, 120
s9(5)......................................76
s9(6)..............................76, 120
s9(7)..........74, 75, 78, 143, 215
s9(8)..............71, 73, 78, 79, 143
s9(9)..............................80, 114
s10...4, 14, 55, 82, 88, 107, 148
s10(1)..........14, 15, 81, 82, 214
s10(3)..........14, 15, 82, 83, 148
s11......4, 12, 14, 28, 34, 44, 55,
    57, 60, 71, 84–88, 140, 142
s11(1)................11, 84–87, 107
s11(2)......................................15
s11(2)(a)......................44, 85
s11(2)(b)........................85, 114
s11(2)(c)......................................85
s11(3)....................15, 16, 86–88
s11(4)......................................87
s12......4, 12, 73, 92, 93, 96, 99,
        142, 215
s12(1)..........11, 89, 91, 140, 142
s12(1)(a)..........................90, 140
s12(1)(b)..........................90, 91
s12(2)......................................91
s12(3)......................................92
s13.....4, 12, 92–94, 96, 99, 152
s13(1)..............................92, 93
s13(2)......................................93
s13(3)....................74, 94, 215
s13(4)....................92, 94, 215
s13(4)(b)......................................92
s13(5)..............................74, 94

Trusts of Land and Appointment
of Trustees Act 1996—*cont.*
s13(6)......................................95
s13(7)......................................93
s13(7)(a), (b)..........................94
s13(8)......................................94
s14......4, 14, 42, 43, 55, 64, 72,
        97–102, 139, 142
s14(1)......................................98
s14(2)......................................97
s14(2)(a)......................................65
s14(3)......................................98
s14(4)..............................98, 114
s15......4, 42, 43, 100, 102, 139,
        140, 143
s15(1)................72, 98, 100, 214
s15(2)..............................94, 99
s15(3)........................11, 99, 100
s15(4)......................................100
s16......4, 55, 71, 103, 114, 122,
        149, 152, 156, 159, 223
s16(1)..........85, 106, 104, 107,
        110–111
s16(2)..............28, 66, 106, 107,
        109–111
s16(3)......28, 66, 106, 108–111,
        116
s16(4)....12, 106, 111–114, 117,
        125, 144, 147, 223
s16(5)......12, 28, 106, 111–114,
        117, 125, 144, 147, 223
s16(6)......................28, 107, 109
s16(7)......................................117
s17..4, 9
s17(1)......................................58
s17(2)–(5)......................101, 143
s17(6)..............................15, 143
s17(6)(a), (b)..........................101
s18..4, 55
s18(1)................14, 82, 85, 101
s18(2)......................................15
Part II..........................4, 7, 123

Trusts of Land and Appointment
of Trustees Act 1996—*cont.*

s19 ......4, 44, 71, 123, 124, 126,
130–136, 144
s19(1)................................12, 124
s19(1)(a)......................124, 125
s19(1)(b) 125, 131
s19(2)..................126, 128, 130
s19(2)(b) 127, 132
s19(3)......................128, 129
s19(3)(d)..............................128
s19(4)..............................129
s20 ....4, 44, 55, 71, 123,
130–134, 136, 140, 145
s20(1)........................12, 14, 131
s20(2)..............................131
s21 .....4, 71, 136, 140, 144, 145
s21(1), (2)..............................132
s21(3)..............................130
s21(4)..............................132
s21(5)..............15, 44, 132, 133
s21(6)......................15, 87, 133
s21(6)(b)..............................134
s21(7)..............................133
s21(8)........................87, 133
Part III..............................4
s22 ....4, 7, 10
s22(1)..............10, 71, 89, 126
s22(2)......................11, 59, 60
s22(3)..........11, 13, 72, 84, 142
s23 ....4, 7, 13

Trusts of Land and Appointment
of Trustees Act 1996—*cont.*

s23(1)..............................13
s23(2)..................13, 15, 34
s23(3)..............................13
s24 4
s24(1), (2)..............................6
s25 ....4, 6
s25(4), (5)..............................114
s26 ....4, 35
s26(1)–(3)..............................6
s27 4
s27(1)..............................4, 40
s27(2)–(4)..............................5
Sched 1..................4, 20, 24, 28
Sched 1, para 1......................28
Sched 1, para 2......................28
Sched 1, paras 3, 4 29
Sched 1, para 5..................138
Sched 1, para 6................25–28
Sched 2................4, 38, 45, 141
Sched 3 ....4, 32–35
Sched 3, para 2(6) ..24, 138, 144
Sched 3, para 3(12), (13).....134,
145
Sched 3, para 5(8)(c) 65, 116
Sched 3, para 6..................86
Sched 3, para 23..........100, 143
Sched 4..........................4, 32–36

Universities and College Estates
Act 1925 29

Table of Abbreviations

The Act	Trusts of Land and Appointment of Trustees Act 1996
AEA	Administration of Estates Act 1925
Emmet	Emmet on Title, 19th edition
EPAA	Enduring Powers of Attorney Act 1985
LPA	Law of Property Act 1925
LP(JT)A	Law of Property (Joint Tenants) Act 1964
LP(MP)A 1994	Law of Property (Miscellaneous Provisions) Act 1994
LRA	Land Registration Act 1925
The new Act	Trusts of Land and Appointment of Trustees Act 1996
PAA	Powers of Attorney Act 1971
SLA	Settled Land Act 1925
TA	Trustee Act 1925
The 1996 Act	Trusts of Land and Appointment of Trustees Act 1996
TLATA	Trusts of Land and Appointment of Trustees Act 1996

References to a Schedule or section number without further attribution will normally be to the 1996 Act.

Chapter 1

Introduction

"This is a worthwhile reform of the technicalities of a complex but important area of the law, which will in the long run make the structure of property settlements and the co-ownership of land simpler and more comprehensible and therefore cheaper to operate for those concerned – which includes everyone who jointly owns a house" [Gary Streeter MP, Parliamentary Secretary, Lord Chancellor's Department].

1.1 General

Politicians' promises, politicians' promises. Cheaper, ha! Well, as another commentator said about another politician more than 30 years ago in – we emphasise – completely different circumstances, "he would say that, wouldn't he?" Perhaps we can review Mr Streeter's summary in a moment, when we have glanced at the substance of the Act. The framework of this introduction will be:

1. To outline, in the most general way possible, the content of the Act.

2. To identify the sections which make up that content.

3. To reproduce and comment on the few but nevertheless important definitions which the Act contains or incorporates.

4. To deal with several words and phrases which are either not defined in the Act at all, or, if they are defined, are only partly defined. Some of these are used so often that the only sensible course is to take them here and where necessary refer back in the later text. We might save a page or two, and we do not want to inflict on readers the same repetitive comments each time those words and phrases recur.

5. Finally we have included a few words about general and recurring issues such as commencement and retroaction.

Readers who habitually hit the main course without preliminaries (but have read the menu so far), please stay with us. This introduction is more than the menu. In outlining the definitions and analysing the recurring words and phrases we will try to highlight their significance on the text of the Act. The detail of some of the later chapters might be hard going without that overall view first.

1.2   The general content of the Act

The general content of the Act, not necessarily in the order of the sections, aims at achieving the following:

1. Replacing the dual alternative systems which currently govern co-ownership, trusts and successive interests with one unitary system. Trusts for sale and strict settlements are replaced by the single, if in some ways flexible, "trust of land".

   That general statement is carried out in the way outlined in (2) and (3) below.

   Replacing trusts for sale by trusts of land has an important consequence. We are of course concerned with traditional settlements and trusts. But we are also concerned with co-ownership. In the same way that co-ownership could only take effect before 1997[1] under a trust for sale, after 1996 it can only take effect as a trust of land. Trusts of land impact on and transform all forms of co-ownership. And in saying that, it means most land in this country – all land held otherwise than by a corporation or sole individual. Mr Streeter was right about that.

2. Phasing out strict settlements. New ones are prohibited, although existing strict settlements can continue.

3. Abolishing statutory trusts for sale. They are replaced with a less familiarly phrased implied trust which imposes no duty to sell. It contains an evenly balanced power to sell and power to retain with neither predominating.

---

1 This assumes that, as presently foreseen, the Act is brought into force on 1 January 1997.

4. Trustees' powers may be delegated to the life tenant. That may be a matter of detail, but the ability to do so forms an important part of the regime. It enables a "trust of land" to mirror, if the parties choose to do so, an essential element of banned-for-future-creation strict settlements.

5. Making important additions to the rights of beneficiaries and to the rights and duties of trustees. For example:

   (a) trustees of land now have the powers of an absolute owner;
   (b) beneficiaries entitled in possession have enlarged statutory rights to be consulted, and of occupation;
   (c) beneficiaries have new rights to direct the appointment (or retirement) of trustees. This applies to all trusts, not only to trusts of land.

   These new features are not compulsory. They may be negatived. Both their existence and the possibility of negativing them have important implications on drafting.

6. Abolishing the doctrine of conversion. We have put it last. But detailed and technical though it is, it has important consequences on the way the rest of the Act is drafted and takes effect. It is a stump which had to be chopped away before the new trusts of land could be planted. In the Act itself it comes almost first, in section 3.

Few parts of the Act are self contained. They are a jigsaw of pieces depending on each other. They also depend on the remaining 1925 property legislation. Parts of this have been repealed, parts have been replaced, parts have been amended. There are pages and pages of "minor and consequential" amendments and part repeals. But subject to all that the 1996 Act is an addition to the 1925 statutes, not something which could exist on its own. It has to be read in the context of the 1925 legislation as now amended.

We promised to review the words in Mr Streeter's comment after outlining the substance of the Act. "Worthwhile" – mainly; "technical", "complex" and "important" – certainly. Whether the reforms will make co-ownership more comprehensible will depend on the legal profession. Enlarging statutory powers and rights may reduce the need for enlargement in the disposition, but increase the possibility of dispositionary restrictions. Drafting changes, yes, drafting simplification, not always. No change at all will be needed to the simple, understandable, form of transfer already used on acquisition by most co-owners, Form 19(JP). And the increased rights and duties of the new regime will require more, not less, advice.

As for the prospect of "cheapness", words still fail us.

1.3   General scheme of the Act

The Act is in three parts. Part I deals with all the purposes except 5(c) above. Part II deals with purpose 5(C). Part III contains supplementary and general provisions. There are then a large number of consequential amendments made to the 1925 legislation, and a number of other minor amendments and repeals, in the four Schedules to the Act.

Part I is sections 1 to 18. Section 1 defines the new concept of "trust of land". Section 2 prevents SLA settlements being made in future, and provides for their being phased out. Section 3 abolishes the doctrine of conversion. Section 4 removes the option to negative the implied power to postpone, and section 5 replaces the statutory trust for sale with the new regime. Sections 6 to 8 deal with the expanded trustees' powers in relation to land, and section 9 with delegation of those powers to beneficiaries. Sections 10 and 11 deal with consents and consultation. Sections 12 to 13 deal with rights of beneficiaries to occupy land. Sections 14 to 15 concern applications to the court and orders relating to trusts of land, and section 16 provides certain protection to purchasers. Sections 17 to 18 contain supplementary provisions.

Part II contains three sections. Sections 19 and 20 confer on beneficiaries in some circumstances the power to appoint and remove trustees of *any* trusts (not just trusts of land). Section 21 contains provisions supplementary to these sections.

Part III comprises six sections. Sections 22 and 23 deal with interpretation, and section 24 with application of the Act to the Crown. Section 25 concerns amendments, section 26 confers power on the Lord Chancellor to make further provision, and section 27 contains the short title, and provisions concerning commencement and the extent of the Act.

There are four schedules. Schedule 1 contains provisions consequential on section 2, Schedule 2 makes amendments to statutory provisions imposing trusts for sale, Schedule 3 makes minor and consequential amendments and Schedule 4 lists repeals.

1.4 The Law Commission's role

This Act is largely the product of two reports of the Law Commission, No 181 on "Trusts of Land", and No 188 on "Overreaching: Beneficiaries in Occupation". The first dates from December 1988 and the second from November 1989. This Act implements practically all the recommendations of the first Report, and one recommendation[2] from the second. The major difference between the Act and the draft Bill annexed to Law Com No 181 is that the Law Commission's Bill would have implemented its changes by amending existing legislation, whereas this Act repeals sections in the earlier legislation and makes fresh provision. As an exercise in clarity and in knowing where to look for your law, the latter is obviously a preferable approach.[3] It is perhaps a pity that it was not taken further, so that the provisions of the 1925 legislation which have been amended *in consequence* of these primary provisions were not also re-enacted in altered form at the same time. Still, half a loaf is better than no bread. Throughout our commentary on the Act, we shall refer back to the Law Commission's views and its draft Bill where appropriate. To assist practitioners, we have also reproduced, at the end of this book, some of the 1925 provisions in their amended form.

1.5 Extent of the Act

The whole Act extends to England and Wales only[4], except for a solitary repeal in the Agriculture Act 1970, which extends only to Northern Ireland.[5] None of the Act applies to Scotland, of course.

1.6 Commencement

None of the Act came into force on the Royal Assent being given on 24 July 1996. Instead, the Act is to come into force when so appointed by the Lord Chancellor by statutory instrument.[6] At the time of writing, it is considered likely that the date appointed will be

---

2 In para 4.27 of the Report.
3 *Cf* HL Deb vol 569, cols 1720-1721, 1 March 1996.
4 S 27(3).
5 S 27(4).
6 S 27(2).

1 January 1997. We have assumed in the text that this will in fact occur. The Lord Chancellor has power by statutory instrument to make such transitional provision as seems appropriate to him[7], subject to annulment by either House of Parliament.[8]

1.7 Other general provisions

There are the usual provisions relating to the various consequential amendments and repeals made by the Act[9] and the short title to the Act. There is also provision that the Crown is to be bound by the Act[10] except in relation to land (a) vested in Her Majesty in right of the Crown or the Duchy of Lancaster or (b) belonging to the Duchy of Cornwall held in that right. In relation to those two categories, the Act does not affect or alter the descent, devolution or nature of those estates or interests in land, except so far as relates to joint tenancies and tenancies in common.[11]

There is also a wide provision, of the kind so beloved of civil servants, extending the power of the Lord Chancellor to make "supplementary, transitional or incidental provision"[12] to *modify an Act of Parliament* (public, general or local – though not private) passed before this Act or in the same session.[13] The technical committee of the Society of Trust and Estate Practitioners in March 1996 objected to the inclusion of this power, saying that this:

> effectively gives the [Lord Chancellor] complete control over English trust and land law. On constitutional grounds there is no reason why a power such as this should appear in this Bill.

But it is still there.

1.8 Framework of this book

This book is divided into a number of distinct parts. After this introductory chapter Chapters 2 to 10 deal with trusts of land, the

---

7 S 26(1).
8 S 26(3).
9 S 25.
10 S 24(1).
11 S 24(2).
12 S 26(1).
13 S 26(2).

subject matter of Part I of the Act. Chapter 11 then deals with appointment and retirement of trustees, the subject matter of Part II of the Act. Each chapter opens with "bullet points" to indicate the main areas covered, and closes with a section of "main practical consequences". Chapter 12 then consolidates these "main practical consequences" into a single rearranged list enabling the practitioner to see where in the book (and the Act) a particular topic is dealt with, if at all.

There are then five appendices: (1) a comparison of procedures between the old and new systems where a will gives a right of residence; (2) a note on assents; (3) a note on conveyancing procedures where there is a sale by survivor of co-owners; (4) a checklist comparing trusts for sale/trusts of land with SLA settlements; and (5) a note on the appointment of trustees. These are followed by the full text of the Act, by a number of the more important provisions (but alas, not all of them) of the 1925 legislation, as amended by the Act and finally by a number of precedents.

1.9 Interpretation

There is comparatively little statutory interpretation provided directly by this Act. Section 1 defines "trust of land" and section 22 defines "beneficiary". Apart from that, section 23 refers on to definitions in Law of Property Act 1925.

1.10 *"Trust of land"*

This crucial definition, central both to the purpose and the mechanics of the Act, is defined in section 1, the very first section. It is short enough to quote it and then briefly comment.

    1.(1)   In this Act -

        (a) "trust of land" means (subject to subsection (3)) any trust of property which consists of or includes land, and

        (b) "trustees of land" means trustees of a trust of land.

    (2)   The reference in subsection (1)(a) to a trust -

        (a) is to any description of trust (whether express, implied, resulting or constructive), including a trust for sale and a bare trust, and

> (b) includes a trust created, or arising, before the commencement of this Act.
>
> (3)   The reference to land in subsection (1)(a) does not include land which (despite section 2) is settled land or which is land to which the Universities and College Estates Act 1925 applies.

Three features of subsection (2) in particular deserve to be stressed.

The manner of creation

It will be a trust of land irrespective of the way it was created. So it can be:

- express;
- implied;
- resulting; or
- constructive.

Some sections of the Act are more specific and refer to a trust created by disposition or to a disposition creating a trust of land.[14] But when "trust of land" is used without further qualification, it includes trusts arising in any of those ways.

The time of creation

It is a trust of land whether or not it was created or arose before the commencement of the Act. The definition is retrospective. That does not mean that the Act affects dispositions by trustees before the commencement of the Act.[15] Nor does it mean that existing strict settlements are reclassified as trusts of land (see s 1(3)).

The type of trust

If it is a trust – *any trust* – of property which consists of or includes land, it will be a trust of land.[16] To make the matter clear beyond argument (and partly to reverse some case law), subsection (2) goes on specifically to include in the definition:

- trusts for sale, and
- bare trusts.

---

14 See 1.17 below.
15 See 1.19 below.
16 S 1(1).

So our trusts of land include:

- trusts for sale of land or including land;
- bare trusts of land or including land; and
- any other trusts of land or including land.

The inclusion of trusts for sale may surprise those who have read that trusts for sale have been abolished. They have not been abolished; they are now members of a larger family. (It is true that *statutory* trusts as trusts for sale have been abolished and replaced, but it is still possible, if usually pointless, to create an *express* trust for sale.[17]) That larger family also includes "bare trusts", which removes a former inconvenience; if a bare trust arose, or if a trust for sale became a bare trust, any statutory powers of trustees for sale did not apply.[18]

It is this larger family, the trust of land, which is the concept behind the new regime. It is to the enlarged trust of land that the enhanced and augmented provisions formerly applicable only to trusts for sale now apply. It is trustees of land who enjoy the wider powers conferred by, and who are subject to the wider duties imposed by, the Act.

Mixed trusts

A "trust of land" does not need to be exclusively of land. It is enough if it *includes* land. Indeed, for some limited purposes a trust which by then is only of the proceeds of sale of land is treated as a trust of land.[19]

That does not however mean that trustees can necessarily treat personalty within the trust in the same way as land. The absolute owner's powers given by section 6 for example are powers "in relation to the land". It pays to check the wording of the section.

1.11 *"Beneficiary"*

Many of the Act's provisions refer to, and confer rights on, "beneficiaries". The word "beneficiary" in this Act bears a restricted meaning compared to the general law. In other words, some who

---

17 See 4.6 below.
18 *Re Wakeman* [1945] Ch 177. See 5.1 below.
19 See s 17 and 5.4, 9.5 below.

would be beneficiaries under the general law are not beneficiaries for the purposes of this Act.

The definition is in section 22:

(1)   In this Act "beneficiary", in relation to a trust, means any person who under the trust has an interest in property subject to the trust (including a person who has such an interest as a trustee or a personal representative).

(2)   In this Act references to a beneficiary who is beneficially entitled do not include a beneficiary who has an interest in property subject to the trust only by reason of being a trustee or personal representative.

(3)   For the purposes of this Act a person who is a beneficiary only by reason of being an annuitant is not to be regarded as entitled to an interest in possession in land, subject to the trust.

This gives rise to at least two problems. One is whether objects of a discretionary trust or power with a trust in default are within the term "beneficiary". The other is whether the *trustees* are.

As to the first problem, we should note that the definition is not qualified by some such phrase as "unless the context otherwise requires". It is absolute. So, to be a "beneficiary" for the purposes of the Act, a person must have "an interest in property subject to the trust". Yet the House of Lords in *Gartside* v *IRC*[20] held that an object of a discretionary trust had no interest in any part of the trust property, at least until the discretion was exercised in his favour. Accordingly, it should seem that, notwithstanding that *Saunders* v *Vautier*[21] can apply to a discretionary trust, the objects of a discretionary trust or power with trust in default are not "beneficiaries" for the purposes of this Act, and do not have the various rights conferred upon such persons.

Turning to the second problem, at first sight the words in brackets in section 22(1) seem to mean that the trustees of a trust of land are included in the definition. This would lead to bizarre consequences. But the words "under the trust" must limit "beneficiary" to a person having a (derivative) equitable interest and hence exclude the trustees of the trust of land. They have no interest "*under* the trust". The reference in brackets to trustees and personal representatives covers the case where an equitable interest under a trust belongs (by devolution or otherwise) to a person who holds it in a fiduciary

---

20 [1968] AC 553.
21 (1841) Cr & Ph 240. See *Re Smith* [1928] 1 Ch 915, *Re Nelson* [1928] 1 Ch 920n.

capacity for the benefit of others (hence the reference in s 22(2) to excluding such a person from the concept of a "beneficiary beneficially entitled").

Beneficiary beneficially entitled

The Act draws a distinction, for some purposes, between "beneficiary" and "beneficiary who is beneficially entitled".[22] The idea is to exclude from the latter category any beneficiary holding his beneficial interest in a fiduciary capacity for others. The way that section 22(2) does this is to use the phrase "only by reason of". This means that a beneficiary holding his interest on trust *for persons including himself* is not excluded, and hence is a *beneficiary beneficially entitled*, even though his beneficial interest under the subtrust is infinitesimal.

Beneficiary entitled to an interest in possession

The Act also makes use of the concept of the beneficiary entitled to an interest in possession.[23] Broadly speaking, the more important rights conferred by this Act on beneficiaries of trusts of land are conferred on those beneficiaries entitled to an interest in possession. There is no definition of "interest in possession" (apart from the negative provision in s 22(3)), and hence it presumably bears its traditional trust law meaning of an interest conferring the right to the present enjoyment of the subject matter of the interest, even though such right is *defeasible* by exercise of a power of appointment or accumulation.[24] Where the right is a right to income, it is a right to the income *produced*, and *net* of trust expenses properly chargeable to income.[25]

The provision in subsection 3 is important because it alters the previous law. Under the LPA an annuitant whose annuity was to be paid out of the income of the land was a person beneficially entitled to possession to the rents and profits of the land and proceeds of sale.[26] Section 22(3) excludes such a person from being treated as a beneficiary entitled to an interest in possession for the purposes of

---

22 See ss 9(1), (4), 11(1), 12(1), and 22(2).
23 See ss 9(1), (4), 11(1), 12(1), and 15(3).
24 *Pearson v IRC* [1980] Ch 1, CA, revsd [1981] AC 753, HL. For inheritance tax purposes it bears a special meaning, as held by the majority of the House of Lords in the *Pearson* case.
25 *Ibid*, [1981] AC 753, 775.
26 *Re House* [1929] 2 Ch 166.

this Act. That does not, of course, mean that such person ceases to be entitled to the annuity. It merely means that he or she cannot exercise the rights conferred on "beneficiaries" entitled to an interest in possession by the Act. The general rights of an annuitant, or of a "beneficiary" simpliciter, are unaffected.

Beneficiary absolutely entitled

If that were not enough, the Act also makes use of the phrase "beneficiary absolutely entitled".[27] This is not defined. In section 7(2) of the Act, the draftsman has used the phrase "absolutely or in trust". This opposition would suggest that "absolutely" means "beneficially". And there is some authority to support that view.[28] But a more usual meaning would be as a measure of the *estate or interest* taken by the grantee, *i.e.* that it was not conditional[29] or limited in any way[30], rather than as a statement of the *capacity* it which it was held. In the context of this Act (s 7(2) apart), this seems the more natural meaning.

Pension trusts

We should specifically deal with the position of beneficiaries of pension trusts. Some concern was expressed on House of Lords Second Reading that certain provisions of the Act might (a) cut across specific statutory provision already made for pension trusts, or (b) confer rights on beneficiaries of such trusts which were inappropriate.[31] As to the former, amendments were made at Committee stage to try to ensure that particular existing provisions for pension schemes "should not inadvertently be thwarted".[32]

As to the latter, the provisions concerned included sections 9 (delegation) 11 (consultation) and 12-13 (occupation of trust land). There can be no doubt that such beneficiaries are "beneficiaries" for the purposes of the Act. But (as we shall see) the provisions referred to only apply to beneficiaries "beneficially entitled to an interest in possession" in the trust property. A pension beneficiary will not

---

27 See ss 6(2), 7(1), 16(4), (5), 19(1), and 20(1).
28 See *Re Ray's Will Trusts* [1936] Ch 520, 526 (but the case is unsatisfactory, for Clauson J held first, that "absolutely" meant "free from any fetter or trust", but second, that the gift so made in that case *was* nonetheless held on trust by the recipient).
29 *Re Pickworth* [1899] 1 Ch 642, 651.
30 *Re Thompson* [1947] VLR 60, 67.
31 See HL Debs, vol 569, col 1725, 1 March 1996.
32 HL Debs, Vol 570, col 1534, 25 March 1996.

qualify until he becomes entitled in possession to benefits as of right under the terms of the trust. When he does become so entitled, typically he either receives assets absolutely (paid as a lump sum or to an insurance company to purchase an annuity) or he receives an annuity from the trustees. In the former case he will cease to be a trust beneficiary; in the latter case he will continue as a beneficiary, but by section 22(3) he is "not to be regarded as entitled to an interest in possession".[33] No doubt it was for this reason that the Lord Chancellor, in House of Lords Committee, considered it unnecessary to table amendments to these provisions.[34]

1.12 *Purchaser*

By section 23(1) the word "purchaser" has the same meaning as in Part I of the LPA. "Purchaser" is defined by section 205(1)(xxi) of that Act for the purposes of its Part I as "a person who acquires an interest in or a charge upon property for money or moneys worth". So it excludes a purchaser for marriage consideration or for a nominal or no consideration (*i.e.* a volunteer). There is also no requirement that a "purchaser" be in good faith.[35]

1.13 *Other definitions*

Two other definitions are given by section 23 of the Act. First, the word "court" is defined by section 23(3) to mean the High Court or a county court. The other provision relating to definition is much wider. By section 23(2) of the Act, subject to the definition of "purchaser" already discussed:

> where an expression used in this Act is given a meaning by the Law of Property Act 1925 it has the same meaning as in that Act unless the context otherwise requires.

1.14 **Other concepts**

In addition to the statutory definitions, there are a number of concepts used throughout the Act which are either undefined or only

---

33 See text to notes 23-26 above.
34 HL Debs, vol 570, col 1534-1535, 25 March 1996.
35 *Cf Midland Bank Trust Co Ltd* v *Green* [1981] AC 513 (definition of "purchaser" for the purposes of the LCA 1925).

partially defined, some of which cause problems. Rather than repeat the discussion constantly, we shall discuss some of them here and then at the appropriate point in the text simply refer back to this discussion.

1.15 *"Charitable, ecclesiastical or public trusts"*

The first is the notion of "charitable, ecclesiastical or public trusts". This is a curious phrase. It did not appear in the Law Commission's bill, although it has often been used before in property legislation, for example in the Settled Land Act 1925 section 29, and in the Trustee Act 1925 section 34. Yet its meaning is obscure. "Charitable trusts" is clear enough. "Ecclesiastical trusts", if not as commonly used a phrase, must mean a trust for charitable ecclesiastical purposes.[36] However, "public trusts" is odd. Some textbooks[37] treat it as a synonym, more or less, for "charitable trust". Yet, as Lord Parker pointed out[38], a trust for the benefit of the public is valid only if it is a charitable trust in the technical sense. A trust which is a public trust but not a charitable one will almost certainly be void. On the other hand, in Scots law, the correct legal term is indeed "public trust", which is valid, and is the equivalent of a charitable trust in English law. The phrase "charitable trust" can be used in Scots law, but popularly is used only to refer to a subdivision of a public trust;[39] But this Act (and indeed the Trustee Act 1925) does not apply in Scotland, so the word "public" is not being used to refer to Scots law.

1.16 *"Function"* and *"function relating to land"*

Next, there are the ideas of a "function"[40] and a "function relating to land".[41] Function is plainly wider than a mere power[42] and must, for example, include a duty which the trustees have. Function relating to

---

36 *See Re Perry Almshouses* [1899] 1 Ch 21, *cf Re St Swithin's Norwich* [1960] P 78.

37 Such as *Lewin on Trusts*, 16th ed at 7-8; *Snell's Equity*, 29th ed, at 143.

38 In *Bowman v The Secular Society Limited* [1917] AC 406, 441, *cf Re Cleveland* [1931] Ch 247.

39 See Wilson and Duncan, *Trusts, Trustees and Executors*, 2nd ed, para 14-02.

40 See ss 6(1), 9(1), (2), (4), 10, 11, 14, 18(1) and 20(1).

41 See ss 10(1), (3).

42 See S 6(1).

land will thus include a duty in relation to the land. In a recent case[43], the Court of Appeal held that LPA section 26(3) applied only to those powers of the trustees which involved "positive acts". Hence, that subsection did not apply to a joint tenant of a periodic tenancy who gave notice of not being willing for the tenancy to continue, so that it came to an end in accordance with the doctrine in *London Borough of Hammersmith & Fulham* v *Monk*.[44] But the words "any function" are general and unlimited.[45] There seems no reason to restrict them to functions which involve "positive acts".

1.17 *"Trust created by a disposition"*

A further concept is that of a trust "created by a disposition"[46], or alternatively a "disposition creating a trust". "Created" just means "brought into legal existence".[47] There is no definition of "disposition" for the purposes of this Act, but, by section 23(2), we are directed to section 205(1)(ii) of the LPA, by which:

> disposition includes a conveyance and also a devise, bequest, or an appointment of property contained in a will.

This definition obviously assumes the use of a document of some sort, although many dispositions may take place without one, *e.g.* the gift of a chattel by delivery. Does the use of the word "disposition" include the case of a declaration of trust by a beneficial owner, who is thereby constituted the first trustee of the trust, or is it confined to the case of *transfer* by the settlor to the trustee? A similar problem arises in LPA section 26(3), but so far as we are aware the courts have never considered it. The word "disposition" seems more natural to describe the transmission of a subsisting interest in property from one person to another, rather than the creation of a separate interest in favour of another person. For example, the grant of a new lease would not normally be regarded as a "disposition" in the absence of specific statutory authority (for such an example see the Housing Act 1985, s 159, defining "relevant disposal"), yet there is no very good reason for distinguishing the two cases in this way. A

---

43 *Crawley Borough Council* v *Ure* [1996] 1 All ER 724.
44 [1992] 1 AC 478.
45 *Cf Henry Briggs & Co Ltd* v *IRC* [1961] 1 All ER 220.
46 See ss 4(1), 8(1), (2), 10(1), (3), 11(2), (3), 17(6), 18(2), 21(5), (6).
47 *Baldwin* v *CIR* [1965] NZLR 1, 6.

proper definition (or the use of a different word) would have put the point beyond doubt. The definition in the LPA is not conclusive; it merely "includes" certain things, thus suggesting the possibility of other matters being included.

1.18 *"Created by more than one person"*

Lastly, there is the concept of a trust being created by more than one person. Does this refer only to the case of two or more persons, *joint* owners of the property *jointly* settling that property, or does it also refer to the case where each of two or more persons separately contributes property to be held by the same trustee or trustees on identical trusts, but as a single fund? Since the former case is rare, it might be thought that the draftsman must have intended to include the latter. It is true that in the latter case the strict analysis is that there are two or more trusts, but in practice no distinction is ever drawn between them, and they are treated as one trust.[48] Indeed, it is exceedingly common in the offshore trust world for a settlement to be made of a nominal sum, say £10, sometimes by way of declaration of trust of the trustee and then for substantial amounts of property to be decanted into the hands of the trustee of the same trusts. In practice, this is always treated as one trust. Similarly, where the question is whether a pre-1991 trust has been "tainted" by the addition of property subsequent to 1991.[49] The legislator there has treated the trust as a single trust and not as two trusts on the same terms. For all these reasons it seems that the concept of a trust being created by more than one person includes the case where two or more persons individually contribute property at different times to be held by the same trustee on the same terms, with the intention that the latter funds should be treated as an accretion to the former. The problem was alluded to, though not resolved, in the debate on House of Lords Report.[50] On Third Reading, however, words were introduced into section 11(3) ("a trust created ... by reference to such a trust") to ensure that that provision, at least, clearly extended to the subsequently added property.[51]

---

48 *Cf Re Rydon's Settlement* [1955] Ch 1.
49 Taxation of Chargeable Gains Act 1992, Sched 5, para 9(4).
50 HL Deb, vol 571, col 962, 22 April 1996.
51 HL Deb, vol 572, col 97, 7 May 1996.

1.19 Retroaction

Many individual sections make specific provision for the retrospective effect of the section, or that it does not apply in some circumstances to documents executed or trusts arising before commencement of the Act. Where they do so we have commented in the text of the relevant chapter.

The general law, the background to those special provisions, will apply where no special provision is made. Perhaps it is stating the obvious. The Act is retrospective in the sense that the definition of "trust of land" in section 1 includes a trust created or arising before the commencement of the Act. Existing trusts, except for existing strict settlements or other trusts specially provided for, have no immunities.

That retroaction however is only in terms of the trusts to which the Act applies. When it comes to *functions*, the exercise of powers and the existence of rights and duties, the Act can only apply from its commencement date onwards. Trustees who leased trust land before commencement for example had only their LPA section 28 or enlarged powers under the trust disposition. Absolute owner powers under the new section 6 only apply from commencement date, and do not validate pre commencement invalid dealings under the old powers. Purchasers, especially of unregistered land, continue to be concerned with the old regime to that extent.

1.20 Use of Parliamentary materials

The recent decision the House of Lords in *Pepper* v *Hart*[52] has completely changed the position regarding the use of Parliamentary materials (and particularly records of debate) in the interpretation of statutes. The old rule was that reference to Parliamentary material as an aid to statutory construction was not permissible.[53] But the majority of the House of Lords in *Pepper* v *Hart* held that reference to certain Parliamentary material as an aid to construction was now to be permitted, where the legislation concerned was ambiguous or obscure, or the literal meaning led to absurdity. But the only material to which reference is henceforth to be allowed is clear statements by

---

52 [1993] AC 593.

53 *Davis* v *Johnson* [1979] AC 264; *Hadmore Productions Limited* v *Hamilton* [1983] 1 AC 191.

a minister, or other promoter of the Bill, leading to the enactment in question, together with any other Parliamentary material needed to understand such statements. Where a clause or other amendment is inserted in a bill at the instance of another person, (*i.e.* not the Government or promoter of the Bill) then we must assume that the clear statement concerned would be that of the promoter of the clause or amendment involved.

Because of the technical nature of the Act, and the lack of "political" judgements to make, there were not many members of either House of Parliament who were able to debate the Bill's merits, and even fewer who wanted to. So the discussion of the Bill was modest by comparison with other legislation. To facilitate reference to such materials as there are, the progress of the Bill is shown below:

House	Stage	Date	Hansard
House of Lords:	1st reading:	1 November 1990	vol 567, col 417
	2nd reading:	1 March 1996	vol 569, cols 1717-1727
	Committee:	25 March 1996	vol 570, cols 1532-1559
	Report:	22 April 1996	vol 571, cols 954-971
	3rd reading:	7 May 1996	vol 572, cols 94-102
House of Commons:	1st reading:	7 May 1996	[not in Hansard]
	SRC	12 June 1996	[not in Hansard]
	2nd reading:	18 June 1996	vol 279, col 787
	Committee:	28 June 1996	[not in Hansard]
	Remaining stages:	16 July 1996	vol 281, col 1052
House of Lords:	Consideration of Commons' amendments	22 July 1996	vol 574, cols 1174-1175
Royal Assent		24 July 1996	vol 282, col 391

Note that there are two series of Hansard, one for the Commons (bound in green), and one for the Lords (bound in red). A few points on Parliamentary procedure can be made for the benefit of anyone who intends to carry out any research. First of all, first readings of Government Bills are purely formal and nothing is said about their contents. Secondly, second readings are concerned with the general principles of the Bill, rather than with details. It is therefore unlikely that a helpful ministerial statement would be found on a point of detail in a second reading debate.

Thirdly, the most detailed discussion of proposed legislation takes place in committee. Although the debate on this Act in the House of Lords committee stage is contained in the House of Lords Hansard (because the committee was a committee of the whole House), the debates of House of Commons Committee Stage are not to be found in House of Commons Hansard, but in an entirely different series of reports altogether, because the committee stage of the Bill was committed to Standing Committee A. Not many libraries keep Parliamentary debates anyway, but of those who do, few keep the reports of standing committee debates.

In fact, the only debates on the substance of the Bill were in the House of Lords: the consideration given by the House of Commons was virtually nil, the only (very minor) exception being the committee stage. The references to House of Commons Hansard just record formally the passing of the particular stages concerned.

Chapter 2

Prohibition on New Settled Land Act Settlements*

- New strict settlements prohibited but existing settlements continue
- Re-settlements, and settlements created under powers of appointment given by existing settlements, are outside the prohibition unless opted into trusts of land
- Charitable, ecclesiastical and public trusts are all trusts of land, whenever they were created
- Cessation of strict settlement when no relevant property is subject to it
- Provisions consequential on section 2

2.1 The background

Not many busy practitioners will mourn Settled Land Act settlements. (We will refer to them from here on as "strict settlements".) What the 1996 Act gives us is not instant abolition, but the prospect of their eventual extinction through rigorous birth control. It will be many years before all existing tenants for life have died, and all existing strict settlements have come to an end. Their increasing rarity will make worse a problem already evident – few practitioners are familiar with their unique rules.

The Lord Advocate[1] in moving the second reading in the Lords commented that strict settlements were redolent of a world already dying in 1925 which has long since disappeared. In 1989 the Law Commission made the case for their abolition or merging with trusts for sale (Law Com No 181). The reasons and problems they cited included:

1. The separate development of strict settlements and trusts for sale was based on historical differences now blurred both by the 1925 legislation and social changes.

---

* S 2 and Sched 1.
1 Not the Lord Chancellor. Confusingly there are three Lords Mackay, and two of them, the Lord Advocate and the Lord Chancellor, figured prominently in the Bill's passage through the Lords.

2. Unless a trust for sale was created, trusts comprising land would inevitably result in a strict settlement. It was the default mechanism and therefore the likely result of creating trusts without, or without competent, advice. They were too easy to create accidentally. They could also arise under a constructive trust, where the implications of the tenant for life having powers of management and complex SLA machinery was probably far from the minds of the parties.[2]

3. It was easy for executors to fail to realise that a will created a strict settlement and then vest the land in trustees instead of the tenant for life – a situation then difficult to disentangle.

4. In addition to the main difference in who had the legal estate and who was entitled to sell, there were also illogical differences of detail between the two systems – for example in deeds of discharge, consents for sale and the effect of not complying with the correct machinery.

5. The subtleties and uncertainties of whether the court would classify rights of residence as creating a strict settlement – and the inappropriateness of SLA powers if they did.

6. The complexity of the Settled Land Act, as exemplified by:

   (a) the prolixity of documentation caused by the requirement for two documents for each transaction;
   (b) the inclusion in strict settlements of many complex interests beyond life interests and interests in remainder;
   (c) the common failure of testators to appoint trustees of the settlement.

7. The inherent conflict of interest between a tenant for life exercising the power of sale and other powers, and the interests of the persons entitled in remainder.

8. Very few new strict settlements are being created, and if the powers of delegation held by trustees of land were broadened, settlors could create a trust of land analogous to an "enhanced" strict settlement.

---

2 See *Bannister v Bannister* [1948] 2 All ER 133 and *Binions v Evans* [1972] Ch 359.

They concluded that the merits of a unitary system outweighed the possible disadvantages of phasing out strict settlements.

2.2 New strict settlements prohibited but existing settlements continue

So as part of the jigsaw of measures outlined in Chapter 1, the first operative section in the new Act clears an enlarged space where the all-embracing trusts of land can flourish by closing strict settlements as an optional mechanism for future dispositions. Existing strict settlements continue. They soldier on under the old SLA regime. SLA tenants for life will not enjoy the enhanced powers of trustees of land under the 1996 Act.

Section 2(1) is short and simple:

> **Trusts in place of settlements**
>
> 2.(1)   No settlement created after the commencement of this Act is a settlement for the purposes of the Settled Land Act 1925; and no settlement shall be deemed to be made under that Act after that commencement.

The ban applies both to settlements created under SLA section 1(1) and settlements deemed to be settlements by that Act. The effect is clear. Suppose testator A does not impose an immediate binding trust for sale but leaves land to his wife for life. If A dies on 31 December 1996 A's gift creates a strict settlement. If he dies on 1 January 1997[3], a trust of land is created.

Despite the prohibition, features of the SLA regime such as the tenant for life having power to deal with the land can be achieved under a trust of land by using the powers of delegation in section 9. That section is discussed later in Chapter 6. It is however an optional revocable course, to be used or abandoned as the trustees decide, not one imposed willy-nilly as it is for strict settlements. For that matter, the traditional dynastic reason for the choice of a strict settlement, preserving land for future generations, is already arguably more effectively carried out by means other than a strict settlement.[4]

---

3 Assuming in both cases that the commencement date of the Act is 1 January 1997.
4 See Law Com No 181 para 4.3, citing the life tenant's power to sell and taxation disadvantages.

2.3 Re-settlements, and settlements created under powers of appointment given by existing settlements, are outside the prohibition

If new settlements are prohibited but existing settlements are to be preserved, the Act needs to say whether a re-settlement counts as a new settlement or not. Here it is simpler to start by quoting section 2(2) and (3):

> (2)   Subsection (1) does not apply to a settlement created on the occasion of an alteration in any interest in, or of a person becoming entitled under, a settlement which -
>
> (a) is in existence at the commencement of this Act, or
>
> (b) derives from a settlement within paragraph (a) or this paragraph.
>
> (3)   But a settlement created as mentioned in subsection (2) is not a settlement for the purposes of the Settled Land Act 1925 if provision to the effect that it is not is made in the instrument, or any of the instruments, by which it is created.

So in general terms a resettlement does not automatically lose strict settlement status. Neither does a settlement created in the exercise of powers of appointment contained in existing strict settlements. (For convenience rather than strictly accurately we will refer to both as "resettlements".) But in both cases the parties can then opt to become a trust of land if they wish by provisions in the resettlement.

An alteration does not always make a new settlement. Where it does, the new settlement may come within subsection (2). To rephrase the subsection, there must be:

(a) either an alteration in any interest in an existing settlement, or
(b) a person becoming entitled under an existing settlement, and (in either case)
(c) a (re)settlement created on that occasion. "Existing settlement" in this context means one existing on 1 January 1997[5] or derived directly or indirectly from it and itself preserved as a strict settlement by section 2(2).

The traditional resettlement was of course carried out when the eldest son, on attaining majority, was induced to bar his reversionary

---

5 Assuming that the commencement date of the Act is 1 January 1997.

entail and substitute a reversionary life interest with remainder to his sons in tail male. The day when the entail could be barred without co-operation from the life interest in possession was therefore postponed for a further generation. In future, transactions whose purpose is to create a new entailed interest will founder because of the prohibition on creating new entailed interests – see Schedule 1, paragraph 5 of the Act, mentioned below under *Provisions consequential on section 2*. So to the extent that resettlements need to create new entailed interests, they will be invalid and wasted. Less use will be made of section 2(2) for that reason.

Where a resettlement falls within subsection (2), subsection (3) allows the resettlement to provide that it is not a settlement for the purpose of the Settled Land Act 1925. Creators of the resettlement have an opportunity to convert to a trust of land if they wish. Bearing in mind that a strict settlement is often not the best vehicle to achieve its assumed purpose of preserving land within a dynasty, especially with the new flexibility attaching to trusts of land, that will sometimes be an option which the parties wish to follow.

The Act is clear on the existence of the option. What is the machinery for following it? Usually the legal estate will be with an SLA tenant for life. If a resettlement is opted out of the SLA, it will be necessary to transfer the legal estate to the trustees of land. How can this be carried out within the powers conferred by the legislation and so as to protect a future purchaser?

A conveyance by the tenant for life would not be within the statutory powers of the tenant for life. But the amendments to SLA section 17 (note the 1996 Act Sched 3 para 2(6)) show the course to be followed.

1. The tenant for life executes a conveyance to the trustees of land in accordance with the proviso to SLA section 17(1) as amended; and

2. The deed of discharge contains a statement in accordance with amended section 17 (1) that the land is subject to a trust of land by virtue of such conveyance.

2.4 Cessation of strict settlement when no relevant property is subject to it

A strict settlement often ends on the death of a life tenant. If the personal representatives of the deceased tenant for life execute a clean assent in favour of the person(s) absolutely entitled, a future purchaser can rely on SLA section 110 and AEA section 36. A section 17 deed of discharge provides protection for the purchaser where the settlement does not end on death – where the conveyance is not by personal representatives, or a former tenant for life owning the legal estate already needs to establish his absolute entitlement so that purchase money need not be paid to trustees of the settlement.

Section 2(4) of the new Act provides for cessation of a strict settlement in different circumstances – when after 1996 there is no relevant property (land or heirlooms) subject to the settlement. Another modest step towards extinguishing existing settlements. Typically if the whole of the settled land (with heirlooms if any) is sold.

> (4)   Where at any time after the commencement of this Act there is in the case of any settlement which is a settlement for the purposes of the Settled Land Act 1925 no relevant property which is, or is deemed to be, subject to the settlement, the settlement permanently ceases at that time to be a settlement for the purposes of that Act.
>
> In this subsection "relevant property" means land and personal chattels to which section 67(1) of the Settled Land Act 1925 (heirlooms) applies.

So:

1. The whole of the settled land with heirlooms is sold after 1996. Result – the end of the strict settlement. If the proceeds are used to buy further land to be subject to the original trusts, there is a trust of land for that further land, not a strict settlement.

That conclusion, which follows from the terms of section 2(4), is reinforced by Schedule 1 paragraph 6 of the Act:

> 6.   Where a settlement ceases to be a settlement for the purposes of the Settled Land Act 1925 because no relevant property (within the meaning of section 2(4)) is, or is deemed to be, subject to the settlement, any property which is or *later becomes* subject to the settlement is held in trust for the persons interested under the settlement. [*emphasis* added]

2. Part only of the settled land is sold after 1996. Result – the strict settlement remains in existence. If the proceeds are used to buy further land, is that land subject to the original strict settlement or to a trust of land on the original trusts? Must the

trustees of the settlement vest the new land in the tenant for life by a subsidiary vesting deed under SLA section 10, or do they hold it themselves under a trust of land? Perhaps the answer is arguable, but ours is below.

The Law Commission were clear. "If an existing settlement acquires more land, that land will be held under the new system." (Law Com No 181 para 8.3). But the terms of clause 13[6] of their draft Bill carrying this effect are not repeated in the Act. Section 2 does not say or imply that. Forget Schedule 1 paragraph 6 – it is limited to a settlement which has ceased. We infer that land bought with SLA funds in a settlement which has not ceased, is subject to the existing strict settlement.

Nothing in the 1996 Act appears to us to stop the unrepealed and unchanged SLA section 10 from applying. The proceeds of sale of settled land are capital money arising under SLA within section 10. Land was retained, so the strict settlement is still in existence. We conclude that in those circumstances the new land must be conveyed to the tenant for life by subsidiary vesting deed under SLA section 10.

The issue is important, not only to solicitors acting for existing settled estates, but to anyone concerned with SLA titles. Can a purchaser safely accept a subsidiary vesting deed, executed after the commencement of the 1996 Act? SLA section 110(2) was not drafted with this point in mind, but it only protects a "purchaser of settled land". What if the land is not settled? Does section 110(2) protect a purchaser of land which appears to be settled but is not?[7] We suggest it will be safer for a purchaser concerned with a post 1996 Act subsidiary vesting deed to satisfy himself that the land is indeed settled within SLA.[7a]

3. Part of the settled land is exchanged for land. Result – the same as (2). above. SLA section 10 applies to land exchanged for settled land just as it applies to land acquired with capital money arising under SLA. The land taken in exchange needs to

---

6 "Land shall not be ... settled land ... by virtue of being subject to a settlement, unless it was ... such land by virtue of being subject to that settlement immediately before the commencement of this Act ...".

7 A question without a conclusive answer. See however Megarry and Wade, Law of Real Property, 5th ed, p 355.

7a Assuming it is not compulsorily registrable, in which case it is a problem for the registrar.

be vested in the tenant for life by subsidiary vesting deed under SLA section 10.

4. The whole of the settled land (or, if part is sold, the whole of the remaining part) is exchanged for land. It is impossible to be categoric about the result but we suggest with diffidence that the land taken in exchange is subject to the strict settlement. It becomes subject to the settlement under SLA section 10 and requires a subsidiary vesting deed. The settlement has not ceased to be a settlement for SLA purposes because, unlike the case of selling the whole, assuming the exchange was simultaneous there has never been a moment when, to use the words of paragraph 6, there is no "relevant property" (*i.e.* land) "... subject to the settlement."

2.5 "Charitable, ecclesiastical and public trusts of land" are all trusts of land, whenever they were created

The question mark over the precise meaning of this phrase has been dealt with already.[8] Nothing more really needs to be added. To save repeating the phrase we will refer to them as charitable etc trusts. They have the advantages of the new system, among them the absolute owner powers mentioned in Chapter 5. Moreover, in the case of charitable etc trusts the powers cannot be limited by the disposition – see section 8(3). (Powers may of course be limited by other statutes relevant to the charity. See e.g. s 6(6) to (8), discussed at 5.6.)

There are other reasons to why charitable etc trusts cannot be treated in the same way as other trusts of land. The existing rules on such matters as numbers of trustees and consents remain unchanged. They are not the subject of these notes. (But see the modest consequential amendment below under *Provisions consequential on s 2.*) And although charitable etc trusts are all now trusts of land, not all parts of the trusts of land regime apply to them. These exclusions will be mentioned in the relevant chapters. Here it is enough to note that among the provisions which do not apply to charitable etc trusts are:

(a) The power to negative or restrict the widened sections 6 and 7 powers (s 8(3)).

---

8 See 1.15.

(b) The duty to consult beneficiaries under section 11.

(c) Provisions protecting purchasers in section 16(2) and (3) – see section 16(6).

It only remains to quote subsection (5):

> (5)   No land held on charitable, ecclesiastical or public trusts shall be or be deemed to be settled land after the commencement of this Act, even if it was or was deemed to be settled land before that commencement.

2.6 Provisions consequential on section 2

These are contained in Schedule 1 of the Act. Paragraph 6, concerned with the acquisition of further property after a settlement ceases to be a SLA settlement, has already been quoted above in 2.3 – Cessation of strict settlement when no relevant property is subject to it. The remaining five paragraphs are concerned with four subjects:

- minors (who have two paragraphs);
- family charges;
- charitable ecclesiastical and public trusts;
- entailed interests.

In some cases it will be enough to summarise their effect.

Minors

Although categorised in Schedule 1 as consequential on section 2 of the Act (prohibition on new strict settlements) paragraphs 1 and 2 are more than that. Provisions dealing with the effect of dispositions to minors were in SLA section 27 and LPA section 19. Those sections are repealed and replaced with one simplified and changed statement in paragraphs 1 and 2. They are short enough to repeat.

> 1.(1)   Where after the commencement of this Act a person purports to convey a legal estate in land to a minor, or two or more minors, alone, the conveyance
> (a) is not effective to pass the legal estate, but
> (b) operates as a declaration that the land is held in trust for the minor or minors (or if he purports to convey it to the minor or minors in trust for any persons, for those persons).

(2) Where after the commencement of this Act a person purports to convey a legal estate in land to –
(a) a minor or two or more minors, and
(b) another person who is, or other persons who are, of full age,
the conveyance operates to vest the land in the other person or persons in trust for the minor or minors and the other person or persons (or if he purports to convey it to them in trust for any persons, for those persons).

(3) Where immediately before the commencement of this Act a conveyance is operating (by virtue of section 27 of the Settled Land Act 1925) as an agreement to execute a settlement in favour of a minor or minors –
(a) the agreement ceases to have effect on the commencement of this Act, and
(b) the conveyance subsequently operates instead as a declaration that the land is held in trust for the minor or minors.

2. Where after the commencement of this Act a legal estate in land would, by reason of intestacy or in any other circumstances not dealt with in paragraph 1, vest in a person who is a minor if he were a person of full age, the land is held in trust for the minor.

Family charges

Paragraph 3 replaces SLA section 1(1)(v). Its short effect is to make it clear that post 1996 instruments imposing family charges – the list is specified – operate as a declaration that the land is held in trust for giving effect to the charge.

Charitable, ecclesiastical and public trusts

Paragraph 4 replaces SLA section 29. Where a conveyance of land is held on charitable, ecclesiastical or public trusts[9] (except land to which the Universities and College Estates Act 1925 applies with its own unique regime):

(a) it must state, if neither section 37(1) nor section 39(1) of the Charities Act 1993 applies to the conveyance, that the land is held on such trusts,

(b) if neither section 37(2) nor section 39(2) of that Act has been complied with and a purchaser has notice that the land is held

---

9 See the discussion of what this phrase means at 1.15.

on such trusts, he must see that any consents or orders necessary to authorise the transaction have been obtained.

Where any trustees or the majority of any set of trustees have power to transfer or create any legal estate in the land, the estate must be transferred or created by them in the names and on behalf of the persons in whom it is vested.

Entailed interests

The creation of entailed interests is no longer possible, though existing ones continue. An attempt to create an entailed interest operates as a declaration of trust absolutely – if the declarant held a fee simple, then of that estate. More specifically:

Where a person purports by an instrument coming into operation after 1996 to grant to another person an entailed interest in real or personal property, the instrument:

(a) is not effective to grant an entailed interest, but

(b) operates instead as a declaration that the property is held in trust absolutely for the person to whom an entailed interest in the property was purportedly granted.

Where a person purports by an instrument coming into operation after 1996 to declare himself a tenant in tail of real or personal property, the instrument is not effective to create an entailed interest.

Main practical consequences of section 2

1. It is no longer possible to create a new strict settlement.

2. When drafting successive interests or other interests within SLA section 1(1), it is no longer necessary to impose an immediate binding trust for sale to avoid creating a strict settlement. New strict settlements can no longer be created.

   (Successive interests were typical of the interests which would trigger a strict settlement, but not of course the only such interests)

3. If concerned with the re-settlement of, or power of appointment under, an existing strict settlement, it is necessary to consider whether to elect to become a trust of land by provision in the re-settlement.

4. If the answer to (2) is yes, the mechanism is:

   (a) The tenant for life executes a conveyance to the trustees of land in accordance with the proviso to SLA section 17(1) as amended; and

   (b) the deed of discharge contains a statement in accordance with amended section 17 (1) that the land is subject to a trust of land by virtue of such conveyance.

5. The sale of all the land and heirlooms in an existing strict settlement will cause the strict settlement to cease.

6. Charitable, ecclesiastical and public trusts of land, whenever created, are all now trusts of land and have the benefit of the enlarged statutory powers of disposal. But they are not subject to the whole of the trusts of land regime (see text 2.5)

7. An entailed interest can no longer be created. Unless the creator has a lesser interest, an attempt to do so will create a fee simple.

Chapter 3

Abolition of the Doctrine of Conversion*

- The reasons for abolition
- Section 3 of the Act and some consequential amendments and repeals in Schedules 3 and 4
- Some practical consequences of abolition – construing and drafting documents

It does not take long to say that the doctrine of conversion is abolished. Technical stuff. It deserves no headlines. If interest to the practitioner governed the order of the chapters, it would come later. But the abolition is dealt with here, early in the book as it is early in the Act, because the content of so many later sections relies on it. If we had failed to cover it now, too many chapters would be full of references to a situation we had not yet explained, that interests formerly treated as being merely in proceeds of sale of land are now regarded as interests in land. So this chapter covers:

- brief justifications for the abolition;
- section 3 of the Act which carries out the abolition, and some consequential amendments and repeals in Schedules 3 and 4;
- a look at some of the practical consequences.

3.1   The reasons for abolition

Where a duty to sell land existed, the doctrine of conversion regarded the land as already sold. So a beneficiary's interest in such a trust was regarded as money, the proceeds of sale, and not land. Conversely where there was a trust for sale of personal property in order to acquire land, the personal property could be treated as land.

It was always an artificial distinction. Its prolonged survival was probably because it was considered to have a role in the concept of overreaching. If a beneficiary was limited to an interest in the proceeds of sale, it justified protecting a purchaser of the *land* from the interests of that beneficiary. But it was never an essential element.

---

* S 3.

Overreaching can depend as comfortably on the distinction between legal and equitable interests and the doctrine of notice. Or overreaching can take place simply because legislation says so. The redundancy of conversion is demonstrated by the fact that it can now be removed without the edifice collapsing.

As the Law Commission point out, the lack of reality in the doctrine of conversion has been recognised and mitigated by the courts. See for example *Williams and Glyn's Bank Ltd* v *Boland.*[1] So the doctrine applied for some purposes but not for others. And it hardly makes sense to tell persons absolutely interested under a trust for sale (where sale may not remotely be contemplated) that they do not own the land, that they have only an interest in the proceeds of sale. Testators who distinguished between real and personal property, not realising the subtle distinctions of the law, will fail to carry out their intentions effectively unless the court construes words used as not carrying their technical legal meaning.[2]

The abolition of the doctrine, like most of the rest of the Act, closely follows the Law Commission's recommendation.

3.2 Section 3 and some consequential amendments and repeals in Schedules 3 and 4

Abolition of doctrine of conversion

3.(1) Where land is held by trustees subject to a trust for sale, the land is not to be regarded as personal property; and where personal property is subject to a trust for sale in order that the trustees may acquire land, the personal property is not to be regarded as land.

(2) Subsection (1) does not apply to a trust created by a will if the testator died before the commencement of this Act.

(3) Subject to that, subsection (1) applies to a trust whether it is created, or arises, before or after that commencement.

Retroaction

Note that subsection (3) applies the abolition of the doctrine to trusts whenever they were created. The possible effect of that provision on the construction of words used in documents, including pre-1997

---

1 [1981] AC 487.
2 The court applied the words in their technical sense in *Re Kempthorne* [1931] 1 Ch 268, *Re Newman* [1930] 2 Ch 409 and *Re Cook* [1948] Ch 212.

documents, is considered below under 3.3 *Practical consequences.* Subsection (2), qualifying that retrospective effect for wills if the testator died before 1997, still leaves the abolition applying to wills made before 1997 if the testator dies after 1996[3]. Some parts of the Act, *e.g.* the enlarged duty to consult under section 11, do not apply at all to wills made before 1997. Section 11 necessitates no rush to review existing wills. But the abolition of conversion under section 2 does apply to pre-Act wills except where the testator dies before 1997, and we will return to that point in *Practical consequences* below.

Consequential amendments and repeals in Schedules 3 and 4

Some of the consequential amendments and repeals to statutes in Schedules 3 and 4 of the Act are needed because of the abolition of conversion. Some have a twin genesis in that abolition coupled with the wider definition of trusts of land, no longer confined to trusts for sale. Schedules 3 and 4 in full are reprinted later and there is no need to examine each provision. But one or two can be mentioned here.

"Land" in statutory definitions

In LPA section 205(1)(ix) undivided shares in land are no longer excluded from the statutory definition. They now rank as "land". References to land in that statute (or in the 1996 Act unless the context otherwise requires – see s 23(2)) now include undivided shares in land.

There are similar changes in LRA section 3(viii) and TA section 68(6). In AEA the LPA definition of land is substituted for the previous reference to the SLA definition. In all of those Acts references to "land" now include undivided shares in land. In SLA itself section 117(1)(ix) undivided shares in land remain excluded except in the phrase "trust of land". And the definition in Land Charges Act 1972 section 17(1) remains unamended.

The exclusion of interests in the proceeds of sale from the definition of "equitable interests" in LPA section 205(1)(x) of course does not reclassify beneficiaries' rights as legal; it arises from the abolition of conversion. A beneficiary's interest under a trust for sale is now in the land and no longer only in the proceeds, but it remains equitable.

---

3 Assuming in all cases that the commencement date of the Act is 1 January 1997.

3.3 Practical consequences

Construing statutes

In construing statutes we have the benefit of the considered consequential amendments and repeals in Schedules 3 and 4 of the Act. Time will tell if any consequence has been overlooked[4] but in general the phraseology used in existing statutes has been adjusted to take account of the abolition of the doctrine of conversion as well as the other changes in the 1996 Act. It is likely to be some time before the less general Acts are reprinted by legal publishers with all the amendments and repeals. In the short term it will be prudent to note up copies of those Acts with the amendments, time consuming though that task is. We hope some modest help will be given by the amended versions of LPA sections 23 to 36 and TA Part III at the rear of this book.

Drafting and construing documents

While the implications of the abolition of conversion has been thought through in statutes, in drafting and construing documents of course it has not. It will need to be remembered, since the change results in some words now having a different meaning to the meaning they bore before the Act:

For example:

A by will gives real estate to X and personal estate to Y.
If A dies before 1997 Y will get any interest in the proceeds of sale of land, X will not.
If A dies after 1996[5] there is no conversion and X will get any interest in the proceeds of sale of land.

The result of the Act on a gift where the testator dies after 1996[6] may reasonably be assumed to be in accordance with the wishes of most testators. Wills should be drafted to take into account the legal meaning of technical expressions, but it is unlikely that a prudently drawn will would actually have relied on the doctrine of conversion to produce an effect which was not immediately obvious – that a gift

---

4 Omissions can be put right by statutory instrument. See s 26.
5 Assuming here and in the preceding line that the commencement date of the Act is 1 January 1997.
6 Assuming the commencement date of the Act is 1 January 1997.

of personal estate would dispose of an interest in the proceeds of sale of land held on trust for sale, and a gift of real estate would not. If, contrary to that assumption, the drafting of any existing wills did rely on the doctrine, then the effect of the gift will be changed if the testator dies after 1996[7]. In those few cases an urgent codicil or new will is needed.

What effect does the Act have on the use of other less technical expressions *e.g.* "land"? This expression has been redefined for the purpose of LPA and other statutes but nothing in the 1996 Act spells out what "land " means in documents. If a testator, say, is entitled to the whole beneficial interest in land subject to a trust of land, a bequest of "land" would now almost certainly include that interest. The position where the testator owns only a part interest in the whole is not the subject of the Act. The question then is whether a bequest of X includes a share or part of X if that is all the testator owns.

This is not the place to examine the answer in detail, but it appears that prima facie a gift of property described in a general way will include any interest in it.[8]

Consequential adjustments to tax legislation

Two minor part repeals in Schedule 4 result from the abolition of conversion.

The part repeal of part of the Inheritance Tax Act 1984 section 237(3) relates to the Revenue's charge over certain assets to recover unpaid tax. While consequential in a sense, it nevertheless imposes an extra liability after 1996. Personal estate is excluded from the charge, and as interests in proceeds of sale under a trust for sale were personalty by the doctrine of conversion, before 1997[9] they were excluded too. With the abolition of conversion, such interests are now land and therefore subject to the charge. The beneficiary has lost an immunity; the Revenue has gained another security.

The repeal of section 110(5)(b) of the Finance Act 1991 concerns stamp duty. Land and interests in the proceeds of sale of land were excluded from the abolition of stamp duty on certain transactions. As such interests are now "land" it is unnecessary to refer to them and the words have been deleted. There is no substantive change in the transactions which attract stamp duty.

---

7 Assuming the commencement date of the Act is 1 January 1997.
8 See *e.g. Williams on Wills*, 7th ed, p 598 and cases there cited.
9 Assuming that the commencement date of the Act is 1 January 1997.

Those are the only amendments to the text of tax legislation made by the 1996 Act. It is not however difficult to think of other tax legislation which distinguishes between land and personal property. Any effect there depends on the framing of the legislation concerned. Any examination of all those implications would be lengthy and time consuming and is not the subject of this book.

Conflict of laws?

The side effects of the abolition of conversion and the 1996 Act in general will not always be negligible in matters with an international dimension. That also is too wide ranging and complex a subject to examine here. But in one area the effect may be less than suspected. Despite the doctrine of conversion, interests in land under trusts for sale are already treated in English law as immovables[10]. The change in their status from personalty to realty should, on that issue, make no difference.

Main practical consequences of section 3

1. In drafting or construing documents, a reference to personal estate will no longer include an interest in the proceeds of sale under a trust for sale.

2. (1) does not apply in a pre-1997 will, but only if the testator died before 1997.[11]

---

10 See *Re Berchtold* [1923] 1 Ch 192.
11 Assuming in both cases that the commencement date of the Act is 1 January 1997.

Chapter 4

Rapprochement of Express and Implied Trusts of Land*

- Express and statutorily implied trusts of land now share mainly the same characteristics
- The statutory power to postpone sale in an express trust for sale is now irremovable
- A trust of land without a duty to sell has been substituted for the former statutory trust in statutory provisions
- How implied and express trusts apply to concurrent and successive interests
- Drafting implications for trusts for sale

4.1 Express and statutorily implied trusts of land now share mainly the same characteristics

What sections 4 and 5 achieve is to bring the characteristics of express trusts and statutorily implied trusts closer. There is no longer a chance of excluding the implied power to postpone sale from the enlarged class of express trusts now categorised as trusts of land; and a statutorily implied trust of land, where it replaces the former statutory trusts, now consists of a power (not a duty) to sell and a power to retain. So that broadly, and subject to qualifications we shall make below, express and statutorily implied trusts of land now share the same characteristics.

That result comes from several interlinked provisions in the Act. They are:

1. The enlarged definition of "trust of land" in section 1.
2. The inclusion, in that definition, of post-1996[1] trusts of many interests previously classified within the now prohibited strict settlement. See Chapter 2.
3. The provisions of sections 4 and 5 and Schedule 2. These are the main subjects of this chapter and they are elaborated below.

---

* Ss 4 and 5 and Sched 2.
1 Assuming the commencement date of the Act is 1 January 1997.

4. The application of the powers of an absolute owner to trustees of land by section 6, discussed below in Chapter 5.

4.2 The relevance of the enlarged definition of trusts of land

Section 1 of the Act has been quoted already in Chapter 1. It defines trust of land as any trust of property consisting of or including land. "Trust" is any description of trust – express, implied, resulting or constructive – and it includes:

(a) a trust for sale; and
(b) a bare trust; and
(c) a trust created or arising before 1997.[2]

While an express trust for sale qualifies as a trust of land it is not the only trust to do so. A trust for sale is a trust of land, but a trust of land is not necessarily a trust for sale. Indeed very often it will not be a trust for sale. Two relevant changes can be identified:

(a) Reclassification of some statutory trusts as express

Some of the express trusts previously qualifying only as statutory trusts because there was no express trust for sale, now rank as express trusts of land in their own right. An express trust of land no longer needs to contain a trust for sale to come within the new regime as an express trust. For example, till 1997 statutory trusts arose on a conveyance of land to trustees, or on a declaration of trust, on trust for beneficiaries in undivided shares without interposing an express trust for sale[3]. Similarly with constructive trusts.[4] After 1996[5], because of the wide definition of trusts of land, the express trusts of that conveyance or declaration and the constructive trust are themselves trusts of land within section 1. The categories of statutorily implied trusts (replacing statutory trusts) have shrunk; the categories of express trusts of land (replacing but also incorporating express trusts for sale) have grown.

---

2 Assuming that the commencement date of the Act is 1 January 1997.
3 Or almost certainly did. It was effected not under LPA s 34, but under SLA s 36(4). See also *Bull* v *Bull* [1955] 1 QB 234 and *Emmet*, 11.148.
4 *Bull* v *Bull* [1955] 1 QB 234.
5 Assuming, here and in the last sentence, that the commencement date of the Act is 1 January 1997.

(b)   Additional trusts of land

Some trusts of land will also arise in circumstances where previously there was neither an express trust for sale nor a statutory trust – for example where there is a bare trust, trustees holding in trust for a single beneficiary absolutely entitled.

4.3   Are trusts for sale of land now abolished or replaced?

As is clear from 4.2,[6] express trusts for sale have not been abolished. They are a sub category of the more widely defined trusts of land. They have been taken over but not put into liquidation. Their continued existence is relevant to the question in 4.6 – Are statutorily implied trusts of land and express trusts of land identical?

But if express trusts for sale of land have not been abolished, trusts for sale have certainly been replaced as the central concept. The tests of whether the trustees have statutory powers, or whether the overreaching provisions of section 27(1) apply, are not whether there is a (narrow) trust for sale. They now depend on whether there is a (wider) trust of land.

Statutory trusts, which were trusts for sale, have indeed been abolished. In some cases the same circumstances will now qualify as an express trust of land. In others the statutory trust is replaced by the new statutorily implied trust, not a trust for sale at all, but a trust of the land with the absolute owner powers for the trustees given by section 6, but without a duty to sell. See 4.7 below.

4.4   The inviolate power to postpone

One of the provisions in section 4(1) which brings express and statutorily implied trusts closer together is that the power to postpone sale of land is now inviolable. Before 1997[7] the power to postpone sale of land was contained in LPA section 25, now repealed and replaced. It was subject to a contrary intention. The power to postpone could be negatived, impliedly[8] or expressly. It was displaced by an express power to postpone.[9]

---

6 And despite statements to the contrary in the parliamentary debates.
7 Assuming that the commencement date of the Act is 1 January 1997.
8 *Re Rooke* [1953] Ch 716.
9 *Re Ball* [1930] WN 111.

The same possibility of a contrary intention (here more specifically requiring an express direction to the contrary in the instrument) also applied to the statutory immunity from liability for postponing sale in the exercise of the trustees' discretion.

Now neither the statutory power to postpone, nor the immunity from liability for postponing sale, can be negatived. They cannot be removed expressly or impliedly, nor displaced by an express power (though conceivably an express power could validly go further than the statutory power.) To quote section 4(1) in full:

> 4.(1)   In the case of every trust for sale of land created by a disposition there is to be implied, despite any provision to the contrary made by the disposition, a powerfor the trustees to postpone sale of the land; and the trustees are not liable in any way for postponing sale of the land, in the exercise of their discretion, for an indefinite period.[9a]

The power to postpone so immutably given is limited, it will be noted, to cases where there is a trust for sale.

Where a trust of land does not impose a trust for sale it is not however necessary, because in that case no duty to sell exists. The trustees as part of their flexible absolute owner powers under section 6 may sell or retain as they wish in their discretion, just as in the statutorily implied trusts (see below). There is no primary duty to sell and therefore no need to qualify it with a power to postpone.

4.5 Retroaction of the section 4(1) changes to powers to postpone

The change takes effect now, that is in relation to discretions exercised after 1996, irrespective of when the trust was created or arose. Trustees who postponed sale without having power to do so before 1997[10] – because the statutory power had been negatived – could at the time have been forced to sell. If the instrument contained a direction negativing their statutory immunity they can be liable now for the results of that delay, for postponing sale at a time when they had no power to do so. But the trustees under the same trust now have an inviolable discretion to postpone and cannot be liable for exercising their discretion after 1996 to do so. The statutory provisions are in section 4(2) and (3).

9a The power is to postpone sale of the *land*. Where the trust is mixed and includes land and personalty, the trust will be a trust of land within s 1(1), but there is no implied power to postpone the sale of the personalty.

10 Assuming that the commencement date of the Act is 1 January 1997.

(2)   Subsection (1) applies to a trust whether it is created, or arises, before or after the commencement of this Act.

(3)   Subsection (1) does not affect any liability incurred by trustees before that commencement.

4.6   Are statutorily implied trusts of land and express trusts of land identical?

The short answer, again despite Parliamentary statements otherwise, is not entirely, and that is because of three factors:

1. Where an express trust comprises a trust for sale, it may possibly tilt the balance between the duty to sell and the power to postpone.
2. The section 4(1) immunity for postponing sale in a trust for sale.
3. An express trust may negative or restrict statutory powers or duties where the 1996 Act allows. In theory it can also enlarge them, but that may not often be necessary in practice because of the new comprehensive statutory powers.

The balance between the duty to sell and the power to postpone

The new statutorily implied trusts are not quite the same as the old statutory trusts. There is now no duty to sell. There is an even balance[11] between the power to sell and the power to retain (see 4.7 below).

That is not always so for express trusts. There may still be an express trust to sell – admittedly, subject to the now inviolable power to postpone, but not always on an even footing with it. These quibbles are only important if the trustees, or the trustees and beneficiaries, disagree about selling or postponing, but then could influence the court's decision under the new sections 14 and 15. The court starts with the principle that on a trust for sale there is a duty to sell and a power to postpone, and so one trustee may call on the others to perform the duty, but all must be agreed if they are to exercise the power.[12]

---

11 In practice, while balance is the avowed intention, the scales are perhaps slightly less than even. In practice retention is the status quo. A trustee content with the status quo need take no initiative. In practice a trustee who wants to sell and disagrees with other trustees needs to apply to the court under s 14. A trustee under the old law who wished to retain could of course refuse to execute a transfer, but in an LPA s 30 application there would often be a duty to sell predominating over a power to postpone.

12 See *Jones v Challenger* [1961] 1 QB 176 at 181 and *Re Mayo* [1943] Ch at 304.

That statement is only a starting point, and will not apply where a trust for sale is only a conveyancing device for co-owners. A collateral object of acquisition other than sale will override the presumption in favour of sale. The case law, some of it conflicting, is not our subject. The legislators thought the new sections 14 and 15 would "carry through the existing provisions of LPA section 30 as it has been applied and developed by the courts, with the amendments necessary to ensure that the court's powers are sufficiently broad and flexible to reflect the nature of the trust".[13]

The new section 15, unlike old LPA section 30, spells out the matters to which the court is to have regard and these include the intentions of the person who created the trust. If the settlor intends that in some circumstances sale must have priority over retention, it is better to state the intentions in the disposition than to rely solely on any surviving implication from a trust for sale. A trust for sale imposed after 1996 *could* be regarded as mere inadvertence caused by a draftsman's unfamiliarity with the 1996 Act or failure to update his precedents. The court still has a general discretion, and the intentions of the creator of the trust are only one of several matters for the court to consider.

Sections 14 and 15 are discussed in Chapter 9. But on the balance between the duty to sell and a power to postpone in an express trust for sale, the 1996 Act does not appear to change the law. Much remains as before. One or two factors are new. The power to postpone now cannot be negatived, and there are specified matters for the court to consider when making a section 14 decision. But the court has not always preferred sale to postponement, and similar reasons in the future will probably produce similar results. Subject to that, there still appears to be a prima facie distinction between the duty to sell and the power to postpone *in an express trust for sale*. The importance of the prima facie principle should, however, not be over stressed. The Parliamentary debate seems to have proceeded on the basis that it no longer applies.[14] It may well be the courts will give

---

13 The words quoted are those of the Lord Advocate in proposing the second reading in the House of Lords.

14 See for example the comments on the second reading of the Bill in the House of Lords on 1 March 1996 of Lord Mishcon, complimented by the Lord Advocate on his extensive knowledge and understanding of this field of law. "Under the new style trust, the trustees ... will hold the legal estates on trust with a power to sell and a power to retain the land rather than having the primary duty of sale as in the existing law." Lord's Mishcon's comment itself was of course not one of the Minister or promoter within the *Pepper v Hart* principle.

it very little weight if they can be persuaded under the *Pepper* v *Hart*[15] decision to apply an evident intention of the legislators.

The section 4(1) immunity for postponement in a trust for sale

The inviolable section 4(1) immunity for postponing sale in a trust for sale (see 4.5) is of course to balance the duty to sell. Do the words "in the exercise of their discretion" prevent it from overriding the general and section 6(5) duty to the beneficiaries? (See 5.3 and 10.1). If not, it appears to give trustees for sale an immunity not given to other trustees.

The ability to negative or restrict statutory powers or duties in an express trust

In several places the Act enables a trust "created by a disposition"[16] to contract out of powers or duties under the Act. And a disposition creating a trust of land may require consents impossible in a statutorily implied trust. The relevant sections are:

(a) section 8(1) (negativing or restricting powers or duties under ss 6 or 7);
(b) section 8(2) (requiring consents for the exercise of ss 6 or 7 powers);
(c) section 11(2)(a) (negativing or restricting the section 11 duty to consult beneficiaries);
(d) section 21(5) (negativing or restricting the ss 19 and 20 powers of beneficiaries to direct appointment and retirement of trustees).

4.7   Substitution of a trust of land without a duty to sell for the former statutory trust for sale in statutory provisions

Statutory trusts were defined in LPA section 35 and arose under certain sections of that Act, AEA and one more specific piece of legislation, the Reverter of Sites Act 1987. Broadly they consisted of a trust for sale of land and they were subject to the power to postpone in LPA section 25.

---

15 [1993] AC 593.
16 See the discussion of this phrase at 1.17.

They have been abolished and replaced. In general terms section 5 substitutes a trust of land (without a duty to sell). That general statement is subject to the more detailed provisions outlined below amending individual sections in Schedule 2. It should also be considered in conjunction with the absolute owner powers now conferred on trustees of land by sections 6 to 8 – see Chapter 5.

4.8 The general provision – section 5

Section 5(1) contains the general reference already quoted to a trust of the land (without a duty to sell), and it incorporates Schedule 2. It reads:

> 5.(1) Schedule 2 has effect in relation to statutory provisions which impose a trust for sale of land in certain circumstances so that in those circumstances there is instead a trust of the land (without a duty to sell).

4.9 The specific provisions – Schedule 2

Many of the amendments detailed in Schedule 2 do not need to be reproduced in this chapter. Their general effect is to replace references to the statutory trusts or trusts for sale by references to trusts for the persons interested in the land. That applies to:

- LPA section 34 (dispositions to tenants in common);
- LPA section 36 (joint tenancies).
(both reproduced as amended at Appendix 7)

In other legislation, the subject matter requires wider ranging amendments. This is the case for the following, although still following the basic principle of replacing the statutory trust for sale with statutorily implied trusts without a duty to sell:

- LPA section 31 (mortgaged property held by trustees after redemption barred)
(reproduced as amended at Appendix 7);
- AEA section 33 (intestacy).

One statute does not form part of the general property legislation and special circumstances make an unmodified trust of land regime unsuitable. This is the Reverter of Sites Act 1987. The amendments have been tailored so that the trustees can sell, holding the proceeds for the putative beneficiaries but without having to consult them or allow them to occupy the land, and with a provision for meeting necessary costs.

4.10 The absence of the trust for sale does not make the land subject to a strict settlement.

Under SLA it was of course important to impose an immediate binding trust for sale if the strict settlement machinery was to be avoided. Failure to do so for successive interests and many other interests produced a strict settlement. Now that the statutory trust for sale has been removed, someone perceived a possible problem. To remove doubts, section 5(2) provides:

> (2)   Section 1 of the Settled Land Act 1925 does not apply to land held on any trust arising by virtue of that Schedule (so that any such land is subject to a trust of land).

4.11 How implied and express trusts apply respectively to concurrent and successive interests

Concurrent interests

One of the main objects behind the new regime is to make co-ownership more realistic, to reflect that most co-ownership of land is for providing a home rather than as an investment. This is achieved partly by the removal of the former mandatory trust for sale with power to postpone (which in express trusts was removable under the pre-1997[17] law); and the substitution of a regime with broadly similar characteristics (whether the trust is express or statutorily implied) and which contain a more evenly balanced power to sell and power to retain. That general statement is of course subject to the minor qualifications discussed already in 4.6.

What are the mechanisms applied by the new regime to concurrent interests?[18] (A similar look at successive interests will be carried out below.)

---

17 Assuming that the commencement date of the Act is 1 January 1997.
18 In all the following references to ("before 1997" or "after 1996", the assumption is that the date of commencement of the Act is 1 January 1997.

(a) **Land is conveyed directly to beneficiaries in undivided shares**
Before 1997
LPA 1925 section 34(2) imposed a statutory trust.
It consisted of a trust for sale with power to postpone.
After 1996
Now there is still a trust implied by statute; not a "statutory trust" properly so called, but the trust for the benefit of the persons interested implied by the amended section 34(2). No trust for sale, but within the definition of "trusts of land".

(b) **Land is conveyed to trustees on trust for beneficiaries in [undivided] shares without the interposition of an express trust for sale**
Before 1997
SLA 1925 section 36(4) imposed a statutory trust.[19] As before, it consisted of a trust for sale with power to postpone.
After 1996
No statutory trust now arises; this express trust is now within the definition of "trust of land".

(c) **The legal estate is beneficially limited to or held in trust for any persons as joint tenants**
Before 1997
LPA 1925 s.36(1), if the disposition did not create a strict settlement, imposed a statutory trust for sale – a trust for sale with power to postpone.
After 1996
LPA 1925 section 36(1) remains unrepealed, the only amendment being to replace the phrase "on trust for sale" with "in trust".
For any express limitation other than an express trust there is only the trust imposed by LPA section 36(1).
For an express trust for joint tenants there is an odd duality. The express trust itself qualifies as a trust of land. But there is an implied trust under section 36(1) too. For most practical purposes the distinction and the overlap do not matter. See however the possibility discussed in 4.6 – that in an express trust the duty to sell, absent from the statutorily implied trust, may be present.

---

19 Or almost certainly did. It was effected not under LPA s 34, but under SLA s 36(4). See also *Bull* v *Bull* [1955] 1 QB 234 and *Emmet*, 11.148.

Successive interests

For example, a conveyance to A and B on trust for C for life.

Before 1997[20]
A strict settlement was created. There was no express trust for sale neither was there a statutory trust for sale. Without a trust for sale the land was settled land.
After 1996
Now such a disposition would create a trust of land.

4.12 Drafting implications

The trust for sale

Many sections of the Act have implications for drafting. We will look at the implications of sections 6 to 8 , the general and other powers of trustees, separately in Chapter 5. These comments here are mainly limited to the changes to the trust for sale made by sections 4 and 5, although since Part 1 of the Act is an interlinked jigsaw of pieces, they depend partly on other changes too.

Should post-Act documents contain trusts for the sale of land or not? It is reassuring that on this question the Act does not appear to lay traps for the unwary. Those who in future impose trusts for sale, or who omit trusts for sale, will include:

(a) those completely unaware of the implications of the Act or that trusts for the sale of land are unnecessary;

(b) people under the impression that all trusts for the sale of land have been abolished[21] or are invalid or illegal;

(c) those who have made a considered and informed decision on whether to impose an express trust for sale.

None is likely to make a serious mistake on this issue based on anything in the new Act. All will come up smelling of roses. In some ways it may not matter.

---

20 Assuming in both cases, here and in the next paragraph, that the commencement date of the Act is 1 January 1997.
21 Apparently like the Lord Advocate in moving the second reading of the Bill in the House of Lords on 1 March 1996. But on that occasion he was no doubt avoiding undue elaboration in the interest of clarity.

But it would be a pity nevertheless if the profession does not make a concerted effort to fulfil one of the ambitions of the Law Commission – not only to make documents easier to explain, but even, in a simple case of co-ownership, capable of being understood by lay persons without explanation. That can hardly be said of the archetypal trust for sale.

How simple the document can be must partly depend on the nature of the transaction. In discretionary or other complex trusts the draftsman will need to consider whether any of the standard powers and duties need to negatived, restricted or enlarged. An express trust for sale may have a marginal influence in supporting a settlor's or co-purchaser's wish that in some circumstances the property should be sold.[22]

In wills we are straying beyond sections 4 and 5, but section 18 gives personal representatives broadly the same rights powers and duties as those given by the Act to trustees. There is no need to create a trust for sale of residue or of other property given to more than one beneficiary. It is perhaps time to review some of the archaic and well worn phrases.

And in a simple case of co-ownership, especially the purchase of a matrimonial or quasi matrimonial home, an express trust for sale is rarely justified. That is probably the practice already, since the purchase document is usually the simple Land Registry Form 19 or Form 19 under Rule 72. Indeed in those simple cases it will not often be necessary or appropriate to mention that word "trust". It connotes to most clients the suggestion, inaccurate in this context, of a life interest. LPA section 34(2) will operate to create a statutorily implied trust where land is conveyed to tenants in common, and section 36(1) will do the same for beneficial joint tenants.

It is true that there is a linked task, necessary[23] if sometimes neglected – defining the type of co-ownership, joint tenants or tenants in common, and if the latter, quantifying their interests. We only mention it here because performing that task might involve the same complex explanations of technical terms we have been trying to avoid. Completing the survivor can/cannot give a receipt line on Form 19(JP) does not quantify a tenant in common's interest nor is it

---

22 See 4.6 and 9.3.

23 See *Springette* v *Defoe* [1992] 2 FLR 388 at 396 and *Huntingford* v *Hobbs* [1993] 1 FLR 736 at 748.

24 See *Harwood* v *Harwood* [1991] 2 FLR 274; *Springette* v *Defoe* [1992] 2 FLR 388 and *Huntingford* v *Hobbs* [1993] 1 FLR 736.

conclusive between the parties whether there is a joint tenancy or tenancy in common.[24] A declaration of trust or separate sharing agreement is preferable to wording in a transfer which will be filed away at the registry. It can be drafted without using the word "trusts". It is also possible, if not quite as easy, to replace "tenant" with a synonym less likely to cause misunderstanding.

The power to postpone

In any trust for sale of land there is an irremovable statutory power to postpone. There will usually be no need for an express one. In a trust of land which does not contain a trust for sale there is no primary duty of sale; the trustees may sell or retain. Again there seems to be nothing to be gained by inserting an express power to postpone.

The main practical consequences of sections 4 and 5

1. The former statutory trusts [for sale] – in the reduced number of cases where they still apply – are replaced by a statutorily implied trust without a duty to sell.

2. The statutory power to postpone is implied in all trusts for sale of land and cannot be negatived.

3. In drafting, a trust for sale may still be employed, although usually it will be inappropriate.

Chapter 5

Powers of Trustees of Land*

- New statutory absolute owner powers for trustees of land
- The rights of the beneficiaries still must influence the exercise of the powers
- The statutory power to purchase land
- Excluding or restricting the statutory powers
- Drafting implications

5.1 Powers under the old regime and their limitations

This is not the place for a full account of the powers of trustees for sale under LPA section 28. They can be studied at length in *Emmet* if a past exercise appears invalid. They are of course the combined powers of a tenant for life and trustees of the settlement under SLA. They remain relevant in checking pre-1997 titles of unregistered land. For the future, that is after 1996[1] and with one exception, they are replaced by the wide ranging provisions of section 6 of the new Act. The exception is that the special, sometimes inconvenient and sometimes overlooked, requirements of the law about trustees' powers of attorney live on. They are discussed in Chapter 10. They have been augmented by new possibilities of delegation under section 9, discussed in Chapter 6.

The essential problem about LPA section 28 and SLA tenant for life powers was that they were complex, fragmented and although wide, in some respects limited. This was so generally recognised that few professionally drawn trusts for sale did not extend them with wider powers, for example and most commonly, all the powers of an absolute owner. A few instances can be given of the limitations of the old statutory powers:

1. When tenants for life or trustees for sale sold, the sale had to be at the best price. This appears to mean they were legally obliged to gazzump where for an individual gazzumping would

---

* Ss 6, 7 and 8.
1 Assuming in both cases that the commencement date of the Act is 1 January 1997.

be regarded as unmitigated greed.[2] The duty to obtain the best price made options dubious, despite the powers to grant options in SLA section 51.[3]

2. Although there were powers to buy land for investment, the courts often treated these restrictively. In *Re Power's Will Trusts*[4] trustees had an express power to invest as an absolute owner. It was held the power did not justify buying land to enable a beneficiary to occupy it. In *Re Wakeman*[5] it was held that, once all the land was sold, the trust for sale ceased[6] and with it the power to invest.

3. Leases could not be granted for more than 50 years (except for forestry, mining or building leases).

4. The statutory power to mortgage was so limited as to be almost useless. It did not authorise mortgaging land to finance its purchase.

These limitations were considerably mitigated in practice:

(a) Enlargements of powers were commonly included in settlements, trusts for sale, conveyances to co-owners and professionally drawn wills. But absolute owner powers by themselves were not always enough – see *Re Power* quoted above.

(b) Even if there is no enlargement, TA 1925 section 17 provides a mortgagee is not concerned to see that money is wanted or as to its application.

(c) Where trustees were beneficially interested, they could combine their legal and beneficial titles to mortgage or lease

---

2 *Battle v Saunders* [1950] 2 All ER 193. The case preceded the terminology of "gazzumping". Fiduciary owners of course owe an overriding duty to act in the interests of the beneficiaries irrespective of the "best price" issue.
3 See *Emmet on Title* 19th ed para 2.122.
4 [1947] Ch 572.
5 [1945] Ch 177. Contrast however *Re Wellstead's Will Trusts* [1949] Ch 296.
6 Compare the express provisions to end a strict settlement in TLATA s 2(4) when all relevant property is sold, discussed earlier at 2.4. That however concerns the ending of the trust's classification as a strict settlement, not the ending of the trust.

freely. That however meant deducing and investigating their beneficial title.

(d) For registered land the registered proprietor has full powers of disposition subject to any restrictions on the register. In practice, which means the practice of the registry, that usually operates to give purchasers from co-owners of registered land freedom from the limitations discussed above.

In the case of a strict settlement a restriction in Form 9 requires capital money to be paid to (named) trustees of the settlement. It also provides that except under an order of the registrar, no disposition by the proprietor of the land is to be registered unless authorised by SLA. This brings the limitations of the powers firmly to the attention of a buyer.

That is not so however for trusts for sale. Unless the transfer or application has indicated that a sole survivor can give a valid receipt for capital money, the registry will note a restriction in Form 62: "No disposition by a sole proprietor of the land (not being a trust corporation) under which capital money arises is to be registered except under an order of the Registrar or of the Court". But that is all. No reference, it will be noticed, to any limitation in the powers of the proprietor under SLA or LPA section 28. The registry regard it as the duty of the applicants for registration to apply for restrictions if powers of disposition are *expressly* limited or require consents, but not apparently to reflect the LPA section 28 limitations. The circular reasoning is that under LRA sections 18, 21 and 25 registered proprietors have full powers in the absence of a restriction in the register.[7] The practice of the registry enables trustees of registered land to make dispositions outside their LPA section 28 powers. It is odd that the practice applied to settled land was not applied to trusts for sale, where trustees enjoy the same powers and are subject to the same limitations. Whether or not that is right, a purchaser can apparently take the absence of the restriction at face value.[8] We are aware of no reported case of the registrar refusing to register a disposition by co-proprietors on the ground of LPA section 28

---

7 See Ruoff and Roper, *Registered Conveyancing* (looseleaf) para 32-05.
8 But note (on a slightly different point) *Walia v Michael Naughton Ltd* [1985] 1 WLR 1115 where the existence of more than one proprietor meant they were trustees, despite the absence of the LRA s 58(3) (Form 62) restriction on the register. A purchaser was entitled to reject a general power of attorney.

limitations unrecorded as restrictions on the register. Although in unregistered titles the limitations were similar, the Land Registry apply an approach to strict settlements which is different from the way they treat trusts for sale. After 1996[9] it will not matter because, express provision apart, trustees of land now have absolute owner powers.

5.2 The new absolute owner powers – the general provision

The new powers are dealt with in sections 6 to 8 of the Act. The detail of those sections and their subsections is commented on below; here we deal with the broad brush general provision in subsection (1).

> **General powers of trustees**
> 6. (1) For the purpose of exercising their functions as trustees, the trustees of land have in relation to the land subject to the trust all the powers of an absolute owner.

"All the powers of an absolute owner"

The phrase not only reproduces one often used in dispositionary enlargements of the former restricted powers. It puts into practice the Law Commission's aim of making the scheme of powers as broadly based as possible. The Act departs from the power-by-power approach of SLA and uses one comprehensive phrase instead. It is one clearly appropriate where the trustees and the owners of the beneficial interests are the same. It has also customarily been used in framing settlements where the legal and beneficial ownerships do not coincide.

The new powers may be limited by the disposition. Settlors who consider them too wide will need to do so. See 5.7. But it is that way round. Settlors now have to limit the new wide statutory power if they wish, instead of enlarging the former limited statutory power. If they do nothing, the wide power will apply.

The subsection goes beyond merely enlarging the powers. It is the foundation of the new balance in trusts of land between the power to sell and the power to retain, so often stressed in the Law Commission report and the parliamentary debate. Yet nowhere is that principle expressed in those words in the new Act. You have to extract it from section 6(1). It depends upon the fact that, subject to

---

9 Assuming that the commencement date of the Act is 1 January 1997.

restrictions in the Act or the disposition or general equitable principles, trustees of land can now do what they like, including retaining or selling.

How far do absolute owner powers go? *Re Power* is an example of a case where the court did not treat absolute powers as absolute. The effect of that decision in relation to buying land for occupation is reversed by section 6(4), discussed in 5.4 below, but are there other implicit limitations to the phrase? Can trustees A and B for example, who hold on trust for C and D, give valuable land away without consideration to E?

There is an overall duty, applying both under the rules of equity and under the Act, to exercise powers properly in the interests of the beneficiaries. See 5.3 below. If the gift to E broke that duty the trustees would be liable to C and D for breach of trust. The donee E would not be a purchaser and so would be unprotected by LPA section 27 or section 16 of the 1996 Act. He would be bound by the trusts in favour of C and D. A purchaser from E depends on protection by LPA section 27 or section 16 of the 1996 Act, discussed in Chapter 10.

"For the purpose of exercising their functions as trustees"

The reference to absolute owner powers is preceded by this phrase. It did not occur in the now repealed and replaced LPA section 28, nor in the Law Commission's draft Bill. We can infer that the insertion of the phrase is deliberate and not merely explanatory. Functions of trustees or functions as trustees are phrases used repeatedly through the Act. They occur not only in this present section 6 but also in sections 9 (delegation), 10 (consents), 11 (consultation), 14 (power of court) 18 (personal representatives) and 20 (incapable trustees). "Function" is not defined either in the Act or in LPA. A typical dictionary meaning of "function" would be an office or purpose, or perhaps more relevantly here, specialised activity of someone holding a particular office. In this Act it could mean office and it could mean all those acts which a trustee must or may carry out – duties as well as powers. Its meaning is wider than "power". The reference is to "functions as trustees" generally, not "functions as trustees of land". See the further discussion at 1.16. But the powers must be "in relation to the land". See below.

It is difficult to be certain, but the subsection's opening phrase probably means no more than that, in exercising their office, trustees have all the powers of an absolute owner.

"In relation to the land"

Functions "in relation to the land subject to the trust" are within the powers. They apply to disposals of that land. Subject to the usual duty to act in the interests of the beneficiaries there is a large range of activities the trustees are authorised to carry out which would not have come within the SLA powers of a tenant for life. To carry out, for example, not only improvements within the old SLA powers, but outside it too.

Are there powers of investment elsewhere?

The new powers which are to be those of an absolute owner, are those "in relation to the land subject to the trust". And there are express powers to invest in new land (see 5.4). But what of investment elsewhere? "Trusts of land" is defined in section 1(1) (a) to include trusts which include land, not necessarily exclusively. See Chapter 1, 1.10. Do the absolute owner powers enable trustees of land (as defined in the Act) to invest in personal property and in doing so to disregard the Trustee Investments Act? The answer is no because of those words "in relation to the land". The absolute owner powers can only be exercised in relation to the land.

It is proposed to deregulate the Trustee Investments Act 1961. If investing in property other than land, then in the absence of a dispositionary wide power of investment, it will not be possible to ignore the current restrictions in the 1961 Act until the deregulation is completed. That may not coincide with the commencement of the 1996 Act.

5.3   Having regard to the rights of beneficiaries

The new absolute owner powers for trustees of land do not exist in isolation. They are subject, as the Lord Advocate put it, "to the requirement to act in accordance with ... the general equitable duties attaching to the position of trustee, and in particular to have regard to the interests of beneficiaries in exercising such powers". He was echoing comments in the Law Commission report. Dicta apply similar statements to trustees' powers in pre-1997[10] law.

In the 1996 Act, to make assurance doubly sure, the draftsman has spelled out the duty in section 6(5).

---

10 Assuming that the commencement date of the Act is 1 January 1997.

(5) In exercising the powers conferred by this section trustees shall have regard to the rights of the beneficiaries.

Notice that the subsection refers only to the "rights" of the beneficiaries. This may be narrower than the "interests" of the beneficiaries which the Lord Advocate quoted as relevant to the equitable principles already established in case law. So while the new provision is declaratory, it is probably not exhaustive. For further discussion of the general equitable duty, see 10.1.

Section 6(5) applies only to the "powers conferred by this section". Further powers of partition are granted by a separate section 7. Does this mean that in partitioning land trustees can ignore section 6(5) and ride roughshod over the interests of the beneficiaries? No, because as well as the overriding equitable principles which would apply, section 7 requires the consent of each beneficiary to be obtained. An extension of section 6(5) would be otiose.

Relationship of section 6(5) with section 11 (the duty to consult)

Chapter 7 covers section 11 of the Act, which imposes a duty to consult certain beneficiaries[11] and to give effect to their wishes. It is narrower than section 6(5) in the class of beneficiaries to whom it relates, but, once established, it imposes wider responsibilities on the trustees. The two duties will sometimes overlap. It is possible for the section 11 duty to consult to be negatived or restricted by the disposition. Indeed, as we say in 5.6 below, it is theoretically possible for the section 6(5) to be negatived too. But where, as will usually be the case, section 6(5) is left intact, it is a duty to be remembered by advisers who have negatived section 11. There is still a duty under section 6(5) and often it will be difficult to have regard to the rights of beneficiaries without consultation with them. Although the section 6(5) duty to "have regard to" those rights is lower than the section 11 duty to give effect to their wishes.

5.4 The power to purchase land

Comprehensive express rights are now included in section 6(3) and (4). The old SLA arbitrary minimum of a 60 year unexpired term for leaseholds has gone. The trustees must of course exercise their

---

11 Those beneficially entitled to an interest in possession.

discretion according to what is reasonably prudent and in the interests of the beneficiaries. Some of the limitations imposed by case law have been eradicated too. The cases demonstrate that even absolute owner powers may not go far enough, especially in buying land. Examples restricting the purchase of land by trustees have been mentioned in 5.1 above. An express power to invest as an absolute owner did not justify buying land to enable a beneficiary to occupy it (*Re Power's Will Trusts*[12]). In *Re Wakeman*[13] it was held that once all the land was sold, the trust for sale ceased and with it the power to invest.

The effect of both decisions is now reversed. *Re Power* is reversed by section 6(3) and (4).

> (3)   The trustees of land have power to purchase a legal estate in any land in England or Wales.
>
> (4)   The power conferred by subsection (3) may be exercised by trustees to purchase land –
>
> (a) by way of investment,
>
> (b) for occupation by any beneficiary, or
>
> (c) for any other reason.

Re Wakeman is reversed by section 17(1). Trustees may still purchase new land even if their original holding has all been sold.

> 17.(1) Section 6(3) applies in relation to trustees of a trust of proceeds of sale of land as in relation to trustees of land.

5.5   Conveying to beneficiaries and partition by trustees

A and B hold land in trust for C and D who are of full age and capacity and absolutely entitled as tenants in common. Section 6(2) enables them to convey it to C and D together whether C and D have required them to do so or not; section 7 enables them to convey it separately, that is partition the land between the two beneficiaries, but in that case only with the consent of both beneficiaries. Two separate options for the same circumstances, although the right to convey without partitioning is not dependent on the beneficiaries being interested as tenants in common. There are detailed differences

---

12 [1947] Ch 572.
13 [1945] Ch 177. Contrast however *Re Wellstead's Will Trusts* [1949] Ch 296.

in the circumstances in which the two powers apply. The circumstances overlap, but they do not wholly coincide.

Conveyance to the beneficiaries – section 6(2)

Before 1997[14] trustees for sale of land had no statutory power of appropriation, although case law sometimes found ways round.[15] Now the power is formalised in section 6(2).

The qualifying circumstances for the power to apply can be considered separately:

(a) There must be land subject to a trust of land. That almost goes without saying.

(b) Each of the beneficiaries interested in the land must be:
  (i) a person of full age and capacity; (the word "person" includes a corporation and the reference to age does not exclude it.[16])
  (ii) who is absolutely entitled to the land. This raises at least two difficulties.

  The first is that "each" of the beneficiaries must be absolutely entitled to the land. It suggests that each of two or more must own the whole. That would be absurd. A less absurd way to treat the phrase is that the beneficiaries must together be entitled to the land, and each must have an absolute interest.

  The second difficulty is the meaning of absolute.[16a] The phrase is "absolutely entitled", not "absolutely and beneficially entitled" (defined in s 22(2) and see 1.11). The words "(whether beneficially interested or not)" in the Law Commission's draft section for partition, now section 7, are absent. "Absolute" can suggest the quantum of the interest, not the capacity of the grantee. "Absolutely" is not a word which means the same in all circumstances. In *In re Ray's Will Trusts*[16b] a gift was to the person who at the testator's death should be abbess of a certain convent, "absolutely". While holding that

---

14 Assuming that the commencement date of the Act is 1 January 1997.
15 See *Re Beverly* [1901] 1 Ch 681.
16 See *In re Earl of Carnarvon's Settled Estates* [1927] 1 Ch 138.
16a See further discussion at 1.11.
16b [1936] 1 Ch 520.

"absolutely" meant free of some fetter or trust in some form, Clauson J held that the gift was not beneficial as it had to be used for the purposes of the convent. But in the following section 7(2) "absolutely" is used in contrast with "in trust", suggesting that there and presumably in section 6 too the draftsman meant absolutely and beneficially. If fiduciary absolute owners of a beneficial interest are excluded it is strange, given the flexible meanings of "absolute" that the phrase defined in section 22(2) was not used. Certainly life or residuary interests do not qualify, and still less where there are objects of discretionary trusts unless an appointment has been made making them absolutely entitled.

The subsection refers to beneficiaries in the plural, but there is nothing to show a contrary intention to the Interpretation Act presumption that singular includes plural and vice versa. Section 6(2) applies to a sole beneficiary as it does to two or more.

At this stage we can quote the subsection in full.

> 6 .(2) Where in the case of any land subject to a trust of land each of the beneficiaries interested in the land is a person of full age and capacity who is absolutely entitled to the land, the powers conferred on the trustees by subsection (1) include the power to convey the land to the beneficiaries even though they have not required the trustees to do so; and where land is conveyed by virtue of this subsection -
>
> (a) the beneficiaries shall do whatever is necessary to secure that it vests in them, and
>
> (b) if they fail to do so, the court may make an order requiring them to do so.

Two further provisions of the subsection can be noted:

1. The power exists irrespective of request by the beneficiaries. Of course the trustees must have regard to the rights of the beneficiaries under section 6(5), but it is hard to see the beneficiaries would often be prejudiced by having the land vested in them. There is also a duty to consult under section 11 (see Chap 7) if that has not been excluded from the trust. It goes further by requiring the trustees to give effect to the wishes of the beneficiaries so far as consistent with the general interest of the trust. See however (2) below which strongly suggests the conveyance may be made without consent.

2. Under section 6(2)(a) the beneficiaries must co-operate in having the land vested in them, and if they fail to do so, the court has power to make an order (s 6(2)(b)). Co-operation is not usually needed for an unregistered conveyance without consideration to take effect, but of course a transfer of registered land needs an application by the new owner to the registry.

Partition by trustees – section 7

Section 7 deals with the corresponding right to partition. It replaces LPA section 28(3). It is simpler to start by quoting section 7 and to continue by noting its differences with section 6(2).

7.(1)   The trustees of land may, where beneficiaries of full age are absolutely entitled in undivided shares to land subject to the trust, partition the land, or any part of it, and provide (by way of mortgage or otherwise) for the payment of any equality money.

(2)   The trustees shall give effect to any such partition by conveying the partitioned land in severalty (whether or not subject to any legal mortgage created for raising equality money), either absolutely or in trust, in accordance with the rights of those beneficiaries.

(3)   Before exercising their powers under subsection (2) the trustees shall obtain the consent of each of those beneficiaries.

(4)   Where a share in the land is affected by an incumbrance, the trustees may either give effect to it or provide for its discharge from the property allotted to that share as they think fit.

(5)   If a share in the land is absolutely vested in a minor, subsections (1) to (4) apply as if he were of full age, except that the trustees may act on his behalf and retain land or other property representing his share in trust for him.

The beneficiaries
Here, as opposed to section 6(2):

(a) Unlike section 6(2), section 7(1) refers to "beneficiaries", not "each of the beneficiaries". The difference suggests there may be a distinction; that perhaps partitioning does not require all of the beneficiaries to be absolutely entitled in undivided shares, only some. (Although it is of course only those beneficiaries who would qualify for partition.) Say for example that a two thirds share under a trust of land is held by A and B in undivided shares absolutely, and the other third share held in trust for C for life with remainder to D. The argument would run that the trustees could partition in respect of A and B, the beneficiaries absolutely entitled.

But that would effectively partition the remaining third too, because the trustees would continue holding not the whole, but the remaining third of the land on the outstanding trusts. The argument produces a strange result, and may not be the correct interpretation. But if it were not intended it is odd that the reference in section 6(2) to "each" of the beneficiaries was not repeated. "Each", at first sight, is more apt for section 7(1), which is concerned with undivided shares, than it is for section 6(2), which is not. Yet it is used in section 6(2) but not in section 7(1).

(b) To qualify for section 7 the beneficiaries must be entitled to undivided shares. Beneficial joint tenancies will not do. If partition for joint tenants is required severance is needed first. Plurality is not an issue here – there must, by the very nature of partition, be concurrent interests.

(c) There is no insistence here that the beneficiary must have capacity. Lack of capacity of a beneficiary will not rule out partition. Presumably consents can be obtained under the Mental Health Act and the conveyance pursuant to the partition can be dealt with by conveying to a trustee or trustees under section 7(2). The apparent requirement for full age is effectively negatived by section 7(5) – the trustees may consent for the minor and hold the partitioned land on his behalf.

Equality money

This is an issue in partition, not of course in section 6(2). Suitable provisions are included for securing it.

Consent

The consent of the beneficiaries must be obtained. Here we have the word "each", but it qualifies "those" beneficiaries – presumably the beneficiaries mentioned in section 7(1), who may perhaps not constitute all the beneficiaries. Consent not to section 7(1), the partition itself and provision for payment of equality money, but the exercise by the trustees of their powers under section 7(2), the conveyance pursuant to the partition. It probably comes to the same thing. There appears to be no statutory requirement the consent should be in writing, but clearly it would be prudent for it to be so recorded.

5.6 Exclusion and restriction of powers

Exclusion and restriction by the disposition – section 8(1) and (3)

The wide powers granted to trustees by sections 6 and 7 are not compulsory. Where the trust of land was created by a disposition, and unless the trust is charitable, ecclesiastical or public[17], they can be negatived or restricted by the disposition. "Created by a disposition", that phrase recurring in the Act is discussed at 1.17. "Negatived or restricted" because the exclusion is "in so far as provision to the effect that they do not apply is made" by the disposition. The exclusion can be partial or apparently total (but on total exclusion see below). This becomes another issue for the settlor and draftsman to consider, only now it is whether and how to restrict wide powers, not whether and how to enlarge restricted ones as it was before. Exclusion will not often be apt for co-purchasers, but occasionally in special circumstances it may warrant consideration there too. See the elaboration of the point in "Drafting Implications" in 5.7 below.

> 8.(1) Sections 6 and 7 do not apply in the case of a trust of land created by a disposition in so far as provision to the effect that they do not apply is made by the disposition.
>
> (3) Subsection (1) does not apply in the case of charitable, ecclesiastical or public trusts.

The possibilities of subsection (1) go further than the obvious. One duty under section 6 is normally uncontentious- that under subsection (5) to have regard to the rights of the beneficiaries. Yet section 8(1) clearly provides that section 6 – and that must mean all or any of section 6 – does not apply to the extent that the disposition says so.

In real life settlors would be unwise to negative section 6(5). It does no more than than encapsulate the essence of what a trustee is supposed to do – look after the interests of the beneficiaries. But a settlor hellbent on exemption would need to be advised that exclusion of section 6(5) alone would achieve little. There would still be the overlapping general equitable duty which the court would not regard as negatived except in the clearest possible terms. And would be understandably reluctant even then.

---

17 See 1.15 for discussion of this phrase.

One last question. Can the exclusion of the powers validly be total? A, a megalomaniac with dynastic ambitions, wishes to preserve his mansion for his family indefinitely. He creates by disposition a trust of land which is not a trust for sale and which does not cause a statutorily implied trust to arise. He gives his 18 month old son a life interest with a remainder which does not vest in interest till 21 years after that son's death. He excludes all sections 6 and 7 powers.

In 50 years time the trustees desperately need to sell. They cannot get beneficiaries' authority because all interests are not vested. How can they sell? An application to the court for an order under section 14 may not be successful – the court's power is to make an order relating to the exercise by the trustees of any of their "functions" – yes that word again see 1.16 – and here the settlor has removed sale from the powers, and presumably therefore from the functions, of the trustees. Would the trustees have any remedy other than applying to the court under TA section 57 for power to sell?

Perhaps there is some principle of public policy which makes total exclusion invalid. But if not, it could just be that the welcome reforms and simplification made by the 1996 Act have perhaps inadvertently facilitated a return to virtual inalienability of land, if that is a course settlors choose. Inalienability, that is, unless a court order is obtained conferring power to sell. It was the problems flowing from the absence of powers to dispose, which led to the 19th century reforming legislation culminating in 1925. A key feature of that legislation was to make land freely alienable to avoid the social ills which were perceived otherwise to have followed. It is that legislation which has now been drastically revised, and in the case of future strict settlements strangled at birth.

Requiring consents before the powers are exercised

In LPA the validity of requiring consents to the exercise of powers is implicit rather than explicit. It was recognised by the provisions in section 26(1) enabling in favour of a purchaser the trustees to perm any two from more consents.

The 1996 Act makes the possibility of consents explicit. The requirement, if it is to be imposed, must be in the "disposition creating the trust" (see 1.17). Linked sections are section 10 (replacing LPA section 58(1) – in favour of a purchaser two consents are enough) (see Chap 7), section 14(2)(a) – power of the court to dispense with consent (see Chap 9), LRA section 58(1) (power of registrar to enter restrictions recording *inter alia* requirements for consent) and possibly LRA section 94(4) as inserted by TLATA 1996 Schedule 3 paragraph 5(8)(c) (further restrictions to protect the rights of beneficiaries).

> 8(2) If the disposition creating such a trust makes provision requiring any consent to be obtained to the exercise of any power conferred by section 6 or 7, the power may not be exercised without that consent.

Other enactments

Sections 6 and 8 contain several slightly confusing references to the effect of other enactments, rules and orders and they are all grouped together here.

Section 8(4) was inserted in committee, mainly because of concerns of the possible effect of the 1996 Act on the Pensions Act 1995. Its aim was to ensure that the ability given by section 8(1) to negative or restrict absolute owner powers, and the ability under section 8(2) to make their exercise subject to consents, do not affect the Pensions Act 1995 section 35(4). This stops the powers of occupational pension scheme trustees from being fettered by provisions requiring consent from the employer.

The wording of section 8(4) however goes beyond that immediate aim.

> (4) Subsections (1) and (2) have effect subject to any enactment which prohibits or restricts the effect of provision of the description mentioned in them.

Subsections 6(6) to (8) deal with conflict between section 6 and certain overriding rules – those imposed by "any other enactment or any rule of law or equity". It includes statutory instruments, court orders and orders of the Charity Commissioners. The subsections make it clear:

(a) that those overriding rules continue to apply despite the widened powers given to trustees by the new regime; and

(b) that the widened powers do not remove restrictions, limitations or conditions imposed by the overriding rules of another enactment.

The subsections themselves are drawn widely, but a specific example is charitable trusts. Land held on charitable trusts is dealt with specially by the Act in several sections. By section 8(3) the dispositionary powers to remove or negative the widened powers does not apply to charitable trusts. They are not subject to the "any two from more" consent provisions of section 10, nor to the purchaser protection given by section 16(2) and (3). On these last two references see Chapters 7 and 10. And of course they are not bound by the statutory restriction to four legal owners.

But, by and large, charitable trusts are subject to the trusts of land regime. Indeed, charitable trusts formerly deemed to be settled land under SLA are converted to trusts of land under section 2(5).

Subsections 6(6) to (8) remove any suggestion that charity trustees are no longer subject to for example the Charities Act 1993 sections 36 to 39. The trustees still have to comply with those sections, and except where protected under the terms of those sections, purchasers from charity trustees need to ensure that they have done so.

It must not be thought that charities are the only target, or even the wider "charitable, ecclesiastical or public trusts" to which the 1996 Act elsewhere refers. Subsections (6) to (8) are drawn in general terms and are capable of having a wide application.

There is one last matter of detail to mention. The continued application of other *restrictions, limitations or conditions* under subsection (8) is only where they are conferred by "any enactment other than this section". "Enactment" is not defined or extended by the Act or by LPA. But the overriding ban on exercising *section 6 powers* in contravention of other rules, applies not only to rules imposed by enactments, but also to those imposed by or any rule of law or equity, statutory instruments, court orders and orders of the Charity Commissioners.

6(6)   The powers conferred by this section shall not be exercised in contravention of, or of any order made in pursuance of, any other enactment or any rule of law or equity.

6(7)   The reference in subsection (6) to an order includes an order of any court or of the Charity Commissioners.

6(8)   Where any enactment other than this section confers on trustees authority to act subject to any restriction, limitation or condition, trustees of land may not exercise the powers conferred by this section to do any act which they are prevented from doing under the other enactment by reason of the restriction, limitation or condition.

5.7 Drafting implications

Enlarging statutory powers

Once the Act is in force, express enlargements of statutory powers for trustees of land are no longer necessary for disposing of or investing in land. But they continue for the present to be necessary if wide powers of investment are needed other than in land.

Restricting statutory powers

This is an option for settlors or co-purchasers except where the land will be held on charitable, ecclesiastical or public trusts. For some possible precedents and suggestions of where they are suitable for consideration, see Precedent.

5.8 Retroaction

Unlike other sections which contain special provisions for specified circumstances, there are no special provisions in sections 6 to 8. So the extent to which the sections 6 to 8 changes are retrospective depends on general principles. See 1.19.

1. The new powers and new regime generally, apply to trusts of land whenever they were created or arose. See the definition of "trust of land" in section 1(1).
2. But in the absence of specific provision the new powers can only apply to *exercises* after the commencement of the Act ie after 1996.[18] The test of validity of exercises before then continues to be the old law.

---

18 Assuming the commencement date of the Act is 1 January 1997.

Main consequences of sections 6 to 8

1. New absolute owner powers replace the former fragmented powers of trustees of land. They include power to buy land for investment or occupation or otherwise.

2. Enlarging the statutory powers for co-owners of land is no longer needed.

3. In investigating unregistered title it is no longer necessary to make sure that post 1996[19] transactions are within the former limited powers. The Act will apply irrespective of when the trust commenced.

4. But a purchaser continues to be concerned:

   (a) to see that pre-1997[20] dealings were within the old law powers, and

   (b) about restrictions or limitations if he has notice of them, irrespective of the date of the dealing.

5. There is a new statutory power to appropriate land and a revised one to partition.

6. The widened powers may be restricted by the disposition creating the trust or made subject to a requirement for consents.

---

19 Assuming the commencement date of the Act is 1 January 1997.
20 Assuming that the commencement date of the Act is 1 January 1997.

Chapter 6

Delegation by Trustees of Land*

- Section 9 is intended to allow beneficiaries under a trust of land to be given much the same powers as a tenant for life under a strict settlement.
- Other powers of delegation are under the Trustee Act 1925 section 25 and the Enduring Powers of Attorney Act 1985
- Who is eligible to be a section 9 attorney
- What powers can be delegated
- Section 9 attorneys cannot give receipts for capital money
- Revocation of the power of attorney
- Duties and liabilities of section 9 attorneys
- Liability of trustees who delegate

Section 9, redrawn, amended and reamended during its passage through Parliament, enables trustees of land to delegate any of their functions as trustees to beneficiaries of full age and beneficially entitled. LPA section 29 is repealed and replaced.

That summary should be set in two contexts:

(a) the intention of the section; and

(b) the alternative mechanisms for powers of attorney by trustees.

6.1 Section 9 is intended to allow beneficiaries under a trust of land to be given much the same powers as a tenant for life under a strict settlement

Section 9 ranges further than the old LPA section 29, which was limited to leasing, accepting surrenders of leases and management. Now trustees can delegate a much wider group of powers and duties – they can delegate "any of their functions".[1] The broadening of the power is not just a minor adjustment to LPA section 29. It results from closing off the strict settlement as a mechanism for future

---

* S 9.
1 But see 6.5 for limitations.

settlors. It is intended to console lawyers and clients who found the features of strict settlements convenient, who might otherwise resent the prohibition on new strict settlements. "The major purpose of this extended power is....to enable a beneficiary under a trust of land to be given much the same powers as a tenant for life under a strict settlement."[2] The aim is to provide an optional facility to mimic some of the characteristics of a strict settlement.

In some ways section 9 goes further than the expressed intention. The trustees themselves now have powers of an absolute owner, not just tenant for life powers under SLA. These are all "functions" which they can delegate under section 9 (subject to possible limitations, discussed below in 6.5). In other ways the situation will be less than equivalent. The trustees retain the legal estate. More importantly, the delegation is revocable. The life tenant will never be sure that the authority the trustees have given him with one hand, will not be removed by the other. A delegated power to sell may be removed at the moment the tenant for life wishes to use it. The trustees can regain the initiative. It is the facade of power which they delegate, not the reality.

6.2 The alternative mechanisms for powers of attorney by trustees

The remaining context in which section 9 delegation should be viewed, is against the other means of delegation open to trustees. In general of course trustees cannot delegate. Delegation needs to be authorised by specific statutory authority. Those restrictions even apply where the trusteeship is a matter of conveyancing machinery, as with beneficial co-owners. Trustees cannot delegate by general power of attorney. Section 9 delegation provides a third category to add to the existing two powers:

(a) under TA section 25 (for a maximum of 12 months); and

(b) an enduring power under the Enduring Powers of Attorney Act 1985.

There is no need to explore these here. Perhaps arbitrarily the place we have discussed them is in Chapter 10, in the context of protection for purchasers. See 10.6.

---

2 Law Com No 181 para 11.1.

6.3 Who may be a section 9 attorney?

The phrase "section 9 attorney" is not used in the Act but we will use it in this chapter as a convenient substitute for the longer expression used in the section: "beneficiary to whom functions are delegated by a power of attorney under subsection (1)". That should save at least several pages!

A section 9 attorney must be *"a beneficiary or beneficiaries of full age and beneficially entitled to an interest in possession."*

Beneficiary or beneficiaries

One, or more than one, beneficiaries may be appointed, but all must pass the test of complying with the definition. Where more than one beneficiary is appointed, it is clear from subsection (4), discussed in 6.9, that the appointment may be:

(a) joint; or

(b) separate; or

(c) joint and separate.

"Separate" is of course the statutory equivalent of the word, archaic in this context, more usually favoured by conveyancers – "several".

Of full age, but what about capacity?

The section 9 attorney must be of full age. That is hardly surprising. It parallels LPA section 20 in relation to trustees. But there is no mention of capacity. Capacity is a requirement for the provisions of several sections of the Act, for example sections 6, 11, 16, 19, 20 and 21, but not apparently here. It is a theoretical rather than a practical issue. Trustees must exercise reasonable care in deciding to delegate the function to the beneficiary (s 9(8) and see 6.11) and their discretion to delegate under section 9 would not be properly exercised by delegating to an attorney who lacked capacity. In practice it would be pointless or dangerous or both. Any person dealing with the attorney would also be vulnerable. If incapacity of the attorney occurred later, no provision is made by section 9, but clearly the trustees should revoke the power.

And beneficially entitled to an interest

This is the phrase defined in section 22(1) and discussed at 1.11.

In possession

Further words, occurring in section 22(3) and defining further who can be a section 9 attorney. The complete phrase, "beneficiary or beneficiaries of full age and beneficially entitled to an interest in possession", (see 1.11) echoes the definition of "tenant for life" in SLA section 19(1). That is consistent with the Law Commission's intentions in proposing the broadened powers of delegation, quoted in 6.1 above. So a person entitled in remainder cannot be a section 9 attorney, nor can the object of a discretionary trust or annuitant for life. He, she or they will normally be the tenant for life.

6.4 Who may appoint?

The Act is clear. It is the trustees of land who may appoint. In spite of the Law Commission's reasoning that "settlors" would be able to create what is in effect an enhanced strict settlement[3], responsibility for appointment is firmly with the trustees. As it was with the Commission's actual recommendatioins and draft Bill – it could hardly be otherwise.

Can the settlor influence the delegation?

A settlor who wishes to mirror SLA machinery as far as possible can express a wish in strong terms that the power of delegation be exercised. But the power of deciding whether to do so is still with the trustees. If they failed to delegate, any person who has an interest in the property could apply to the court under section 14 (see Chap 9). The applicant would usually be the life tenant. The settlor would not be eligible unless he had retained an interest in the trust property. The court could make an order relating to the exercise by the trustees of any of their "functions", which we suggest includes the power of delegation under section 9. The court would have regard to the matters in section 15(1) which include the intentions of the person who created the trust.

Can a settlor go further, and so structure the settlement that delegation is virtually inevitable? Time, and the ingenuity of property and trust practitioners, will tell. One possible course may however be inherently self-defeating. This would be to use the power under

---

3 See Law Com No 181 para 1.6.

section 8 of restricting and negativing section 6 absolute owner powers, by providing that they were only to be exercised while a section 9 delegation is in force. In terms as simple and drastic as that the direction could stultify the settlement – there might for example be no beneficiary eligible as attorney. But in addition the powers of trustees are to delegate "any of their functions as trustees". They could hardly delegate powers which had been removed from their own competence to exercise.

6.5 What powers can be delegated?

The trustees may delegate "any of their functions as trustees which relate to the land". "Functions" we have discussed at 5.2 and 1.16. Clearly a wide range of powers and duties may be delegated.

In practice we suggest, partly for reasons connected with capital money – see below – and partly on grounds of prudence and commonsense, that a general comprehensive power of attorney will not often be appropriate. It may be better to specify the powers delegated: powers of management no doubt, and perhaps powers of dealing subject to limitations and restrictions. The trustees will need to bear in mind that they will be liable for failing to exercise reasonable care in deciding to delegate the function (s 9(8) see 6.11). There may well be practical limits on what should be delegated. The power of attorney should be tailored to fit the circumstances. *It should in any event exclude the right to receive or give receipts for capital money.* (See below).

Interaction with rights to occupy

Section 12, discussed in Chapter 8, gives certain beneficiaries statutory rights of occupying the trust property. The beneficiary who is so entitled must have the same qualifications, except full age, as a beneficiary to whom the trustees can delegate powers under section 9. He must be a "beneficiary who is beneficially entitled to an interest in possession". Usually they will be the same person. Often occupation will coincide with the need to receive additional delegated powers – the occupier of the family farm may be a typical example.

In practice it is rare for trustees to enter into a licence agreement with an occupying beneficiary. In any but the simplest case, however, it will often be sensible unless rights and duties are comprehensively defined by the will or settlement. Where do the powers implicit in occupation, for example, run out and need to be augmented by delegation of some of the trustees' functions under section 9? A licence agreement specifying the duties could accompany a section 9 power of attorney specifying the powers of an occupying beneficiary.[3a] They would have the advantage of clarifying where powers and responsibilities end. Without them it will not always be easy to know.

No sub delegation by the section 9 attorney

Two legal limits on what may be delegated emerge from section 9(7). The first relates to subdelegation. While subsection (7) puts section 9 attorneys in the same position as trustees in relation to the exercise of the functions delegated, they are not to be regarded as trustees for the purpose of any enactment permitting the delegation of functions by trustees. So section 9 attorneys cannot subdelegate:

(a) under section 9; or

(b) under TA section 25; or

(c) under the Enduring Powers of Attorney Act (assuming we are right in treating this as an "enactment permitting the delegation of functions by trustees").

Can trustees delegate the ability to receive, and give receipts for, capital money?

The second limit relates to capital money. We consider that section 9 attorneys cannot give receipts for capital money. It is not however a self evident conclusion. Section 9(1) entitles trustees to delegate "any of their functions as trustees which relate to the land". If it stopped there, the answer to the question just asked would be yes, since the wording of subsection (1) seems wide enough. If that were indeed the answer, there would be further problems about overreaching, especially for a sole section 9 attorney.

But the answer is "no", because the matter does not stop there, and there are further provisions in section 9(7) which are relevant. It provides that section 9 attorneys are in the same position as trustees in relation to the exercise of their delegated powers, "but not for other purposes including in particular for the purpose of any enactment ... imposing requirements relating to the payment of capital money". Such an enactment is LPA section 27 which includes

---

3a The trustees have power under s 13(3) and (5) to impose conditions of occupation. See 8.7.

the words "capital money shall not be paid to ... fewer than two persons as trustees".

It is true that LPA section 27(2) is in negative rather than positive terms and it is mainly directed at the numbers of the trustees. But by implication its reverse, positive, side does require capital money to be paid to trustees, and section 9(7) does say that section 9 attorneys are not to be regarded as trustees for this purpose. It would have been clearer to have said directly that trustees cannot delegate their competence to give receipts for capital money[4], but this appears to be the somewhat indirect effect of section 9(7).[5] The result is not beyond all shades of doubt, but it is certainly the safer conclusion to work on. And if it is wrong, grave problems would arise in relation to overreaching by a sole section 9 attorney.

Perhaps we should repeat the conclusion we have just struggled to reach. **Section 9 attorneys cannot receive or give receipts for capital money.**

The conveyancing implications

If the power to sell has been delegated, the section 9 attorney will not, in accordance with the last paragraph, be authorised to receive or give a receipt for the proceeds of sale. The transfer will therefore look much like a transfer by the tenant for life of a strict settlement, with the attorney executing the transfer under the power, but with the trustees being necessary parties to give a receipt for the proceeds of sale.

The purchaser does not need to investigate the eligibility of the section 9 attorney[6] – see section 9(2), 6.12 and 10.6.

6.6 Section 9(1)

Except for the words "by power of attorney" – see 6.7 below – we have now analysed every word in section 9(1). It is time to reproduce the complete subsection:

---

4 As was suggested by Lord Mishcon in the debate on the third reading in the House of Lords.
5 If further support for that view is needed see the words of the Lord Chancellor in moving a redrafted s 9 on 25 March 1996: "capital money must still be paid to or by the direction of two trustees or one trustee being a trust corporation, and the beneficiary is not to be taken as trustee, or acting by the direction of trustees, simply by reason of having had functions delegated to him."
6 Unless he has knowledge that the attorney is not eligible.

Delegation by trustees

9.(1) The trustees of land may, by power of attorney, delegate to any beneficiary or beneficiaries of full age and beneficially entitled to an interest in possession in land subject to the trust any of their functions as trustees which relate to the land.

6.7   How may the delegation be carried out?

Power of attorney

Delegation must be, in the words of section 9(1) just quoted, "by power of attorney". Under section 9(3) it must be by all the trustees jointly.

It may be for any period or indefinite, and may not framed as an enduring power under the Enduring Powers of Attorney Act (subss (5) and (6), reproduced below).

(5) A delegation under subsection (1) may be for any period or indefinite.

(6) A power of attorney under subsection (1) cannot be an enduring power within the meaning of the Enduring Powers of Attorney Act 1985.

6.8   Revocation other than by the attorney ceasing to be eligible

Voluntary revocation

Under section 9(3) the power of attorney, unless expressed to be irrevocable and to be given by way of security, may be revoked by any one or more of the trustees. Implicitly the power of revocation remains whether the power is granted for any period or indefinitely. As we have pointed out already, this is a serious qualification in terms of the power of the attorney.

Involuntary revocation by appointment of a new trustee

Revocation does not occur if one of the appointing trustees dies or ceases to be a trustee. The appointment of a new trustee however automatically revokes the power of attorney. Assuming a transaction gives rise to capital money the appointment of a new trustee would be shown on the title of the trustees to give a receipt. In cases where no capital money is paid the person dealing with the attorney should enquire if there have been new trustees since the power was executed, although in that situation there would perhaps be less risk of loss if it tranpired the attorney's authority had ceased. See further 6.12 and 10.6 for the steps a purchaser should take for protection against revocation.

> (3)   A power of attorney under subsection (1) shall be given by all the trustees jointly and (unless expressed to be irrevocable and to be given by way of security) may be revoked by any one or more of them; and such a power is revoked by the appointment as a trustee of a person other than those by whom it is given (though not by any of those persons dying or otherwise ceasing to be a trustee).

6.9 Revocation by reason of the attorney ceasing to be eligible

If a section 9 attorney ceases to be a person[7] beneficially entitled to an interest in possession in land subject to the trust, the power is revoked. The Law Society was concerned, and through them their lordships were much exercised, over the effect of the original Bill on joint and several attorneys. Or as section 9(4) has it, joint and separate attorneys. These concerns have been addressed in the present form of subsection (4). It is now clear enough to quote without repetition by paraphrase:

> (4)   Where a beneficiary to whom functions are delegated by a power of attorney under subsection (1) ceases to be a person beneficially entitled to an interest in possession in land subject to the trust
>
> (a) if the functions are delegated to him alone, the power is revoked,
>
> (b) if the functions are delegated to him and to other beneficiaries to be exercised by them jointly (but not separately), the power is revoked if each of the other beneficiaries ceases to be so entitled (but otherwise functions exercisable in accordance with the power are so exercisable by the remaining beneficiary or beneficiaries), and

---

7 The word "person" used here, instead of the word "beneficiary" used in s 9(1), is probably not important. "Beneficiary" is used in the opening words of the subsection and "person" must relate to it. We suspect the variation is stylistic rather than significant, that the parliamentary draftsman wished to avoid referring to a beneficiary ceasing to be a beneficiary beneficially entitled. If so, we can hardly blame him.

(c) if the functions are delegated to him and to other beneficiaries to be exercised by them separately (or either separately or jointly), the power is revoked in so far as it relates to him.

6.10 Duties and liabilities of section 9 attorneys

These are the subject of the first half of section 9(7). It is close to the wording of LPA section 29(3), now repealed.(We have already quoted from the second half in 6.5.) In exercising their delegated functions, section 9 attorneys have the same duties and liabilities as trustees.

(7) Beneficiaries to whom functions have been delegated under subsection (1) are, in relation to the exercise of the functions, in the same position as trustees (with the same duties and liabilities); but such beneficiaries shall not be regarded as trustees for any other purposes (including, in particular, the purposes of any enactment permitting the delegation of functions by trustees or imposing requirements relating to the payment of capital money).

6.11 Liability of the trustees for defaults of section 9 attorneys

The wording of what is now subsection (8) was much debated. Mark 1 followed the Law Commission and left the trustees fully responsible for the acts of the attorney. It was pointed out this meant liability without control and would have resulted in the power of delegation becoming a dead letter. Following representations on behalf of the Law Society, Mark 2 provided the trustees' liability should only arise if it was not reasonable for the trustees to delegate the function to the attorney. After further negotiations Mark 3, the present subclause, emerged under which the liability of the trustees for default of the section 9 attorney is only if the trustees did not exercise reasonable care in deciding to delegate the function to the attorney. It is not quite the reinstatement of LPA section 29(3)[8] which the Law Society

---

8 The (now repealed) LPA s 29 read: "The persons delegating any power under this section shall not, in relation to the exercise or purported exercise of the power, be liable for the acts or defaults of the person to whom the power is delegated, but that person shall, in relation to te exercise of the power by him,be deemed to be in the position and to have the duties and liabilities of a trustee".
The counterpart of the words starting "but that person " to the end of the subsection is now s 9(7) of the 1996 Act.

had wanted, but it is probably close to stating the general law on the trustees' duties[9] in the exercise of their powers.

It suggests that trustees need to consider carefully:

(a) whether they delegate at all;

(b) if so, the functions which they delegate; and

(c) the suitability of the attorney. Of course, they have little choice in selecting the attorney since often there will only be one beneficiary who is eligible.

Subsection (8) reads:

> (8)   Where any function has been delegated to a beneficiary or beneficiaries under subsection (1), the trustees are jointly and severally liable for any act or default of the beneficiary, or any of the beneficiaries, in the exercise of the function if, and only if, the trustees did not exercise reasonable care in deciding to delegate the function to the beneficiary or beneficiaries.

6.12 Protection for later purchasers and persons dealing with a section 9 attorney

Section 9(2) deals with a limited problem – that purchasers and other persons relying on the power of attorney, cannot check whether a section 9 attorney is eligible without investigating the beneficial trusts. Accordingly the person dealing with the attorney is protected if he has no knowledge of ineligibility, while a later purchaser needs a statutory declaration from the person who dealt with the attorney. The person dealing with the attorney should not try to investigate the extent of the attorney's beneficial interest unless facts within his knowledge put him on notice.

Subsection (2) is not reproduced in this chapter because we have dealt with it in Chapter 10,[10] which deals generally with protecting the purchaser. Here we stress that:

(a) section 9(2) protection is only on eligibility of the attorney to be appointed;

(b) a later purchaser needs, before or within three months after his purchase, a section 9(2) declaration from the person who dealt

---

9 See *Speight* v *Gaunt* (1885) 9 App Cas 1.
10 See 10.5.

with the attorney *irrespective of how long elapsed between the execution of the power and its exercise*;

(c) the later purchaser needs to rely on PAA protection against revocation. Here a declaration is only needed if more than 12 months elapse between the execution of the power and its exercise.

6.13 Transitional provisions (s 9(9))

Despite the repeal of LPA section 29, an existing section 29 delegation lives on – it is not revoked by the 1996 Act.

> (9)   Neither this section nor the repeal by this Act of section 29 of the Law of Property Act 1925 (which is superseded by this section) affects the operation after the commencement of this Act of any delegation effected before that commencement.

Main practical consequences of section 9

1. An approximation of strict settlement powers and responsibilities can be achieved by delegation of trustees' powers to the life tenant.

2. Wide powers can be delegated but the power of attorney should be tailored to the circumstances.

3. The attorney cannot be authorised to give receipts for capital money. If the life tenant is authorised to sell, the trustees must join in the transfer to give a receipt.

4. A section 9 attorney has the same duties and liabilities as trustees.

5. Trustees are liable to exercise reasonable care in delegating.

Chapter 7

Consents and Consultation

- No need for more than two consents
- Minors and mental patients
- Changes to rules on consultation
- Transitional provisions and "opting in"

7.1 Consents: introductory

It was common, under the trust for sale regime, to find that the trustees for sale could not actually *sell* the land concerned without the consent of some other person. Typically this would be the settlor's or testator's widow, who would have a life interest. Some trusts for sale went further, and required the consent of the third party to the exercise of other, or indeed all statutory, powers vested in the trustees. In this way it was possible to replicate many of the structural features of the SLA settlement *without* vesting the legal estate in the tenant for life. But Parliament provided against an excess of caution by providing, in LPA section 26(1), that, where the consent of more than two persons was required by the disposition for the sale or for the exercise of any other powers of the trustees, then, in favour of a *purchaser* (as defined), the consent of any two such persons would be sufficient, even though as against beneficiaries of the trust it might still represent a breach of trust. The purpose of this provision was therefore simply protection of purchasers and not at all protection of trustees.

7.2 Consents: new provisions

The Law Commission originally recommended amendments to section 26, to cover the change from trust for sale to trust of land. But the 1996 Act repeals section 26 and, by section 10(1), purports to make entirely new (although similar) provision in relation to trusts of land. It provides:

> If a disposition creating a trust of land requires the consent of more than two persons to the exercise by the trustees of any function relating to the

land, the consent of any two of them to the exercise of the function is sufficient in favour of a purchaser.

The first point that requires to be noticed is the use of the words "a disposition creating a trust of land". This phrase has aleady been discussed.[1] The second point is that a *disposition* is an action disposing of something, not an action *requiring something*. So we must be intended to read "*terms* of a disposition".

Thirdly, whereas section 26(1) referred to the execution of a trust for sale, *i.e.* the sale, and the exercise of any *powers* vested in the trustees, section 10(1) refers to the exercise of any *function* relating to the land. The use of "function" was recommended by the Law Commission, and appeared in their draft Bill. But it is not defined, either by this Act or by the LPA.[2] However, as discussed earlier[3], it must be wider than "power", including in particular any action which the trustees are *obliged* to take (*i.e.* where they have no discretion).

Fourthly, the effect of the provision is to protect *purchasers*, not to relieve the trustees from liability for any breach of trust which they may commit in exercising any "function".[4] "Purchaser" of course has the same meaning as in Part I of the LPA[5], *i.e.* a person who acquires an interest in or a charge upon property for money or money's worth.[6]

Fifthly, section 26(1) does not apply to trustees of land held on "charitable, ecclesiastical or public trusts".[7] This curious phrase has already been discussed.[8]

Sixthly, unlike most of the provisions of this Act, section 10 does not apply to personal representatives.[9] Lastly on this provision, note that this is a mandatory rule, and obviously it cannot be excluded by provision to the contrary in the trust.

7.3   Consents: minors (and the mentally incapable)

Subsection (3) provides for the case where a person whose consent is required is not of full age:

---

1 See 1.17 above.
2 Let in by s 23(2).
3 See 1.16 above.
4 See *Waller* v *Waller* [1967] 1 WLR 451.
5 See s 23(1) of this Act: 1.12 above.
6 See s 205(1) (xxi) of the 1925 Act.
7 S 26(2).
8 1.15 above.
9 S 18(1).

Where at any time a person whose consent is expressed by a disposition creating a trust of land to be required to the exercise by the trustees of any function relating to the land is not of full age -

(a)   his consent is not, in favour of a purchaser, required to the exercise of the function, but

(b)   the trustees shall obtain the consent of a parent who has parental responsibility for him (within the meaning of the Children Act 1989) or of a guardian of his.

This is narrower than LPA section 26(2) (which it replaces), for that provision extended also to persons lacking capacity by reason of mental disorder. A receiver of the property of such a person, appointed under section 99 of the Mental Health Act 1983, may be authorised to consent to the exercise by trustees of their powers.[10] There is therefore a means of obtaining consents where the beneficiary is mentally incapable, and the trustees will need to obtain this, just as they need to obtain parental consent for minors. The difference between LPA section 26(3) and the new section 10(3) relates solely to purchasers. Under the old law purchasers were not concerned with consents for either minors or the mentally incapable. This immunity for purchasers is continued under section 10(3) for minors, but it is not continued for the mentally incapable. Purchasers must see that the receiver gives consent.

7.4 Applications to the court

Under the LPA, section 30, if a particular consent could not be obtained (for example because the relevant person refused[11]), application could be made to the court for an order dispensing with the need for the consent. Under the new Act, this is also possible, by applying under section 14, which is discussed later.[12]

7.5 Consultation: general

Section 26 of the LPA covered both consents and consultation with beneficiaries. The latter topic is in this Act covered by a separate

---

10 See ss 99(2), and 96(1)(k) of that Act.
11 Re *Beale's Settlement Trusts* [1932] 2 Ch 15.
12 See Chap 9.

section, namely section 11. The general rule regarding consultation is set out in subsection (1):

> The trustees of land shall in the exercise of any function relating to land subject to the trust -
>
> (a)   so far as practicable, consult the beneficiaries of full age and beneficially entitled to an interest in possession in the land, and
>
> (b)   so far as consistent with the general interest of the trust, give effect to the wishes of those beneficiaries, or (in case of dispute) of the majority (according to the value of their combined interests).

This is similar to LPA section 26(3), but there are a number of differences.

7.6 Consultation: changes from old law

First, there is the obvious difference of terminology consequent upon the change from trust for sale to trust of land. Secondly, section 26(3) did not make clear exactly what the trustees were to consult the beneficiaries about, whereas the new section 11(1) refers expressly to "the exercise of any function". In one case[13], the Court of Appeal held that section 26(3) applied not only to the execution of the trust for sale, but also to every exercise of the powers vested in the trustees. However, they further held that it only applied to "positive acts", and hence did *not* apply to a joint tenant of a periodic tenancy who gave notice of not being willing for the tenancy to continue, so that it came to an end in accordance with the doctrine in *London Borough of Hammersmith and Fulham* v *Monk*.[14] The words "any function" are general and unlimited.[15] There seems no reason for them not to apply to the situation in the Court of Appeal case if the facts should recur.

Thirdly, section 26(3) applied to an annuitant whose annuity was paid out of the income of the land.[16] But annuitants are expressly excluded, by section 22(3) of this Act, from being beneficiaries entitled to an interest in possession, and hence trustees will not have to consult them under this Act. It is unclear why this change has been made. The Law Commission does not discuss the point. It is possible

---

13 *Crawley Borough Council* v *Ure* [1996] 1 All ER 724.
14 [1992] 1 AC 478.
15 *Cf Henry Briggs & Co Ltd* v *IRC* [1961] 1 All ER 220.
16 *Re House* [1929] 2 Ch 166.

that the draftsman foresaw difficulties with, *e.g.* pension trust beneficiaries who had became entitled to annuities.[17]

Fourthly, by section 11(2)(c), section 11(1) does not require trustees to consult beneficiaries before conveying the land to them under section 6(2), discussed above.[18] (Of course under the old law, there was no such power for trustees to do so without a request or at least the agreement of the beneficiaries.) Fifthly, whereas section 26(3) of the LPA applied to personal representatives holding land on trust for sale[19], section 11 does not.[20]

An apparent difference between section 26(3) and section 11(1) turns out on closer inspection not to be one. Section 26(3) expressly provided that a purchaser was not to be concerned to see that consultation had in fact taken place. Section 11 omits any such provision. However section 16(1) makes similar provision in respect of section 11(1).

7.7 Consultation: transitional effect

A final question on section 11 is its transitional effect. Section 26(3) applied to an express trust for sale only if the disposition so provided. Following a Law Commission recommendation[21], section 11(2)(a) reverses the position, so that the general rule for the future is that section 11(1) does *not* apply to the extent that the disposition so provides, *i.e.* you must "opt out". (This is comparable with the provision that the powers conferred on trustees by ss 6 and 7 of the Act can also be excluded by the terms of the disposition creating the trust.[22]) But section 11(2)(b) provides further that section 11(1) does not apply "to a trust created or arising under a will made before the commencement of this Act". These words were not in the bill as originally presented, but were added at House of Lords Report stage.[23]

At first sight the dichotomy is a little odd. One might read the provision as dealing with (i) trusts *created* before commencement, and (ii) trusts arising under wills *made* before commencement. But it

---

17 *Cf* 1.11 above.
18 See 5.5 above.
19 See s 205(1)(xxix) of that Act.
20 S 18(1).
21 Para 13.5 of Law Com No 181.
22 See 5.6 above.
23 HL Debs, vol 571, col 961, 22 April 1996.

makes no sense to lump these together, and subsection (3) deals separately with at least some of the trusts in (i). So the better reading must be (i) trusts created under a will, and (ii) trusts arising under a will, in either case the will being *made* before the commencement of the Act. The wording was based on that in the Family Law Reform Act 1969[24], and is apparently intended to extend to trusts created by assents by personal representatives to beneficiaries.[25] A will of course speaks from death. So it is not when it is *made* that it comes into effect, but when the testator *dies*. Hence on this view a trust made by will and executed before commencement is excluded, though the testator might die many years after commencement. Yet if the same testator revoked that will after commencement, and replaced it with another will (containing, let us say, an identical trust) the trust is within section 11. Presumably, as a codicil republishes a will from the date of the codicil, the same result would follow if the testator after commencement did not replace the will, but by codicil merely altered an irrelevant detail. This point was made by Lord Mischon in Committee, in making an amendment (later withdrawn) which would have excluded the effect of the republication unless the codicil adopted the new rules.[26]

7.8 Consultation: "opting-in" existing trusts

There is a third aspect to the transitional provision. It is that section 11(1) does not apply to trusts already in existence at commencement, or trusts created thereafter by reference to such a trust, unless they are "opted in". By section 11(3):

> Subsection (1) does not apply to a trust created before the commencement of this Act by a disposition, or a trust created after that commencement by reference to such a trust, unless provision to the effect that it is to apply is made by a deed executed -
>
> (a)   in a case in which the trust was created by one person and he is of full capacity, by that person, or
>
> (b)   in a case in which the trust was created by more than one person, by such of the persons who created the trust as are alive and of full capacity.

---

24 Sched 3 para 6.

25 HL Debs, vol 571, col 961, 22 April 1996.

26 HL Debs, vol 570, col 1542, 25 March 1996.

These provisions were substituted in House of Lords Committee, for provisions requiring existing trusts to be "opted out" within one year of commencement.[27]

A number of points arise under section 11(3). First there is the question of "disposition", which is discussed elsewhere.[28] Secondly there is the point that provision that section 11(1) is to apply "is made". Presumably this covers *implied* as well as *expressed* inclusion. Thirdly, the inclusion of section 11(1) must be made by *deed*, even though the original trust was created by writing, or even orally. Presumably the making of such a deed does not affect anything done or not done before the deed was made. In relation to the similarly worded power of *exclusion* in section 21(6) of the Act, section 21(8) makes this point expressly. But there is no parallel provision here in section 11. Fourthly, if such a deed is executed, it is irrevocable, whatever it says.[29]

Fifthly, the "opting-in" procedure also applies to a trust "created ... by reference to" a pre-Act trust. The words "by reference to" are very wide.[30] What do they cover in this context? In moving the amendment which introduced these words into the Bill, the Lord Chancellor said that they were to ensure that a gift of further property post-commencement on the same trusts as, and as an accretion to, an existing trust should be treated on the same basis as the existing trust for the purposes of the transitional provisions. Although such a gift is often treated simply as part of the original trust[31], Lord Mackay plainly saw it as something separate, and specifically referred to the subsequent gift as "a referential trust". [32] But a trust may be "referential" and yet distinct.[33] Suppose a trust is made by A for his children. Then B makes a trust, with a different trustee, for *his* children. If B's trust instrument incorporates by reference all the provisions of A's trust instrument, except those dealing with the parties and the definition of the class of beneficiaries, surely B's trust is "created by reference to" A's trust? It

---

27 HL Debs, vol 570, cols 1540-1541, 25 March 1996.
28 See 1.17 above.
29 S 11(4).
30 See *e.g. Kirby* v *Manpower Services Commission* [1980] 1 WLR 725, 730-731, in a very different context.
31 See 1.18 above, and in particular *Re Rydon's Settlement* [1955] Ch 1.
32 HL Debs, vol 572, col 97, 7 May 1996.
33 *Cf Harvela Investments Ltd* v *Royal Trust Company of Canada (CI) Ltd* [1986] 1 AC 207 (sealed bid for shares for sum ascertainable by reference to highest rival bid).

is certainly not understandable without reference to it.[34] A third case. Suppose A's trust confers a wide power of appointment, which is exercised so as to create a subtrust, with new trustees, a much narrower class of beneficiaries, and maybe a different proper law, so that for CGT purposes, at least, there is plainly a new trust.[35] The new trust is also "created by reference to" A's trust. Perhaps this is a candidate for the *Pepper* v *Hart* treatment?[36]

The last point on this provision is the question of who should make the deed. Section 11(3) refers to the person or persons who "created" the trust. The meaning of this phrase is discussed elsewhere, and in particular whether or not it extends to the case where different persons settle property on the same terms at different times.[37]

Main practical consequences of sections 10 and 11

1. Whatever the trust says, no more than two consents are needed to the exercise of *any* trustee function relating to the land, in order for a purchaser to be protected.

2. But although a minor's consent is not needed to protect a purchaser, that of the receiver of a mentally incapable person is.

3. Trustees of land must now consult beneficiaries of full age and beneficially entitled in possession about the exercise of *any function* in relation to the land.

4. But annuitants no longer count for this purpose.

5. Those creating trusts of land for the future can "opt out" of the consultation obligation; existing trusts can be "opted in".

---

34 *Cf Bank of Nova Scotia* v *Yoshikumi Lumber Ltd* (1992) 99 DLR (4th) 289, 389, dealing with referential bids.
35 *Bond* v *Pickford* [1983] STC 517; *Roome* v *Edwards* [1982] AC 279.
36 See 1.20 above.
37 See 1.18 above, and also 11.11 below.

Chapter 8

Rights of Occupation

- Beneficiaries' rights to occupy
- Trustees' powers to limit rights
- Imposition of conditions
- Compensation for excluded beneficiaries

8.1 General

Beneficial co-owners have always been entitled in principle to occupy land so co-owned, and the introduction of the statutory trust for sale in 1925 did not alter that position.[1] But the Law Commission[2] thought there was some doubt, and recommended putting the beneficiaries' rights of occupation on a statutory footing.[3] This Act, like the Law Commission's Bill, seeks to implement that idea.

The primary provision is section 12(1):

> A beneficiary who is beneficially entitled to an interest in possession in land subject to a trust of land is entitled by reason of his interest to occupy the land at any time if at that time -
>
> (a)   the purposes of the trust include making the land available for his occupation (or for the occupation of beneficiaries of a class of which he is a member or of beneficiaries in general), or
>
> (b)   the land is held by the trustees so as to be so available.

8.2 Who is a "beneficiary"?

The problems begin with the words "a beneficiary". Section 22(1) defines this to mean a person who has an interest in property under the trust. This definition is discussed elsewhere[4], but since the House of Lords held[5] that an object of a discretionary trust had no interest

---

in any part of the trust property, at least until the discretion was exercised in his favour, the objects of a discretionary trust are not beneficiaries for this purpose. "Beneficiary who is beneficially entitled" has already been considered.[6] But this section wants more. It depends on there being a beneficiary beneficially entitled *to an interest in possession* in the land.[7] As we have seen[8], a person beneficially entitled to an annuity charged on the land is not to be regarded as so entitled. The position of beneficiaries under pension trusts has also already been considered.[9] It is unlikely that they would have a interest in possession unless or until they were entitled to an annuity, and then (as we have seen) they are specifically excluded. So discretionary objects, beneficiaries who hold their interests on trust for others, pension trust beneficiaries and annuitants have no statutory rights of occupation.

8.3 Conditions to be satisfied: *purposes*

The right of the beneficiary to occupy depends on either of two conditions being satisfied, designated (a) and (b) in the subsection. The first (para (a)) depends on the *purposes* of the trust, and not on the actual property position. The notion of the *purposes* of a beneficiary trust is a difficult one. Generally the law has seen the purpose of a beneficiary trust as being *to benefit the beneficiary*. The *mode* of benefiting him was usually irrelevant. Indeed, if the settlor attempted to dictate how the beneficiary was to be benefitted, that could be ignored.[10] So in English law there was normally no need to distinguish between the *purposes* of such trust and the notion of benefiting the beneficiary generally.

That said, there could be circumstances in which the court looked at the "purposes" of a trust. Or, more likely, it would look at the purposes for which a particular land transaction was carried out, which transaction just happened, through the operation of the 1925 legislation, to produce a trust for sale.[11] These "purposes" were then

---

6 See 1.11 above.

7 *Cf* s 9(1), which uses the same words, but adds "of full age".

8 See 1.11 above.

9 See *ibid*.

10 See *Re Skinner's Trusts* (1860) 1 J&H 102; *Re Bowes* [1896] 1 Ch 507; *Re Lipinski's Will Trusts* [1976] Ch 235.

11 See *e.g. Re Buchanan-Wollaston's Conveyance* [1939] Ch 738; *Jones v Challenger* [1961] 1 QB 176.

used as justification for enforcing or not enforcing the primary trust (*i.e.* to sell) in the trust for sale.

All this has now been made much more explicit. The right to occupy requires that the *purposes* of the trust include making the land available for his occupation or for that of the class of beneficiaries. Since it has not been common in the past for settlors to express their purposes in creating a trust (except in letters of wishes, uncommon in this kind of trust), the courts will have to work this out from all the circumstances. Settlors and testators creating trusts for the future would be well advised to make the matter plain.

8.4 Conditions to be satisfied: *availability*

The other alternative (para (b)) is that the land is held so as to be *available*. It is not altogether clear what this is intended to extend to. But it concentrates on the *factual* position, *i.e.* the land is *so*. It must cover the case where, whatever the purposes of the trust, it is available for occupation by the beneficiary. But "availability" is not a clear cut concept. What if the property is to be sold in a few weeks, a couple of months, a year? Is it "available" or not? Suppose the property is a hotel. Can a beneficiary claim to use an unoccupied room for the night?

Subsection (2) reinforces the point by providing that section 12(1):

> does not confer on a beneficiary a right to occupy land if it is either unavailable or unsuitable for occupation by him.

"Unavailable" is simply the converse of "available'" and similar comments apply. "Unsuitable" is, if anything, even more difficult to get a grasp on. No standards are laid down by reference to which suitability is to be judged, nor from whose standpoint (if anyone's) this should be done. After all, if the beneficiary *wants* to occupy certain land, it cannot be said to be "unsuitable" from his point of view, unless you are prepared to say that someone else knows better for him than he does, an attitude with an old fashioned taste in these days of increasing self determination.

8.5 Exclusion from right to occupy

Finally, there is the problem of many beneficiaries simultaneously claiming the right to occupy. The Law Commission recognised this problem, and recommended that the trustees should have a discretionary power to exclude or restrict occupation rights where more than one beneficiary had the right to occupy.[12] This is now found in section 13, to which section 12 is expressly made subject.[13]

Section 13(1) begins simply enough:

> Where two or more beneficiaries are (or apart from this subsection would be) entitled under section 12 to occupy land, the trustees of land may exclude or restrict the entitlement of any one or more (but not all) of them.

The general rule, where private trusts are concerned, is that, in the absence of different provision made in the terms of the trust, trustees must be unanimous in order to exercise any power.[14] There is nothing in the Act to alter that rule here. So if there are two, three or four co-owners of land, holding on trust for themselves, they cannot exercise this power to exclude one (or more) of their number from the right to occupy unless they are unanimous.

In exercising the powers of exclusion or restriction, subsection (4) requires the trustees to take into account:

(a)   the intentions of the person or persons (if any) who created the trust,

(b)   the purposes for which the land is held, and

(c)   the circumstances and wishes of each of the beneficiaries who is (or apart from any previous exercise by the trustees of those powers would be) entitled to occupy the land under section 12.

Of these, paragraph (b) is the only one to call for express comment. This is that here the trustees are not directed to have regard to the purposes of the *trust*, which was the matter we considered under section 12. Instead, they are to have regard to the purposes for which *the land is held*, which is a test rather closer to that considered by the courts in the case law.[15] Presumably, if pension funds trustees thought there was any risk that that beneficiaries were included in the scope of the right of occupation, and the land concerned were "available", this power could be exercised so as to exclude the right of occupation.

Notice that the power of exclusion or limitation is expressly stated to be in relation to "the entitlement" to occupy where such beneficiaries are "entitled under section 12 to occupy". What is not

---

12 Law Com No 181, para 13.4.

13 See s 12(3).

14 *Luke v South Kensington Hotel Company* (1879) 11 Ch D 121; *Re Mayo* [1943] Ch 302; *Re Butlin's Settlement Trusts* [1976] Ch 251.

15 Such as *Re Buchanan-Wollaston's Conveyance* and *Jones* v *Challenger*, note 11 above.

clear is whether the power is exercisable in relation to an entitlement to occupy *not* under section 12. Suppose a beneficiary entitled in possession is a trustee of his interest for his minor children. He has no statutory right to occupy under section 12. But suppose that the trust *expressly* conferred a right of occupation on that beneficiary (thus enabling him to live there with his children). Can the trustees exclude or restrict that right under section 13? It would seem not, for the words *"the entitlement"* refer back to the words "entitled under section 12", and he is entitled, not under section 12, but under the express terms of the trust. One solution is to say that "the entitlement" means "*any* entitlement, *however* arising", but this strains the wording. Another is to say that section 12 *replaces* any express right of occupation, now or future, so that the purported express grant of the right by the settlor/testator is ineffective. That does not seem right either.

8.6 Exclusion: limitations

But the trustees' power under section 13(1) is not unlimited: subsection (2) forbids them to:

(a)   unreasonably exclude any beneficiary's entitlement to occupy land, or

(b)   restrict any such entitlement to an unreasonable extent.

Probably there was no alternative to using such vague terminology if (apparently) substantive justice was to be done to each individual case. But these unfortunate words will be productive of much litigation. Every beneficiary who finds him or herself on the receiving end of an exclusion or restriction under section 13(1) from the trustees will look for a weapon to beat the trustees with. They will not have far to look. And family litigation is the worst sort.

Moreover, subsection (7) provides that:

The powers conferred on trustees by this section may not be exercised -

(a)   so as to prevent any person who is in occupation of land (whether or not by reason of an entitlement under section 12) from continuing to occupy the land, or

(b)   in a manner likely to result in any such person ceasing to occupy the land,

unless he consents or the court has given approval.

The width of the words in (a) at first sight seems enough to cover persons who are not beneficiaries at all (including both lawful occupiers, such as tenants, and unlawful ones such as squatters) as well as those who are beneficiaries. But for the exercise of the powers in section 13 to prevent a person from continuing to occupy the land, it must be a *beneficiary*, for these powers extend only to beneficiaries' entitlement to occupy the land. So a beneficiary in possession can only be deprived of that possession with his consent or the approval of the court.

The trustees must have regard to certain matters in exercising their powers under the section to restrict or exclude beneficiaries' entitlement to occupy land[16], and the court must have regard to the same matters if asked to approve a restriction or exclusion in relation to a beneficiary in possession.[17] Additionally, the court will have to have regard to the circumstances and wishes of the beneficiaries entitled to occupy.[18] However, these circumstances are not stated to be exclusive, but merely inclusive. In other words, the court can – and may indeed have to – take into account other matters.

Again, there is in (b) the reference to the purposes for which the land is held. But there is also (in (a)) the separate reference to the intentions of the settlor or settlors. But as the purposes for which the land is held may well be found by looking at the intention of the settlor or settlors, it is not necessarily the case that these will be different. Although the Law Commission's Bill was drafted slightly differently, the same dichotomy occurs in the Act as in their Bill.

8.7 Exclusion: conditions and compensation

Lastly, the trustees have power, by section 13(3), to:

> impose reasonable conditions on any beneficiary in relation to his occupation of land by reason of his entitlement under section 12.

By section 13(5), these *include* conditions requiring him:

(a)   to pay any outgoings or expenses in respect of the land, or

(b)   to assume any other obligation in relation to the land or to any activity which is or is proposed to be conducted there.

---

16 S 13(4).
17 S 13(8).
18 S 15(2).

But where the trustees have exercised their powers to exclude or restrict entitlement of a beneficiary, then section 13(6) makes clear that the conditions which may be imposed on beneficiaries in occupation *include* conditions requiring the latter beneficiaries to:

(a)   make payments by way of compensation to the beneficiary whose entitlement has been excluded or restricted, or

(b)   forego any payment or other benefit to which he would otherwise be entitled under the trust so as to benefit that beneficiary.

In exercising their powers under this section trustees will have to be careful not accidentally to destroy a beneficiary's interest in possession for inheritance tax purposes.[19]

8.8 Occupation, exclusion and delegation

The rights of occupation, the power of exclusion (on terms), and the power of delegation[20] are not intended to be kept completely separate. They may be used all at the same time, if circumstances require. So, for example, the trustees of a trust owning a farm may delegate to one beneficiary of several entitled in possession certain powers of management of the property, as if he were the tenant for life under an SLA settlement, and he may occupy pursuant to the statutory right on terms that he farm the land in such and such a way, and that he compensate the other beneficiaries whose statutory right has been excluded by the trustees.

---

19 *Cf Pearson* V *IRC* [1981] AC 753.
20 Discussed above, in Chap 6.

Main practical consequences of sections 12 and 13

1. The right of a beneficiary beneficially entitled in possession under a trust of land to occupy the land is put on a statutory basis for the first time.

2. But *either* making the land available for occupation must be one of the trust's purposes, or the land must be held by the trustees so as to be available for such occupation. And the trustees have power to exclude or restrict the exercise of the statutory right if there are two or more persons entitled to occupy, but they can impose conditions on the occupant, including compensation to be paid to the excluded.

3. Settlors and testators creating trusts for the future should make it clear whether the purpose of the trust includes making land available for occupation by a beneficiary or class of beneficiaries.

Chapter 9

Powers of the Court

- Wider powers conferred on court
- Factors to which court must have regard
- Special regime for trustees in bankruptcy
- Powers extended to trusts of proceeds of sale

9.1 Introductory

Under the old scheme of the trust for sale, the court had power to make orders in relation to the sale of the property.[1] The courts used this to give effect, broadly, to what they thought to be the "purposes" of the trust.[2] But this power was something of a blunt instrument. It only permitted orders connected with *sale* of the property, reflecting its role in the context of the trust for sale. Having freed the conveyancing system from the use of the trust for sale device, section 30 is therefore completely replaced by a new provision, section 14 of the 1996 Act. This confers wide power on the court. Subsection (2) provides:

> On an application for an order under this section the court may make any such order -
>
> (a)   relating to the exercise by the trustees of any of their functions (including an order relieving them of any obligation to obtain the consent of, or to consult, any person in connection with the exercise of any of their functions), or
>
> (b)   declaring the nature or extent of a person's interest in property subject to the trust,
>
> as the court thinks fit.

9.2 Scope of section 14

It will immediately be seen that the scope of this provision is not restricted to orders about sale, and is thus very much wider than

---

1 LPA, s 30.
2 See 4.6 and 8.3 above.

LPA, section 30. But the court cannot under this section make an order for appointment or removal of trustees.[3] It is specifically provided that anyone who is a trustee of land or who "has an interest in property subject to a trust of land" may apply to the court.[4] It is not clear whether an annuitant whose annuity is paid out of the income of the property is entitled to apply to the court. Notwithstanding that an annuitant is not to be regarded, *for the purposes of the Act*, as entitled to an interest *in possession* in that property, the better view is that such a person is within section 14.[5] This view is strengthened by the fact that, as first introduced into the House of Lords, the Bill referred here to "a trustee of land or a beneficiary under a trust of land". This was amended in House of Lords Committee[6] expressly to widen the range of persons who could apply to the court, in particular to cover a creditor of a beneficiary who obtained a charging order over his interest under the trust. If such a person is to be included, then so must be an annuitant.

There is also a transitional provision, so that the powers of section 14 are available to the court whether the "application ... is made before or after the commencement of this Act".[7] This is presumably a reference to the fact that an application is usually treated as "made" when the originating process is issued, or at the latest served, rather than when the court actually hears the application.[8] It would make no sense to provide that the section 14 powers were available to the court on a hearing which took place *before* the commencement of the Act.

9.3   Factors to which court must have regard

However, unlike section 30, the draftsman has not left the court's discretion under this Act completely untrammelled. Section 15(1) stipulates that the court must have regard to the following matters (although not exclusively):

(a)   the intentions of the person or persons (if any) who created the trust,

(b)   the purposes for which the property subject to the trust is held,

---

3 S 14(3).
4 S 14(1).
5 Cf *Re House* [1929] 2 Ch 166.
6 HL Debs, vol 570, cols 1542-1543, 25 March 1996.
7 S 14(4).
8 Cf *Carmel Exporters (Sales) Ltd* v *Sea-land Services Inc* [1981] 1 All ER 984, 992-993.

(c)   the welfare of any minor who occupies or might reasonably be expected to occupy any land subject to the trust as his home, and

(d)   the interests of any secured creditor of any beneficiary.

By and large these reflect concerns evidenced in the caselaw under the trust for sale system.[9] The Law Commission's draft Bill however included specific reference to the rights of adult beneficiaries entitled in possession, to chargees under the Charging Orders Act 1979, and to "any other matters appearing to the court to be relevant".[10] The second of these has been widened in this Act to "any secured creditor", and the third was probably thought unnecessary to be spelled out.

But section 15(2) *does* refer specifically to the interests of beneficiaries entitled to occupy the land under section 12, and requires the court on an application relating to the exercise of the trustees' powers under section 13 to have regard to their circumstances and wishes. Section 15(3) imposes a requirement on any other kinds of application (except one under section 6(2)) to have regard to the circumstances and wishes of any beneficiaries *of full age* and entitled to an interest in possession. In the case of dispute, the trustees are to have regard to the majority by value. But it is clear that in neither case is the court *bound* by these circumstances and wishes. They are simply a factor to be taken into account.

It will be interesting to see how the courts treat the case law on LPA section 30 in relation to applications under section 14. The Lord Advocate, introducing the Bill on Second Reading in the House of Lords, plainly thought that they would apply it.[11] The most important difference is that the old law depended on there being a *trust* for sale, with *power* to postpone sale. So the predominant legal characteristic was clear from the outset, and the section 30 case law was built up on the question in what circumstances it was right to override that characteristic. But the new law is balanced: unless an express trust for sale is created, there is *power* to sell and *power* to retain. Yet the case law contained a number of useful ideas, such as the collateral purpose which should not be frustrated[12], the purpose now incapable of fulfilment[13] and so on. Time will tell.

---

9 See 4.6 and 8.3 above.
10 See Law Com No 181, paras 12.9 and 12.10, and cl 6 of the Bill.
11 HL Debs, vol 569, col 1719, 1 March 1996.
12 *Re Buchanan-Wollaston's Conveyance* [1939] Ch 738.
13 *Jones v Challenger* [1961] 1 QB 176.

9.4 Applications by trustee in bankruptcy

There is a separate regime where the section 14 application is made by a trustee in bankruptcy. Section 15 itself does not apply.[14] Instead, there is a new section 335A inserted into the Insolvency Act 1986.[15] The section provides, first, that the application should be made to the court having jurisdiction in relation to the bankruptcy.[16]

Section 335A(2) then provides:

> On such an application the court shall make such order as it thinks just and reasonable having regard to -
>
> (a)   the interests of the bankrupt's creditors;
>
> (b)   where the application is made in respect of land which includes a dwelling house which is or has been the home of the bankrupt or the bankrupt spouse or former spouse -
>
>> (i)   the conduct of the spouse or former spouse, so far as contributing the bankruptcy,
>>
>> (ii)   the needs and financial resources of the spouse or former spouse, and
>>
>> (iii) the needs of any children; and
>
> (c)   all the circumstances of the case other than the needs of the bankrupt.

But subsection (3) then makes clear that the interests of the bankrupt's creditors are paramount where the application is made after the end of one year from the first vesting of the bankrupt's property in the trustee, *unless* the circumstances are exceptional. This is the same provision as that found in sections 336(5) and 337(6) of the Insolvency Act 1986.

Again, it is provided that the court's powers under this section are exercisable whenever the application was made', *i.e.* the originating process issued.

These provisions are in line with the Law Commission's recommendations[17] and their draft Bill (although enacted in a slightly different form of drafting).

---

14 See s 15(4).
15 See Sched 3, para 23 of the 1996 Act.
16 Subs (1).
17 See Law Com No 181, paras 12.11 and 12.12.

9.5 Trust of proceeds of sale

Unlike LPA section 30, section 14 applies also to a trust of *proceeds of sale of land* as it applies to a trust of land.[18] For this purpose, such a trust is defined as one where the property

> consists of or includes -
>
> (a)   any proceeds of a disposition of land held in trust (including settled land), or
>
> (b)   any property representing any such proceeds.[19]

For this purpose, the "disposition" includes one before this Act comes into force.[20] However, despite the words in brackets in paragraph (a), any trust which despite section 2 of this Act is still a settlement for the purposes of the SLA is excluded from being a trust of proceeds of sale of land.[21] So if there is a "disposition" of settled land[22] resulting in capital money arising, it is necessary to check and see if the trust remains an SLA settlement. If it does not, then it will be a trust of proceeds of land, and an application can be made to the court under section 14. But if it *does* remain an SLA settlement, then it is not such a trust, and section 14 cannot apply. For the purposes of these provisions, "trust" is widely defined, and covers *any* description of trust, whenever created or arising.[23]

Finally, one limitation: whereas LPA section 30 applied to *personal representatives* holding land on trust for sale[24], section 14 does not do so.[25]

---

18 S 17(2).
19 S 17(3).
20 S 17(6)(a).
21 S 17(5).
22 Including heirlooms: s 17(6)(b).
23 S 17(4).
24 See s 205(1)(xxi) of that Act.
25 S 18(1).

Main practical consequences of sections 14 and 15

1. The court's powers have been extended to cover disputes about the exercise of any of the trustees' functions or about the nature or extent of beneficiaries' interests.

2. The court must now have regard to a number of factors, including the intentions of the settlor/testator, the purposes of holding the property, and the interests of minors and secured creditors.

3. The pre-Act case law under LPA section 30 will still be relevant, though not determinative.

4. There is a new statutory regime for dealing with applications by the trustee in bankruptcy of a beneficiary for an order for sale of the property.

5. The section 14 procedure applies to trusts of *proceeds of sale* of land, just as it applies to trusts of land.

Chapter 10

Protection for Purchasers*

- Continuation of existing LPA section 2(1)(ii) and (2) (overreaching) and LPA section 27 protection
- New additional protection reflecting risk areas new to the changed regime
- New deed of discharge provisions avoiding the need for purchasers to investigate the equities following conveyance to beneficiary on termination of the trust
- Need for statutory declaration within three months of a purchase to protect purchaser relying on delegated powers under section 9

10.1 The existing continuing LPA section 27 and section 2(1)(ii) and (2) protection

The existing overreaching provisions in LPA 1925 section 2(1)(ii), 2(2) and section 27 continue to govern the new regime, subject only to consequential amendments. Before we deal with LPA section 27, a point needs to be made about the changed context. Trustees have a duty, not just to act within their statutory or express powers, but to exercise them in the interests of the beneficiaries. Before the 1996 Act came into force, the statutory powers of trustees for sale were limited, but they had after all a *duty* to sell.

The balance now has changed. A trust for sale is unlikely. Trustees relying on what is now a statutorily implied trust have no duty to sell. Of course they now have the powers in relation to the land of an absolute owner. But as the power has expanded the importance of the duty to act in the interests of the beneficiaries has grown too. Trustees can no longer shelter behind a duty to sell. Whether an action is within their powers is usually easy to decide; but the issue between them and the beneficiaries, of whether it is a proper exercise of their discretion, can be a matter of opinion. Does that ever concern a purchaser too? In this changed context LPA section 27 now needs to be read.

---

* S 16.

LPA section 27, originally protecting purchasers buying from trustees for sale with a duty to sell, differs markedly from SLA section 110, protecting purchasers from a tenant for life who had a power but no such duty. Is section 27 adequate in the changed regime of trusts of land? Neither section 27 nor SLA section 110 appear to target directly whether discretions are exercised properly. Perhaps it is implicit a purchaser is not concerned. If it is implicit, the reference to section 6(5) in section 16(1) is unnecessary.[1] But with the new statutory absolute owner powers the increased role of the duty to the beneficiaries may be a source of litigation. As amended by the new Act, LPA section 27 reads:

> Purchaser not to be concerned with the trusts of proceeds of sale which are to be paid to two or more trustees or to a trust corporation

Oddly, the new Act has not amended the heading. The new wording of subsection (1), however, now goes beyond trusts of proceeds of sale.

> 27(1) A purchaser of a legal estate from trustees of land shall not be concerned with the trusts affecting the land, the net income of the land or the proceeds of sale whether or not those trusts are declared by the same instrument as that by which the trust is created.

The new provisions extend to the trusts themselves and not just the proceeds of sale. This is an amendment consequential on the abolition of the doctrine of conversion in section 3.

> (2)   Notwithstanding anything to the contrary in the instrument (if any) creating a trust of land or in any trust affecting the net proceeds of land if it is sold, the proceeds of sale or other capital money shall not be paid to or applied by the direction of fewer than two trustees, except where the trustee is a trust corporation, but this subsection does not affect the right of a sole personal representative as such to give valid receipts for, or direct the application of, proceeds of sale or other capital money, nor, except where capital money arises on the transaction, render it necessary to have more than one trustee.

The section is not drawn so as to make it clear that the subsection (1) protection is dependant on following the subsection (2) formalities (two or more trustees to receive capital money). Nevertheless that is how it has been construed.[1a] See also section 2 (1)(ii) quoted below.

---

1 See 10.3 below. S 16(1) protects purchasers from the failure of the trustees to follow the statutory duty in s 6(5). It does not however in terms relieve purchasers from checking whether the trustees have followed the general equitable duty to much the same effect.

1a Compare *City of London Building Society* v *Flegg* [1988] AC 54 with *Williams & Glyn's Bank* v *Boland* [1981] AC 487.

Section 23 of the LPA has been repealed. It was an important support for LPA section 27. It deemed in favour of a purchaser that a trust for sale subsisted until the land had been conveyed to ... persons interested in the proceeds of sale. The rationale for the repeal is that it is no longer needed. "Trust of land" is now defined to include any trust (of any description, including a bare trust) of property which consists of or includes land. So that now it is still a "trust of land" even though there is a bare trust arising, for example, because the beneficial interests of several beneficiaries become vested in one adult beneficiary. The purchaser does not need to assume that the trust is still subsisting.

LPA section 2 also has some relevance. It is subject to consequential amendments, but unchanged in substance.

> **Conveyances overreaching certain equitable interests and powers**
> 2 (1) A conveyance to a purchaser of a legal estate in land shall overreach any equitable interest or power affecting that estate, whether or not he has notice thereof, if - ...
>
>> (ii) the conveyance is made by trustees of land and the equitable interest or power is at the date of the conveyance capable of being overreached by such trustees under the provisions of subsection (2) of this section or independently of that subsection and the requirements of section 27 of this Act respecting the payment of capital money on such a conveyance are complied with; ...
>
> (2) Where the legal estate affected is subject to a trust of land, then if at the date of a conveyance made after the commencement of this Act by the trustees, the trustees (whether original or substituted) are either -
>
> (a) two or more individuals approved or appointed by the court or the successors in office of the individuals so approved or appointed; or
>
> (b) a trust corporation,
>
> any equitable interest or power having priority to the trust of land shall, notwithstanding any stipulation to the contrary, be overreached by the conveyance, and shall, according to its priority, take effect as if created or arising by means of a primary trust affecting the proceeds of sale and the income of the land until sale.
>
> (3) *(The list of equitable interests and powers excluded from subsection (2) remains unchanged)*

Subsection (2) deals with equitable interests or powers *having priority to* the trust of land, not those arising under the trust. While the subsection is the subject of consequential amendments, it is

outside the main focus of this work. It is limited to conveyances by
trustees appointed or approved by the court or their successors in
office, and consequently rarely applies.

The more general provisions in subsection (1)(ii) also apply
however whenever the equitable interest is capable of being
overreached independently of subsection (2).

10.2 Trustee Act 1925 section 17

Section 17 of the Trustee Act 1925 does not rate a mention in some
of the shorter conveyancing texts. But as it is concerned with trustees
it is relevant to our subject, trusts of land. Its range is not wide, but it
offers protection not given elsewhere:

> 17.   **Protection to mortgagees dealing with trustees**
>
> No purchaser or mortgagee paying or advancing money on a sale or
> mortgage purporting to be made under any trust or power vested in
> trustees, shall be concerned to see that such money is wanted; or that no
> more than is wanted is raised, or otherwise as to its application thereof.

10.3 New protection of purchasers of unregistered land in section 16(1) to (3)

The new additional provisions in section 16(1) to (3), reproduced
and commented on below, like section 16(4) and (5) (see 10.4 below)
do not apply to registered land. Provisions comparable to section
16(5) protecting the registrar when registration of title takes place,
however, are dealt with separately below.

Subsections (1) to (3) are necessitated by the new regime because
it creates, mainly as between the trustees and those beneficially
interested, new, or wider, or clarified requirements on trustees and
the possibility of limitations in the trust instrument. Conveyancing
would grind to a halt if purchasers' solicitors had to check what
additional limitations exist and that all limitations or requirements,
statutory or personal to the trust, had been observed.

Beneficiaries' rights, consent for partitioning and duties to consult beneficiaries

Section 16(1) makes it unnecessary for a purchaser to check whether
the trustees have followed:

(a) the direction in section 6(5) to have regard to the rights of the beneficiaries in exercising their enlarged general powers under section 6 (s 6(5));[1b]

(b) the direction to obtain beneficiaries' consent before partitioning land under section 6(2) (s 6(3)); or

(c) the widened general duty to consult beneficiaries and give effect to their wishes in exercising any function (s 11(1)).

Protection of purchasers

16(1) A purchaser of land which is or has been subject to a trust need not be concerned to see that any requirement imposed on trustees by section 6(5), 7(3) or 11(1) has been complied with.

Statutory requirements and rules of law or equity

Section 16(2) protects purchasers from invalidity caused by:

- contraventions of section 6(6) (overriding effect of other enactments or any rule of law or equity); or
- section 6(8) (the need to comply with restrictions, limitations or conditions imposed by another enactment)

if the purchaser has no actual notice of the contravention.

16 (2) Where -

(a) trustees of land who convey land which (immediately before it is conveyed) is subject to the trust contravene section 6(6) or (8), but

(b) the purchaser of the land from the trustees has no actual notice of the contravention,
the contravention does not invalidate the conveyance.

The contravention which does not invalidate the conveyance is that of section 6(6) or (8). It is suggested that this does not relieve a purchaser from the need to see where necessary that the requirements of any other enactments or rule of law is complied with.

Limitations under section 8 of statutory absolute owner powers under sections 6 and 7

Section 16(3) gives protection again for a purchaser with no actual notice, this time against "limitations" by virtue of section 8. That word is presumably intended to include:

1b There is however a wider general equitable duty to have regard to the interests of the beneficiaries, and this does not appear to be covered by the protection given by s 16(1). See 10.1.

- section 8(1) – the enlarged absolute owner powers in section 6 and the power of partition in section 7 are not to apply in so far as provision to that effect is made by the disposition, and
- section 8(2) – the disposition may require consent to be obtained to the exercise of any section 6 or section 7 power.

Note however the reverse implication. A purchaser who has actual notice of the limitation or need for consent must investigate whether the disposal conforms with the limitation or that consent was given as appropriate. If consent was required, section 10 will apply, replacing the comparable provisions in LPA section 26, now repealed. In favour of a purchaser the consent of any two is enough if the disposition requires a larger number.

The need for the new protection originates in the enlargement of the statutory trustees' powers we have discussed in Chapter 5. Now the statutory norm for the powers of trustees of land is the power of an absolute owner under section 6(1). When drafting the trust instrument, instead of enlarging limited statutory powers as was usual, settlors and their advisers may have imposed restrictions on the enlarged statutory power. The limitations are no longer in the statute but they may be in the trust instrument. But a purchaser – and this is the point of section 16(3) – may assume, in relation to a post-1996 dealing, that the wide statutory power applies unless a limitation has been brought to his notice.

That is not the case for transactions before 1997[1c]. The old law applied for these and a purchaser continues to be concerned now, in checking parts of a title which are before 1997, that the dealing was within statutory or dispositionary powers as they then existed.

Duty to bring limitations to the notice of purchasers

There is a further provision in section 16(3) which needs to be stressed, only indirectly concerned with protecting purchasers, more directly prescribing duties of trustees. If section 8 limitations exist, it is the duty of trustees to take reasonable steps to bring them to the notice of any purchaser from them. The duty is to take reasonable steps rather than absolute. But in a simple case of limitations in the trust disposition, reasonable steps would surely consist of sending a copy of them to the purchaser or his solicitors if he was represented.

1c Assuming, here and in the previous and following sentences, that the commencement date of the Act is 1 January 1997.

16 (3) Where the powers of a trustee of land are limited by virtue of section 8 -

(a)   the trustees shall take all reasonable steps to bring the limitation to the notice of any purchaser of the land from them, but

(b)   the limitation does not invalidate any conveyance by the trustees to a purchaser who has no actual notice of the limitation.

Actual notice

In all three subsections the reference is to "actual" notice, one stage more emphatic than the "knowledge" which relieves a purchaser under section 9(2) (see 10.6). Constructive notice will not be enough. Does "actual" notice include imputed notice, that is where the purchaser's agent has the knowledge? We are not aware of authority on the point, but it would be strange if a purchaser could take free on the grounds of his solicitor's omission to tell him. It would imply the trustees should only communicate with the purchaser direct – an absurd consequence.

Charitable, ecclesiastical or public trusts of land

Under section 16(6) subsections (2) and (3) do not apply to land held on charitable, ecclesiastical or public trusts.[2] As before we will reduce this to "charitable etc trusts". The implications need to be explored:

(a) In the case of subsections (2) and (3) purchaser protection does not apply for charitable etc trusts. Those subsections concern statutory requirements and rules of law or equity, and limitations under section 8 of statutory absolute owner powers under sections 6 and 7.

(b) The loss of protection in respect of section 8(1) – allowing the disposition to negative or restrict enlarged absolute owner powers in section 6 and the power of partition in section 7 is not a real loss, because section 8(1) does not apply to charitable etc trusts anyway.

(c) But for section 8(2) (consents) and the requirements of other enactments or rules of law or equity, subject to any express

---

2 For a discussion of what this phrase means, see 1.15.

provisions in the particular legislation, a purchaser from a charitable trust is concerned to see that the requirements are complied with, and that necessary consents are obtained.

(d) Section 16(1) applies to charitable as it does to other trusts. It concerns beneficiaries rights, consent for partitioning and duties to consult beneficiaries. The nature of the duties which it covers is such that they are unlikely to apply to a charity. Be that as it may, a purchaser who has no actual knowlege of a contravention is not concerned, whether the trust is charitable or not.

Invalidity and the need to overreach as well

There is another difference between the subsections. Section 16(2) and (3) protect purchasers against *invalidity* caused by contraventions of their subject matter if the purchaser has no actual knowledge of the contravention or limitation. The transaction will still be valid in favour of a purchaser who does not know of the contravention or limitation. That does not always mean that the purchaser will take free of the beneficial interests. For that freedom to operate the purchaser needs to rely on the overreaching effects of LPA 1925 section 27. In particular the purchaser, to gain the protection of both sections, must be a purchaser of a legal estate and must pay capital money to at least two trustees or a trust corporation.

Section 16(1) uses a different phrase, "need not be concerned to see" – slightly less emphatic than the corresponding phrase in LPA section 27(1) "shall not be concerned with the trusts affecting ...", which for section 27 has a wide effect if section 27(2) (payment of capital money) is observed. Clearly the purchaser is not entitled to enquire about the subjects covered by section 16(1), and probably would be unwise to enquire. The subsection does not say in so many words that the transaction is valid in favour of a purchaser but perhaps that is implicit, or at least the subsection further supports a purchaser who relies on the more general protection in sections 2 and 27.

But suppose somehow the purchaser is actually aware the trustees are in breach of the duties referred to in section 16(1). In the case of subsections (2) and (3) actual knowledge removes the purchaser's protection. Does actual knowledge have a similar effect for subsection (1)? Would it make the transaction invalid, or if not, leave the purchaser a constructive trustee for the abused beneficial interests? The wording is not the same as AEA 1925 section 36(7), where, in favour of a purchaser, an assent or conveyance in respect of a legal estate by a personal representative is to be "taken as sufficient evidence" that the disposition is to the right person. On that wording however *Re Duce and Boots Cash Chemists (Southern) Ltd Contract*[2a] shows that a buyer was entitled to object to the title when the abstract and recitals in the assent both showed that the assent was to the wrong person – the remainderman instead of the tenant for life.

Perhaps it is a theoretical quibble, because in practice a purchaser actually aware of a contravention would and should insist on compliance.

10.4 The new deed of discharge on termination of the trust

It is convenient to consider subsections (4) and (5) together. Where unregistered land is conveyed to beneficiaries on termination of the trust, section 16(4) creates a duty on the trustees to execute a deed of discharge, and section 16(5) protects a purchaser who has relied on such a deed without actual knowledge of a mistake.

The subsections provide a completely new deed of discharge procedure for trusts of land. Unlike subsections (1) to (3) the provision is not made necessary by the new regime. It is welcome law reform occupying (though unfortunately not completely filling) a previous gap in the legislation. For settled land there are already comparable provisions for a deed of discharge on termination of the settlement in SLA 1925 section 17.

For trusts for sale of land, however, until 1997[3] a conveyance to the beneficiaries brought the equities on to the title. Practitioners sometimes overlooked this exception to the curtain principle. A purchaser from such beneficiaries needed to investigate their equitable entitlement.

"There is no formal provision for the termination of a trust for sale. This means that purchasers of land which has been subject to a trust for sale may be put in the position of having to investigate the trusts in order to ascertain the trust for sale has ended." – Law Com No 181 paragraph 3.9 – quoting their October 1985 Working Paper.

(Except where the trustees were holding on trust for themselves as joint tenants and there is only one survivor. Here a purchaser could

---

2a [1937] Ch 642.
3 Assuming that the commencement date of the Act is 1 January 1997.

rely on a conveyance as beneficial owner under the Law of Property (Joint Tenants) Act 1964, but since the reform of covenants for title under the Law of Property (Miscellaneous Provisions) Act 1994 can now only rely on a statement that the seller is solely and beneficially interested.)

The difficulties of bringing the equitable interest on the title often made it more convenient to prolong the trust on paper after its real life was spent. The trustees would continue to hold in trust for the person absolutely entitled until a sale of the property was requested by that person. A purchaser could then rely on LPA section 23 – in favour of a purchaser the trust for sale was deemed to be subsisting – and on the overreaching effect of LPA sections 2 and 27. If a surviving tenant in common became entitled to the whole beneficial interest, for example as beneficiary under the will(s) of the deceased co-owner(s), one conveyancing option is to abstract the terms of those wills. But that leaves a purchaser vulnerable to undisclosed dealings with the equitable interest. An assent of that equitable interest is of little value, since it is not in respect of a legal estate and so does not carry the presumption under AEA 1925 section 36 that it is in favour of the correct person. A safer course is for the surviving trustee/legal owner, although the only person beneficially entitled, to appoint a second trustee when selling to obtain the benefit of LPA sections 2 and 27 and avoid the need to prove or investigate the equitable interest to justify selling as sole owner.

The same considerations sometimes made it expedient for personal representatives to retain land in that capacity rather than vest it in themselves or others as trustees. If there was an elderly person with a right of residence, for example, the personal representatives might be better advised not to assent to themselves as trustees on trust for sale – if that is what the settlement had created. If they did so they could not later convey to the person ultimately entitled on the death of the life tenant without bringing the equities on the title. By retaining the land as personal representatives they could assent in favour of the person ultimately entitled when the life tenant died, and a later purchaser could in relation to that assent rely on AEA section 36.

Most of those manoeuvrings will in future no longer be necessary. Those reasons for delaying or avoiding vesting property in trustees as trustees, in order to avoid the ultimate transfer from the trustees to the person absolutely entitled and the consequent need to prove his beneficial entitlement, no longer hold good. When it is time to vest land in the persons absolutely entitled it is simply a question of executing a section 16(4) deed of discharge at the same time as the conveyance. Purchasers can then rely on the protection given by section 16(5).

At this stage we can quote the two subsections:

> 16(4) – Where trustees of land convey land which (immediately before it is conveyed) is subject to the trust to persons believed by them to be beneficiaries absolutely entitled to the land under the trust and of full age and capacity -
>
> (a)   the trustees shall execute a deed declaring that they are discharged from the trust in relation to that land, and
>
> (b)   if they fail to do so, the court may make an order requiring them to do so.
>
> 16(5) – A purchaser of land to which a deed under subsection (4) relates is entitled to assume that, as from the date of the deed, the land is not subject to the trust unless he has actual notice that the trustees were mistaken in their belief that the land was conveyed to beneficiaries absolutely entitled to the land under the trust and of full age and capacity.

It follows from the wording of the subsections that a surviving trustee-tenant in common who becomes entitled to the whole beneficial interest cannot execute an effective section 16(4) deed of discharge. Section 16(4) only applies where trustees of land convey it to the beneficiary believed to be absolutely entitled. It does not operate where such a beneficiary already is the legal owner, *e.g.* as surviving trustee, so no conveyance is needed. In that one case it will still be safer to appoint a second trustee when selling or receiving capital money and to rely on the overreaching effect of LPA sections 2 and 27.

To what extent is section 16 (4) and (5) retrospective?

If, before the Act came into force, A and B, say in January 1996, conveyed land previously subject to a trust for sale to C, the person absolutely entitled, can C now call for a deed of discharge, and if one is executed, can a purchaser from C rely on it?

Almost certainly the answer to both questions is "no". "Trust of land" is defined of course to include such trusts created or arising before the commencement of the Act. That, however, is not the issue. The question is not whether section 16 applies to trusts created before the commencement of the Act, but whether section 16 is capable of applying to actions by trustees before the Act commenced. Some sections make specific provision to clarify the retrospective element or lack of it – for example sections 2(1), 2(5), 3(2) and (3), 4(2) and (3), 9(9), 11(2)(b), 14(4) and 25(4) and (5). No such provision occurs in section 16. So it is necessary to construe the words used, applying the presumption against legislation having retrospective effect. Clear words are needed to justify a retrospective effect, and such indications as there are in section 16 suggest the opposite.

The duty to execute a deed of discharge is triggered "where trustees of land convey ..." Not "where trustees of land *have conveyed*". The implication of the present tense is to limit the duty imposed by section 16(4) to such a conveyance carried out after the Act commenced. So the duty to execute the deed of discharge, and the power of the court to order execution, does not apply to a conveyance completed in 1996, or 1926, or indeed to any conveyance before 1 January 1997.[4]

If that is correct, then section 16(5) cannot help a purchaser after a pre-Act conveyance to a beneficiary. Suppose having completed the conveyance before commencement, the trustees execute a deed of discharge voluntarily after commencement, perhaps because of difficulty in proving strictly the beneficial entitlement of the person to whom the land was conveyed. Section 16(5) protects a purchaser of land "to which a deed under subsection (4) relates". But if the deed of discharge was not required by subsection (4), the land could not be land "to which a deed under subsection (4) relates". So the purchaser would be outside the terms of, and unprotected by, section 16(5) .

10.5 Protection – new provisions for registered land

The existing overreaching provisions in LPA 1925 section 2(1)(ii), 2(2) and section 27 apply both to registered and unregistered land and have been quoted earlier as slightly amended by the new Act. Section 16, also quoted earlier, does not apply to registered land. Nevertheless subsections have been added to LRA 1925 section 94 partly reflecting the new regime, and partly reflecting section 16(4), and these will be detailed below.

First, a brief reminder why section 16 protection provisions are considered unnecessary for registered land. It is trite to say the Land Registry does not recognise trusts. References to trusts are, so far as practicable, to be excluded from the register and neither the registrar

---

4 Assuming that the commencement date of the Act is 1 January 1997.

nor any person dealing with a registered estate or charge is to be affected with notice of a trust (LRA section 74). The Registry cannot enter notice of interests capable of being overreached by the proprietor (LRA section 49(2)). Under LRA sections 20(1) and 23(1) disposals of registered land are subject to registered incumbrances and overriding interests (and to the covenants and conditions of the lease if leasehold) but free of all other interests whatsoever.

Certainly in practice co-proprietors of registered land were rarely prejudiced by the limited statutory powers of trustees in the few cases where the trust instrument had not enlarged them. "In practice" because proprietors of registered land are assumed to have full powers of disposition unless restrictions are noted on the register, and in practice restrictions were not registered against co-proprietors (although they were against strict settlement tenants for life) to record the former limited statutory powers of disposal, unless the disposition contained an express limitation or requirement for consent.[5]

But nevertheless trusts of land, as they now are, do impinge on registered land to some extent. Unless the land is held beneficially as joint tenants the Registry should be asked to register the commonplace specific restriction required by LRA section 58(3) (Form 62) that no disposition by a sole proprietor of the land (not being a trust corporation) under which capital money arises is to be registered except under an order of the Registrar or of the court. Applications to register and Form 19(JP) require information on whether this restriction is applicable. It reflects that LPA section 27, about numbers of trustees, applies to registered land.[6] LRA section 58(1) as it stands contains a more general provision enabling restrictions to be registered about consents or requiring that some "other matter or thing is done".

Lack of good faith will apparently remove protection[7] as will fraud.[8] And the provisions about overriding interests make a purchaser vulnerable to equitable interests if the beneficiary is in occupation. Sale by two or more may overreach (*City of London Building Society* v *Flegg*).[9] The risk of overriding interests looms larger in a constructive trust, when the restriction against dispositions

---

5 See 5.1.
6 See LRA s 95.
7 *Peffer* v *Rigg* [1977] 1 WLR 285.
8 *Lyas* v *Prowsa Developments Ltd* [1982] 1 WLR 1044.
9 [1988] AC 54.

by sole proprietors is unlikely to have been made. *Williams and Glyn's Bank Ltd* v *Boland*[10] is notorious, but less famously the purchaser in *Hodgson* v *Marks*[11] was subject to the beneficial interest of the occupying lady who had voluntarily transferred her legal estate to the vendor but without intending a gift.

The new subsections to LRA section 94 – Land held in trust (see Sched 3 para 5(8)(c))

(4)   There shall also be entered on the register such restrictions as may be prescribed, or may be expedient, for the protection of the rights of persons beneficially interested in the land.

This' is a brand new provision. It did not appear in the Law Commission's original draft Bill and does not appear to have been discussed or even referred to in the parliamentary debates on the Bill. It is presumably intended to clarify the registrar's ability to note such restrictions despite LRA section 74. At [??] no such restrictions have been prescribed.

Possibly the content of such regulations will include restrictions to record any limitations on powers of disposal or requirements for consent under section 8 which, for unregistered land, the trustees are directed by section 16(3) to take reasonable steps to bring to the notice of any purchaser. If so, there appears to be an overlap with LRA section 58(1).

Section 16(3) imposes a duty on the trustees to take reasonable steps to bring limitations under section 8 to the notice of purchasers. That duty does not apply to registered land and there is no need for it to do so. If restrictions are registered a purchaser will have notice of them and will need to see they are complied with. If no restriction is registered a purchaser can assume, under normal registered land principles, that the registered proprietors have full powers of disposal. In general, and subject to the limited inroads on the principle already quoted, a purchaser of registered land does not need to be protected from limitations of which he has no actual knowledge.[12]

---

10 [1981] AC 487.

11 [1971] Ch 892.

12 Although if restrictions are registered, notice will be deemed. It will of course be actual or imputed if the purchaser's solicitor has carried out the basic precaution of inspecting office copy entries and making a Land Registry search.

(5)   Where a deed has been executed under section 16(4) of the Trusts of Land and Appointment of Trustees Act 1996 by trustees of land the registrar is entitled to assume that, as from the date of the deed, the land to which the deed relates is not subject to the trust unless he has actual notice that the trustees were mistaken in their belief that the land was conveyed to beneficiaries absolutely entitled to the land under the trust and of full age and capacity.

The wording closely follows section 16(5), this time protecting the registrar rather than a purchaser of unregistered land. Note however that it cannot apply to land where the title was registered at the time of the [conveyance]. The deed of discharge needs to be executed under section 16(4), and section 16 does not apply to registered land (s 16(7)); so a deed of discharge of registered land could not be under section 16(4). The only application of the new subsection must be to a conveyance of unregistered land and deed of discharge, followed later by an application to register the title. It is at that stage that the registrar could rely on the new subsection.

10.6 Protection of purchaser relying on the exercise of delegated powers

Limitations on powers of attorney by trustees

Advisers of trustee donors of powers of attorney, even where they are beneficial owners too, and purchasers relying on such a power, need to take special care. It is well known that trustees are subject to the principle of delegatus non potest delegare and cannot use a general power of attorney under the Powers of Attorney Act 1971. This is so even where the trustee is a beneficial owner. In *Walia* v *Michael Naughton Ltd*[13] the fact there was more than one proprietor meant they were trustees, despite the absence of the LRA section 58(3) restriction on the register. A purchaser was entitled to reject a general power of attorney.

Powers of attorney outside the 1996 Act

The forms of powers of attorney open to trustees independently of the 1996 Act are:

1. *A power of attorney under TA section 25 as amended by PAA 1971 section 9*

---

13 [1985] 1 WLR 1115.

It is no longer limited to absence abroad but the period may not exceed 12 months.

(a) In favour of a person dealing with the donee of the power the acts of the donee are not invalidated by the donor's failure to give notice of the power to the other trustees etc within one month under TA section 25(4).

(b) Where a power of attorney has been revoked and a person, without knowledge of the revocation, deals with the donee of the power, the transaction between them is, in favour of that person, as valid as if the power had been in existence. (PAA section 5(2))

(c) Where the interest of a purchaser depends on whether a transaction between the donee of a power of attorney and another person was valid by virtue of subsection PAA section 5(2) it is conclusively presumed in favour of the purchaser that the person did not at the material time know of the revocation of the power if:

– the transaction between that person and the donee was completed within 12 months of the date on which power came into operation; (PAA section 5(4)(a)) or

– that person makes a statutory declaration, before or within three months after completion of the purchase, that he did not at the material time know of the revocation of the power. (PAA section 5(4)(b))

For a TA section 25 power the alternative in PAA section 5(4)(b) of a statutory declaration is never needed, since a section 25 power is bound to be limited to a 12 month period and so must always be exercised within that period. A section 25 power may not be in favour of the only other co-trustee.

2. *An enduring power under the Enduring Powers of Attorney Act 1985, using the prescribed form*

Before the power is registered with the court:

PAA section 5 protection so far as applicable applies in favour of third persons as quoted in (1) (a) and (b) above.

After registration of the enduring power with the court a purchaser's protection goes further. He may be protected against invalidity too:

9 – (3) Any transaction between the attorney and another person shall, in favour of that person, be as valid as if the power had then been in existence, unless at the time of the transaction that person had knowledge

of any of the matters mentioned in subsection (2) above
(i.e. invalidity, revocation or expiry)

9 – (4) Where the interest of a purchaser depends on whether a transaction between the attorney and another person was valid by virtue of subsection (3) above it shall be conclusively presumed in favour of the purchaser that the transaction was valid if

(a)   the transaction between that person and the attorney was completed within twelve months of the date on which the instrument was registered; or

(b)   that person makes a statutory declaration before or within three months after completion of the purchase that he had no reason at the time of the transaction to doubt that the attorney had authority to dispose of the property which was the subject of the transaction.

Again this declaration is therefore only needed where the disposal by the attorney is delayed, but this time after *12 months from registration* of the power.

Section 9(6) and Schedule 2 of EPAA give further protection in cases where the instrument failed to create a valid enduring power and the power has been revoked by the donor's mental incapacity. Broadly, a purchaser is protected if he neither knew of the invalidity nor that the donor has become mentally incapable. (This does not obviate the need to examine the power carefully. If, for example, the current prescribed form was not used a purchaser could not claim he did not know of the invalidity.)

The attorney may, subject to the power, exercise trusts, powers or discretions vested in the donor as trustee and may "without the concurrence of any other person give a valid receipt for capital or other money paid." The relationship of this with LPA section 27 which requires capital money to be paid to not less than two trustees, is unclear. No express provision prohibits a trustee from giving an enduring power to a co-trustee. But it is safer to assume that a receipt given solely by that co-trustee, partly as attorney and partly on his own behalf, will lose the benefit of the overreaching powers in section 27.

Delegation under the 1996 Act section 9

To those complex niceties is now added a third possibility, that of delegation under TLATA 1996 section 9. That subject has been covered earlier in Chapter 6; we are here only concerned with the provisions in section 9(2) to protect purchasers, afterthoughts introduced in the Bill at report stage and amended at third reading. They fall short of complete self-contained protection.

> 9 – (2) Where trustees purport to delegate to a person by a power of attorney under subsection (1) functions relating to any land and another person in good faith deals with him in relation to the land, he shall be presumed in relation to that other person to have been a person to whom the functions could be delegated unless that other person has knowledge at the time of the transaction that he is not such a person.
>
> And it shall be conclusively presumed in favour of any purchaser whose interest depends on the validity of that transaction that that other person dealt in good faith and did not have such knowledge if that other person makes a statutory declaration to that effect before or within three months after completion of the purchase.

Section 9 envisages invalidity or revocation of a section 9 power in four circumstances:

(a) section 9(2) the section 9 attorney is not a person to whom powers could validly be delegated;

(b) section 9(3) express revocation by any one or more of the trustees;

(c) section 9(3) revocation by the appointment of a new trustee (but not death or retirement of existing trustees);

(d) section 9(4) revocation because the section 9 attorney ceases to be entitled to a beneficial interest in possession.

There is a fifth possibility – the supervening mental incapacity of a trustee, since a section 9 power of attorney cannot be an enduring power (s 9(6)).

It is only in relation to (a) that section 9(2) protects a purchaser. It protects against initial invalidity because the section 9 attorney is not eligible or the person dealing lacked good faith; it does not protect against subsequent revocation.

It is easy to see why the protection is required. A purchaser could not check the qualification of the delegatee, in particular that he was beneficially entitled to an interest in possession, without investigating the equitable interests, and the whole thrust of the Act is to reinforce the intention of the 1925 legislation that these should not concern a purchaser. And as for checking the good faith of a predecessor!

A declaration by the person dealing with the delegatee is always required before or within three months after that person's sale. There is no automatic dispensing with the need for a declaration if the exercise of the power by the attorney is within 12 months from the power (as it is under PAA) or from registration (as it is under EPAA).

The subsequent purchaser appears to be conclusively protected if the declaration is obtained whether he knows of invalidity or not. He has nevertheless to be a "purchaser". In the 1996 Act "purchaser" has the same meaning as in LPA Part I (see 1.12). In that definition, unlike the definition for the rest of LPA, "good faith" is not a requirement. The person dealing with the attorney, whose own protection does not require a declaration, nevertheless loses it if he has knowledge at the time of the transaction that the attorney was not qualified. He also loses it if he lacks good faith. Interestingly however the phrase is not used in the comparable provisions in PAA.

How can a subsequent purchaser following the exercise of a power of attorney under section 9 also be protected from the possibility of revocation? By relying on PAA. So such a purchaser needs to see that:

1. In any event the person dealing with the attorney makes the declaration under section 9(2) before or within three months after that person's sale (the purchaser's purchase). That declaration only gives protection against invalidity of the transaction because of the ineligibility of the attorney.

2. It will usually be necessary for a purchaser to obtain protection against the possibility of revocation too.

3. If the original transaction with the attorney was within 12 months of the power no further action is required. (PAA section 5(4)(a))

4. If it was not, a further declaration under PAA section 5(4)(b) is needed from the person dealing with the attorney, again before or within three months after that person's sale (the purchaser's purchase).

It will normally be convenient to amalgamate requirements (1) and (4), using the words required by each statute, in the same declaration.

Main practical consequences of section 16 and other adjustments to purchaser protection

1. Protection by LPA section 27 continues. Purchasers still need to ensure capital money is paid to at least two trustees or a trust corporation. If they do so equitable interests under the trust of land will still be overreached.

2. Trustees who convey unregistered land to a beneficiary on termination of the trust must now execute a deed of discharge. This will protect a subsequent purchaser. Such disposals before 1997[14] bring the equities on the title.

3. Where a purchaser relies on the exercise of a delegated power under section 9:

   (a) Section 9(2) protection is only on eligibility of the attorney.

   (b) A later purchaser needs, before or within three months after his purchase, a section 9(2) declaration from the person who dealt with the attorney *irrespective of how long elapsed between the execution of the power and its exercise.*

   (c) The later purchaser needs to rely on PAA protection against revocation. Here a declaration is only needed if more than 12 months elapse between the execution of the power and its exercise.

---

14 Assuming that the commencement date of the Act is 1 January 1997.

Chapter 11

Appointment and Retirement of Trustees

- New beneficiaries' powers to appoint and remove trustees
- New power to remove mentally incapable trustee
- "Opting out" by the settlor
- Partial solution to the "two individuals" discharge trap

11.1 Introduction

Part II of the Act deals with an entirely distinct topic, the appointment and retirement of trustees. This is perfectly general, and is not confined to trusts of land. Under the existing law, apart from express powers in the trust instrument, powers to appoint substitute and additional trustees are conferred by TA section 36(1), (6), on those nominated for the purpose or (if there are no such persons willing to act) the continuing or existing trustees. In addition there is power for an existing trustee to retire without replacement, in section 39 of that Act. The court has power to appoint and remove trustees under section 41.

The 1996 Act makes two main changes to the existing law. First, as the law stands, the beneficiaries of a trust have as such no right to appoint or remove trustees.[1] They can – if of full age and capacity, and acting unanimously – terminate the trust and require the trustee to convey as they require. But that may not suit their book. And it may incur a tax charge. Accordingly, section 19 of the Act gives beneficiaries a right in certain cases to appoint and remove trustees. Secondly, where a trustee is mentally incapable of acting, but there is no one else who is both able and willing to appoint a substitute trustee, as the law stands it is necessary for application to be made to the court. So section 20 of the Act gives beneficiaries a like right to appoint a new trustee in his place.

These changes were recommended by the Law Commission[2], and were originally contained in clause 18 of the draft Bill, although the

---

1 *Cf Re Brockbank* [1948] Ch 206.
2 In para 9.1 of Law Com No 181.

enacted provisions are very differently formulated. The final form of section 19 was in fact introduced only at the Report stage of the Bill in the House of Lords[3], the version in that Bill as originally presented itself having been significantly amended at Committee Stage.[4]

Taken together, these two provisions may seem to represent a significant shift in the balance of power in the trusts. But in reality it is not so. These powers only apply where the beneficiaries are in a position to terminate the whole trust anyway. All these provisions enable is an alteration in the trusteeship which could effectively be managed by a termination and resettlement on a new trustee. It enlarges the beneficiaries' negotiating position very slightly, by not requiring the beneficiaries to go to the expense of incurring a potential tax charge, but that is about all. Let us look at the new law in more detail.

11.2 Section 19(1)

Section 19(1) reads:

> This section applies in the case of a trust where -
>
> (a)   there is no person nominated for the purpose of appointing new trustees by the instrument, if any, creating the trust, and
>
> (b)   the beneficiaries under the trust are of full age and capacity and (taken together) are absolutely entitled to the property subject to the trust.

11.3 Construction problems

Both these paragraphs raise construction points. The section can apply equally to a trust declared orally, as to one created by instrument. An oral trust which makes no provision for any person to have power to appoint new trustees is one where is no person nominated for that purpose "by the instrument (if any) creating the trust", for the simple reason that there is no instrument. But what about the (admittedly rare) case of an oral trust which *does* contain such provision? On the strict wording paragraph (a) is equally satisfied, because the nomination is not made "by the instrument (if

---

3 HL Debs, vol 571, col 969, 22 April 1996.
4 HL Debs, vol 570, cols 1543-47, 25 March 1996.

any) creating the trust". So the beneficiaries and the person nominated *both* have the power to appoint new trustees, and may vie with each other in an untrustlike manner.

Secondly, if a person *was* nominated, but has died, then there "*is* no person nominated": the Lord Chancellor was clear, in introducing this clause, on the policy objective here.[5]

Thirdly, we should notice the reference to appointing *new* trustees. To satisfy paragraph (a), the power referred to seems to be the power to appoint a trustee or trustees *in substitution* for existing trustees. (This was clear in clause 18 of the Law Commission's draft Bill.) If it is merely a power to appoint trustees *in addition to* the existing trustees, that is not enough.[6]

Turning to paragraph (b), we see the reference to the beneficiaries being "of full age and capacity". By what law is that to be tested: English law, the law of the beneficiary's domicile or the law of the situs of the trust property[7] (if different)? Suppose an English law trust with beneficiaries domiciled in Italy and property in Jersey. By English law full age is attained at 18, by Jersey law it is attained at 20, and by Italian law it can be obtained for some purposes from 16. Since we are here concerned with a statutory power conferred by English law on beneficiaries, it would seem most sensible to judge full age and capacity by English law too[8], even though this may cause difficulty in some cases.

But there is an even more serious problem with paragraph (b). For that power (and therefore the section) to apply, the "beneficiaries" must together be "absolutely entitled to the property". Does this apply to a discretionary trust, or to a trust where there is a trust in default of appointment? If the term "beneficiary" were not defined, there would be no doubt. The general law is that where all the possible objects of a trust (including discretionary objects of a power with a trust in default) are of age and capacity and unanimously require the transfer of the trust property as they direct, the trustees must comply.[9] The so called rule in *Saunders v Vautier*[10] applies just as much to discretionary trusts and powers as to fixed trusts. But the

---

5 HL Debs, vol 571, col 968, 22 April 1996.
6 Although compare TA s 41, which uses "new trustee" in both senses.
7 The words "of full age and capacity" occur also in ss 6(2) and 16(4), (5), but there they are dealing with English land, and hence English law will apply. *This* provision, by contrast, applies to all trusts governed by English law, whatever and wherever the property.
8 *Cf Re Kehr* [1952] 1 Ch 26.
9 *Re Smith* [1928] 1 Ch 915, *Re Nelson* [1928] 1 Ch 920n.
10 (1841) Cr & Ph 240.

draftsman of the Act (unlike in the Law Commission's Bill) has defined the term "beneficiary" to mean a "person who under the trust has an interest in property subject to the trust".[11]

Yet the House of Lords[12] held that an object of a discretionary trust had no interest in any part of the trust property, at least until the discretion was exercised in his favour. Accordingly, it should seem that, notwithstanding that *Saunders* v *Vautier* can apply to a discretionary trust, the power for beneficiaries to appoint and remove trustees under section 19 cannot.[13]

One other point on "beneficiary" already discussed is whether, because of the drafting, the *trustees* of a trust of land are included in the definition. Here that would lead to bizarre consequences. But (as earlier considered[14]) the better view is that the words "under the trust" must limit "beneficiary" to a person having a (derivative) equitable interest, and hence exclude the trustees of the trust of land.

11.4 Direction to trustee(s)

Assuming however that we have a trust to which section 19 applies, what is the right conferred on the beneficiaries? Section 19(2) reads:

> The beneficiaries may give a direction or directions of either or both of the following descriptions -
>
> (a)   a written direction to a trustee or trustees to retire from the trust, and
>
> (b)   a written direction to the trustees or trustee for the time being (or, if there are none, to the personal representative of the last person who was a trustee) to appoint by writing to be a trustee or trustees the person or persons specified in the direction.

So a "direction" needs to be given. It must be in writing. But there is, curiously, no requirement that it be signed. There seems no doubt that it could be handwritten, typewritten or printed. Although an audio or video tape recording of such a direction could be a "document" for some purposes[15], it would be an abuse of language to say that the information it undoubtedly contains is "written".

---

11 S 22(1), discussed at 1.11 above.

12 In *Gartside* v *IRC* [1968] AC 553.

13 *Cf* Lord Mishcon on Second Reading in the House of Lords: HL Debs, vol 569, cols 1721-2, 1 March 1996.

14 See 1.11 above.

15 For example the law of evidence or discovery in civil procedure: *Grant* v *Southwestern and County Properties Ltd* [1975] Ch 195.

The fact that the direction has to be given "to" a trustee means, in the absence of specific provision in a particular trust, that the direction must come to his knowledge. So if a direction is sent to an individual trustee's home or office it cannot be said to be "given" to him, unless and until it actually comes to his knowledge. Query whether it must come *physically* to him as well. If it were possible to give a direction *orally* the need for a physical object to reach the trustee would be redundant. The trustee's spouse could tell the trustee by telephone of the written direction received at their home, and the "direction" would have reached the trustee. But the requirement is for a *written* direction to be given to the trustee, so it seems that the document must itself reach the trustee.

11.5 Awkward cases

In the case of the beneficiaries seeking to appoint a trustee, under section 19(2)(b), it could be that there is no trustee in office. If the last trustee has died, the direction is to be given to his personal representative. That is fine as far as it goes, but what happens if that trustee died domiciled in a jurisdiction where there are no personal representatives? If there are trust assets in England and Wales, the Public Trustee may be the appropriate person to give the notice to.[16] If the trust assets are in a jurisdiction not knowing the concept then this procedure will not apply, and it will be necessary to apply to the court under TA section 41 for a new trustee to be appointed. Similarly, if the last trustee has died, but it is not known if he left a will or not (and perhaps his family are not responding to enquiries), it will be impossible to be sure that the correct person is being given the direction. Even if the identity of the unnamed executor is known it will not be safe to rely on the doctrine of relation back until probate has been given, for that named person may subsequently renounce probate, or may simply do nothing in relation to it.

A further problem arises in relation to a corporate trustee which is dissolved. A company cannot have a personal representative. Probably on dissolution the trust property vests in the Crown, though not as bona vacantia[17], and the Crown has no duties in connection with it.[18] A new trustee can be appointed by the court

---

16 Administration of Estates Act 1925, s 9 (as amended).
17 *Pryce-Jones v Williams* [1902] 2 Ch 517.
18 *Re General Accident Assurance Corporation* [1904] 1 Ch 147.

under the TA section 41, and vesting orders can also be made under sections 44 and 51 of that Act.

11.6 Duty to retire

Directions under s19(2) can be of two kinds: directing a particular trustee or trustees to *retire*, and directing the current trustees (or personal representative of the last trustee) to *appoint* a particular person as trustee. Dealing first with the former case, the duty cast on a trustee directed to retire is set out in s19(3):

> Where -
>
> (a)   a trustee has been given a direction under subsection 2(a),
>
> (b)   reasonable arrangements have been made for the protection of any rights of his in connection with the trust,
>
> (c)   after he has retired that there will be either a trust corporation or at least two persons to act as trustees to perform the trust, and
>
> (d)   either another person is to be appointed to be a new trustee on his retirement (whether in compliance with a direction under subsection 2(b) or otherwise) or the continuing trustees by deed consent to his retirement,
>
> he shall make a deed declaring his retirement and shall be deemed to have retired and be discharged from the trust.

So it is a duty to make a deed declaring his retirement, which discharges him from the trust. But there are three pre-conditions. Two are easily dealt with. Either another person is to be appointed trustee in his place *or* the continuing trustees' consent to the retirement. This means that if the beneficiaries want to act *against* the trustees' wishes, they must make arrangements for substitute trustees to be appointed in their place. One wrinkle is that paragraph (d) says that "another person *is to be* appointed". This does not require that the substitute is appointed at the same time as the retiring trustee retires, much less that it should happen by the same document. It postulates the possibility of a trustee being under a duty to retire though no appointment of a substitute may yet have occurred by the time that he does so. This seems odd.

The second pre-condition is the familiar requirement that after the retirement there must be either a trust corporation or at least two persons to act as trustees to perform the trust. This is taken from TA

1925, sections 37(1)(c) and 39, and before that sections 10(2)(c) and 11 of the Trustee Act 1893. But the 1925 legislation as originally enacted required a trust corporation or at least two *individuals* to remain to perform the trust. The 1893 Act only required *persons*, not *individuals*. The 1996 Act here goes back to the 1893 Act, and for good measure amends the 1925 Act as well.[19]

The third pre-condition is the making of "reasonable arrangements" for the protection of "any rights" of the trustee who is to retire. This was not in the Law Commission's Bill. Plainly this covers reimbursement of liabilities properly incurred. By TA section 30(2) he is entitled to an indemnity for this, and under the general law to a lien on trust property operating as a first charge, coming before the beneficiaries' interests.[20]

This lien is not a common law possessory lien, but an equitable lien, and so is not lost if possession is given up (although of course the assets may be dissipated in non-traceable form). It is hard to see that any arrangement giving the trustee less protection than that which he would have under the general law could be regarded as reasonable for this purpose. On the other hand, since the statute does not expressly or impliedly abrogate that equitable lien, why is there any need to make any separate arrangement at all? Why not simply rely on that? Does this mean that the lien is *impliedly* abrogated by the Act? That would seem hard. Or does the Act require that the trustees should receive protection *over and above* the general law? After all, until this Act, a trustee was in a strong position. Subject to the terms of the trust he could decide whether, and when to retire, and if the beneficiaries wanted him to go he could bargain for whatever protection he though proper. Perhaps the better view is that the general law lien is unaffected, but this provision is added to restore some balance to the trustee's weakened position. He must go, but he has a basis for claiming more in terms of security than the general law would given him.

When a trustee *does* retire under section 19(3), both he and the continuing (and any new) trustees are under a duty to do anything necessary to vest the trust property in the continuing (and any new) trustees.[21] This is based on TA section 37(1)(d) and section 39(2).

---

19 See 11.12 below.
20 See *Re Oxley* [1914] 1 Ch 604, *Lewin on Trusts*, 16th ed 1964, 213 and 282, and cases there cited.
21 S 19(4).

11.7 Duty to appoint

All of that dealt with the beneficiaries' first kind of direction under section 19(2), to require a trustee or trustees to *retire*. Where a direction is given to require a particular person or persons to be *appointed* trustee or trustees this Act is silent as to the effect. Presumably the existing trustee or trustees must comply with the direction. The question is, how do they do so? The draftsman seems to have assumed that section 19 confers power to appoint, for section 21(3) applies section 36(7) of the Trustee Act 1925 "to a trustee appointed under section 19 or 20 as if he were appointed under that section". But there are no words in section 19 expressly conferring such a power. Perhaps it is to be implied, and some support may be obtained for this view from the similar words used at the end of section 20, discussed below. But if it is to be implied, then it is implying a lot from very little. It would have been very simple for the draftsman to say as much expressly, but he unfortunately chose not to do so. If it is *not* implied, how else can it be achieved?

The Law Commission[22] assumed that the trustees would make the appointment under their existing powers, and clause 18 of their Bill was drafted on that basis. *Ex hypothesi*, there is no person (including the trustee) with the express power to appoint new trustees. The statutory powers of appointing new and additional trustees are contained in TA section 36(1), (6). Now, these powers *are* conferred, in default of other persons nominated for this purposes, on the trustees. The power under section 36(1) may not be available, as it only applies where one or more of the pre-conditions laid down in that subsection is satisfied, and if one of these is satisfied in the case where the beneficiaries require a trustee to be appointed, this will be purely coincidental. So the power to appoint additional trustees under section 36(6) will be that used, and the appointment will work, not because section 19(2) of the Act says so, but because section 36(6) of the 1925 Act says it will. So if, for any reason[23], that power is not available, the trustees would seem to have no power to comply with the beneficiaries' direction. If the power to appoint additional trustees has been conferred on some one else, he or she must be asked to exercise it. Only if he or she is unwilling to do so can the trustees exercise it.

---

22 In para 9.1 of Law Com No 181.
23 For example because it has been excluded by the trust instrument: TA s 69(2).

11.8 Mentally incapable trustee

Section 20 of the Act deals with appointing a substitute for a trustee who is mentally incapable of acting. Subsection (1) sets out three pre-conditions as follows:

> This section applies where -
>
> (a)   a trustee is incapable by reason of mental disorder of exercising his functions as trustee,
>
> (b)   there is no person who is both entitled and willing and able to appoint a trustee in place of him under section 36(1) of the Trustee Act 1925, and
>
> (c)   the beneficiaries under the trust are of full age and capacity and (taken together) are absolutely entitled to the property subject to the trust.

The first condition is self-explanatory. As for the third, it is identical to section 19(1)(b) of the Act and the points made above in relation to that provision will apply to this. The second condition needs further comment.

First, there could be no person able and willing to appoint under section 36(1) of the 1925 Act, even though an express power to remove and appoint trustees is conferred by the terms of the trust. An appointment under an express power would not be an appointment under section 36. Secondly, section 20 will usually only apply where the incapable trustee or trustees are the only trustee or trustees. If there is a mentally capable trustee, he or she will have power to substitute a trustee under section 36(1). Thirdly, section 20 can apply where section 19 cannot, for example where there is a person with power to appoint new trustees (so s 19 cannot apply), but he or she refuses to exercise his or her powers.

When the section does apply, the beneficiaries may give a written direction to any one of three persons requiring that person to appoint by writing the person or persons specified in the notice to be a trustee or trustees in place of the incapable trustee.[24] The three persons are the trustee's receiver, an attorney acting under an enduring power of attorney which has been registered, and a person authorised pursuant to Part VII of the Mental Health Act 1983. None of these persons has power (s 20 apart) to appoint a substitute trustee. This suggests that the power to do so must be contained in

---

24 S 20(2).

the words of the section itself. If this is right, it strengthens the argument in relation to the similar wording in section 19(2)(b), discussed above.

11.9 Supplementary provisions

There are some provisions and limitations common to directions under both section 19 and section 20. None of them appeared in the Law Commission's Bill. First, a direction by several beneficiaries can be given either jointly, or individually by each of them.[25] In the latter case, of course, each beneficiary must specify the same person or persons to be appointed or to retire, as the case may be.[26] If any of them withdraws the direction before it has been complied with, it ceases to be such a direction.[27]

One limitation is that, by section 21(4),

> A direction under section 19 or 20 must not specify a person or persons for appointment if the appointment of that person or those persons would be in contravention of section 35(1) of the Trustee Act 1925 or section 24(1) of the Law of Property Act 1925 (requirements as to identity of trustees).

Both of these provisions require that, where there is a trust of land and a trust of the proceeds of sale of that land, those trustees must be the same persons. Presumably a direction given in breach of the obligation in section 21(4) of the 1996 Act is simply not a "direction" within section 19, and hence the trustees have no duty to comply with it.

11.10 "Opting out"

A second, more significant limitation on the rights conferred by sections 19 and 20 is that they can be excluded by the settlor in at least some cases. Section 21(5) provides that:

> Sections 19 and 20 do not apply in relation to a trust created by a disposition in so far as provision that they do not apply is made by the disposition.

---

25 S 21(1).
26 S 21(2).
27 *Ibid.*

This is curiously worded. First, it only applies to a trust "created by a *disposition*". This is discussed elsewhere.[28]

Secondly, it refers to "provision" being "made" that section 19 should not apply. Presumably this covers *implied* as well as *expressed* exclusion.

Thirdly, for the power to be excluded, such provision must be made "by the disposition". But a disposition, being the *action* of disposing of something, would not normally *provide* anything. So presumably it should be read as provision made by the *terms* of the disposition. Does this cover an *oral* disposition? Whilst it would be unusual for an orally declared trust to make any provision at all in relation to powers of appointment and removal of trustees, it could be done.

11.11 Pre-Act trusts

Of course section 21(5) can only apply to trusts created after the Act came into effect. This would leave pre-Act trusts at a disadvantage. So section 21(6) provides a partial solution:

> Sections 19 and 20 do not apply in relation to a trust created before the commencement of this Act by a disposition in so far as provision to the effect that they do not apply is made by a deed executed -
>
> (a)   in a case in which the trust was created by one person and he is of full capacity, by that person, or
>
> (b)   in a case in which the trust was created by more than one person, by such of the persons who created the trust as are alive and of full capacity.

The same points arise under section 21(6) as under section 21(5), both in relation to the meaning of disposition, and to provision being made. But it will be noted that such provision must be made *by a deed*, even though the original trust was created by writing or even orally. The deed will be irrevocable, whatever it says.[29] It does not affect anything done before execution, to comply with the directions under sections 19 or 20, though if such a direction had not by then been complied with, it ceases to have effect.[30]

Who makes the deed? This is a very interesting question. Parliament has not permitted *the trustees* to exclude sections 19 and

---

28 See 1.17 above.
29 S 27(7).
30 S 21(8).

20 (no doubt all the well advised ones would). Nor is it provided that the beneficiaries (or any of them) should be able to do so, although of course they could contract amongst themselves that they should not exercise the powers in sections 19 and 20. Instead, the Act focuses on the *settlor*. If there was only one person who created the trust, and that person is still alive and of full capacity, then he or she is the (only) person who can execute the deed. If that person is dead or not of full capacity, then there is no one who can execute the deed on his or her behalf, and in particular not the personal representatives or the receiver of a mental patient's property. This has the merit of simplicity, though at the cost of potential injustice.

Where the trust was created by more than one person, the position becomes more complex. The deed must be executed by such of those persons as are alive and of full capacity. It is notable that the wording does not refer to "settlor" or to "more than one settlor". Instead, it refers to the trust being "created by more than one person". Does this refer only to the case of two or more persons, *joint* owners of the property, *jointly* settling that property? Or does it also refer to the case where each of two or more persons separately contributes property to be held by the same trustee or trustees on identical trusts, but as a single fund? We considered the problem above, and concluded that the draftsman must have intended to include the latter.[31]

If the case of settlement of two or more piece of property on identical trusts is to be included in section 21(6)(b), it might offer an easy escape from sections 19 and 20 for the trustees of a trust where the settlor has already died. One of the trustees simply adds a further small amount of property to the trust fund out of his free assets. He has helped to create the resultant "mixed" trust fund, and as the only one of the creators of the trust still to be living, he can make the deed excluding sections 19 and 20. To avoid the possibility that the mixed trust might be treated as created only when the money was added (which might occur after the Act came into force) the trustees may think of contributing such additional funds *before* the coming into force of the Act.

11.12 Amendment to existing law

A final, rather minor change is made to the existing law by Schedule 3 paragraph 3(12), (13). Under the Trustee Act 1893, sections

---

31 See 1.18 above.

10(2)(c) and 11, a trustee was not discharged from his trust unless after his retirement there were at least two *persons* or a trust corporation (as defined) to continue as trustees. By the time of TA, sections 37(1)(c) and 39, because of amendments made by the Law of Property Act 1922, this had become "two *individuals* or a trust corporation". It was never quite clear why it was thought desirable to alter the rule at all. It may have had something to do with the fact that, until the Bodies Corporate (Joint Tenancy) Act 1899, a corporation could not be a joint tenant, so before then it would be most unlikely to be one of two or more trustees. The "two individuals" rule caught out many whose trusts were purportedly exported from the United Kingdom to purely corporate trustees offshore. The problem is less serious since Knox J decided (in effect)[32] that it was possible to exclude the operation of the rule in the trust instrument. Nevertheless, the opportunity has been taken in the present Act to change the law on this point back to 1893, and to rejoin Ireland, Gibraltar and other jurisdictions which made no change in 1925. Incidentally, the amendment was not in the Bill as originally introduced into Parliament, but made only on Third Reading in the House of Lords, as the Lord Chancellor said, to "ensure consistency with" section 19![33]

---

32 In *LRT Pension Trust Co Ltd v Hatt* [1993] PLR 227.
33 See HL Debs, vol 572, col 99, 7 May 1996.

Main practical consequences of sections 19 to 21

1. Where the beneficiaries can put an end to the trust (not being a discretionary trust), they can instead now direct a particular trustee or trustees to retire and/or direct the trustees to appoint a particular person or persons to be trustee(s).

2. If a trustee has become mentally incapable, then such beneficiaries can require his receiver, his attorney under an enduring power or a person authorised under the Mental Health Act to appoint a substitute trustee ot trustees.

3. But both of these new rights can be excluded by the trust instrument or, in pre-Act trusts, by a subsequent deed made by the settlor.

4. It will no longer be necessary to have two individual trustees remaining in post after the retirement of a trustee for him to be discharged: it will be sufficient that there are two trustees, individual or corporate.

Chapter 12

Consolidated Key Provisions and Main Practical Consequences of the Act

At the end of Chapters 2-11 we have tried to identify some "main practical consequences" of the section or sections covered by the chapter. This chapter brings these together.

It is not just to save the practitioner who is looking for practical consequences from the trouble of flipping through ten separate chapters. The aim is to present an overall, less fragmented view; and to group those consequences in a re-arranged order reflecting the concerns of the practitioner, rather than in the sequence of the sections of the Act.

Our list cannot possibly be exhaustive. It represents the thoughts of two solicitors asking themselves: "What difference will the Act make in practice to the client, to the conveyancer, to the solicitor drafting wills or settlements and to solicitors negotiating or litigating over co-ownership of or other trusts of land?" Readers and rival commentators will come up immediately with many other answers and further consequences will emerge in time.

But with that disclaimer we hope the following will be useful to the practitioner. We have followed the same cryptic staccato style as at the end of each chapter. As some consequences apply across two or more of the headings we have used, there is some duplication. For the detail and the explanation, reference will be needed to the chapter concerned.

Key provisions and consequences specially relevant to drafting

Express trusts for sale unnecessary

1. It is no longer necessary to impose an immediate binding trust for sale, either:

(a) to trigger the powers and duties of a trust for sale; [s 1, **Chap 1**] (*any* trust of or including land will be subject to the trusts of land regime) or

(b) to avoid creating a strict settlement [s 2, **Chap 2**].

Express trusts for sale still possible

2. But an express trust for sale may still be employed although usually it will be inappropriate [ss 1, 3 & 4, **Chap 4**].

Prohibition on new strict settlements

3. New strict settlements can no longer be created [s 2(1), **Chap 2**].

Re-settlement

4. If concerned with the re-settlement of, or power of appointment under, an existing strict settlement, it is necessary to consider whether to elect to become a trust of land by provision in the re-settlement [s 2(3), **Chap 2**].

5. If the answer to (2) is yes, the mechanism is:

(a) the tenant for life executes a conveyance to the trustees of land in accordance with the proviso to SLA section 17(1) as amended; and

(b) the deed of discharge contains a statement in accordance with amended section 17(1) that the land is subject to a trust of land by virtue of such conveyance. [**Sched 3 para 2(6), SLA s 17, Chap 2**]

New entails abolished

6. An entailed interest can no longer be created. Unless the creator has a lesser interest, an attempt to do so will create a fee simple [**Sched 1 para 5, Chap 2**].

Relegation of trustees' powers to tenant for life

7. An approximation of strict settlement powers and responsibilities can be achieved by delegation of trustees' powers to the life tenant [s 9, **Chap 6**].

8. Wide powers can be delegated but the power of attorney should be tailored to the circumstances [s 9, **Chap 6**].

New absolute owner powers

9. New absolute owner powers for trustees of land replace the former fragmented powers of trustees for sale. They include power to buy land for investment or occupation or otherwise [ss 6(1), (3), 9(4), **Chap 5**].

10. Enlarging the statutory powers for co-owners of land is no longer needed [ss 6-8, **Chap 5**].

Negativing or restricting powers

11. The widened powers may be restricted by the disposition creating the trust or made subject to a requirement for consents [s 8(1) and (2), **Chap 5**].

Relevant matters on decisions by the court

12. In an application under section 14 the court must now have regard to a number of factors, including the intentions of the settlor/testator, the purposes of holding the property, and the interests of minors and secured creditors [s 15, **Chap 9**].

13. The relevance of the intentions of the settlor/testator means that consideration should be given to expressing these when the trust is created [s 15, **Chap 9**].

Areas for consideration when drafting

14. Areas which need consideration in drafting a new trust include:

(1) whether to impose a trust for sale (because if imposed, a trust to sell may still predominate over the inviolate power to postpone sale); [ss 1, 4, **Chap 4**]

(2) whether to demonstrate an intention of the person creating the trust which will be relevant on a section 14 application, for example giving priority to sale over retention or vice versa in defined circumstances; [ss 6-8, 14-15, **Chaps 5 & 9**]

(3) whether to negative or restrict any of the absolute owner powers in sections 6 and 7; [s 8(1), **Chap 5**]

(4) whether to impose a requirement for consent(s) for the exercise of any power; [ss 8(2), 10, **Chaps 5 & 7**]

(5) whether to demonstrate an intention that the section 9 powers of delegation be exercised; [ss 9, 15, **Chap 5**]

(6) whether to negative or restrict the duty under section 11 to consult beneficiaries; [s 11, **Chap 7**]

(7) whether to indicate the purposes of the trust include making land available for occupation by beneficiaries within section 12(1)(a); [s 12(1), **Chap 8**]

(8) whether to negative or restrict the power of beneficiaries to direct the appointment or retirement of trustees under sections 20-21; [s 21, **Chap 11**]

Abolition of doctrine of conversion

15. In drafting or construing documents, a reference to personal estate will no longer include an interest in the proceeds of sale under a trust for sale [s 3, **Chap 2**].

This does not apply in a pre-1997 will, but only if the testator dies before 1997 [s 3(2), **Chap 2**].

Key provisions and consequences specially relevant to administering trusts and advising trustees and beneficiaries

Retroaction

1. The new regime of trusts of land applies to *any trusts* of land whether or not they were created before the commencement of the 1996 Act, except existing strict settlements [ss 1,2, Chaps 1, 2].

Balance between sale and retention

2. The former statutory trusts [for sale] – in the reduced number of cases where they still apply – are replaced by a statutorily implied trust without a duty to sell [s 5, Sched 2, Chap 4].

3. The statutory power to postpone is implied in all trusts for sale of land and cannot be negatived [s 4, Chap 4].

Charitable etc trusts of land

4. Charitable, ecclesiastical and public trusts of land, whenever created, are all now trusts of land and have the benefit of the enlarged statutory powers of disposal. But they are not subject to the whole of the trusts of land regime (see text at 2.5) [s 2(5), Chap 2].

New statutory powers of an absolute owner

5. New statutory absolute owner powers for the trustees of land replace the former fragmented powers of trustees for sale. They include power to buy land for investment or occupation or otherwise. They may be negatived or restricted in the disposition creating the trust [s 6(1), (3), (4), Chap 5].

6. There is a new statutory power to appropriate land and a revised one to partition [ss 6(2), 7, **Chap 5**].

7. The powers must be exercised having regard to the rights of beneficiaries [s 6(5), **Chap 7**].

Consultation

8. Unless the right has been negatived trustees of land must now consult beneficiaries of full age and beneficially entitled in possession about the exercise of *any function* in relation to the land and must give effect to their wishes [s 11, **Chap 7**].

But annuitants no longer count for this purpose [s 22(3), **Chap 7**].

Beneficiaries' right of occupation

9. The right of a beneficiary beneficially entitled in possession under a trust of land to occupy the land is put on a statutory basis for the first time [s 12, **Chap 8**].

10. But *either* making the land available for occupation must be one of the trust's purposes, or the land must be held by the trustees so as to be available for such occupation [s 12(1), **Chap 8**].

11. And the trustees have power to exclude or restrict the exercise of the statutory right if there are two or more persons entitled to occupy, but they can impose conditions on the occupant, including compensation to be paid to the excluded [s 13, **Chap 8**].

Extended powers of the court

12. The court's powers have been extended to cover disputes about the exercise of any of the trustees' functions or about the nature or extent of beneficiaries' interests [s 14, **Chap 9**].

13. The pre-Act case law under LPA section 30 will still be relevant, though not determinative [s 15, **Chap 9**].

14. There is a new statutory regime for dealing with applications by the trustee in bankruptcy of a beneficiary for an order for sale of the property [**Sched 3 para 23, Chap 9**].

15. The section 14 procedure applies to trusts of *proceeds of sale* of land, just as it applies to trusts of land [s 17(2)-(6), **Chap 9**].

16. The court must now have regard to a number of factors, including the intentions of the settlor/testator, the purposes of holding the property, and the interests of minors and secured creditors [s 15, **Chap 9**].

Mimicking a strict settlement by delegating trustees' powers to the life tenant

17. An approximation of strict settlement powers and responsibilities can be achieved by delegation of trustees' powers to the life tenant [s 9, **Chap 6**].

18. Wide powers can be delegated but the power of attorney should be tailored to the circumstances [s 9, **Chap 6**].

19. The attorney cannot be authorised to give receipts for capital money. If the life tenant is authorised to sell, the trustees must join in the transfer to give a receipt [s 9(7), **Chap 6**].

20. A section 9 attorney has the same duties and liabilities as trustees [s 9(7), **Chap 6**].

21. Trustees are liable to exercise reasonable care in delegating [s 9(8), **Chap 6**].

Resettlements of strict settlements

22. If concerned with the re-settlement of, or power of appointment under, an existing strict settlement, it is necessary to consider

whether to elect to become a trust of land by provision in the re-settlement [s 2(3), **Chap 2**].

23. If the answer to (22) is yes, the mechanism is:

   (a) the tenant for life executes a conveyance to the trustees of land in accordance with the proviso to SLA s 17(1) as amended; and

   (b) the deed of discharge contains a statement in accordance with amended section 17(1) that the land is subject to a trust of land by virtue of such conveyance [**Sched 3 para 2(6)**, SLA s 17, **Chap 2**].

Ending strict settlement by selling all the land and heirlooms

24. The sale of all the land and heirlooms in an existing strict settlement will cause the strict settlement to cease [s 2(4), **Chap 2**].

Deed of discharge necessary on conveyance of unregistered land to beneficiary

25. Trustees who convey unregistered land to a beneficiary on termination of the trust must now execute a deed of discharge. (This will protect a subsequent purchaser. Such disposals before 1997 bring the equities on the title.) [s 16(4), (5), **Chap 10**].

Appointment and retirement of trustees – generally and at the instance of the beneficiaries

26. Where the beneficiaries can put an end to the trust (not being a discretionary trust), they can, unless the power has been negatived, instead now direct a particular trustee or trustees to retire and/or direct the trustees to appoint a particular person or persons to be trustee(s) [ss 19, 21, **Chap 11**].

27. If a trustee has become mentally incapable, then such beneficiaries can require his receiver, his attorney under an enduring power or a person authorised under the Mental Health Act to appoint a substitute trustee or trustees [**ss 20, 21, Chap 11**],

28. It will no longer be necessary to have two individual trustees remaining in post after the retirement of a trustee for him to be discharged: it will be sufficient that there are two trustees, individual or corporate [**Sched 3 para 3(12), (13), Chap 11**].

Key provisions and consequences specially relevant on the purchase of land currently or formerly held by trustees of land

New absolute owner powers

1. New absolute owner powers for trustees of land replace the former fragmented powers of trustees for sale [s 6(1), (3), (4), Chap 5].

Enlarging the statutory powers for co-owners of land is no longer needed.

Investigating powers of trustees

2. In investigating unregistered title it is no longer necessary to make sure that post 1996 transactions are within the former limited powers. The Act will apply irrespective of when the trust commenced. [ss 1(2), 6-8, Chap 5].

3. But a purchaser continues to be concerned:

   (a) to see that pre-1997 dealings were within the old law powers, and

   (b) about restrictions or limitations if he has notice of them, irrespective of the date of the dealing [s ??, Chap ??].

LPA section 27 protection and paying capital money to at least two trustees

4. Protection by LPA section 27 continues. Purchasers still need to ensure capital money is paid to at least two trustees or a trust corporation. If they do so equitable interests under the trust of land will still be overreached [LPA s 27, Chap 9].

5. An attorney with powers delegated under section 9 cannot be authorised to give receipts for capital money. If the life tenant is authorised to sell, the trustees must join in the transfer to give a receipt [s 9, **Chap 6**].

Section 16 deed of discharge on termination of trust

6. Trustees who convey unregistered land to a beneficiary on termination of the trust must now execute a deed of discharge. This will protect a subsequent purchaser. Such disposals before 1997 bring the equities on the title [s 16(4), (5), **Chap 9**].

Disposals under delegated powers in section 9

7. Where a purchaser relies on the exercise of a delegated power under section 9:

   (a) section 9(2) protection is only on eligibility of the attorney; [s 9(2), **Chap 9**]

   (b) a later purchaser needs, before or within three months after his purchase, a section 9(2) declaration from the person who dealt with the attorney *irrespective of how long elapsed between the execution of the power and its exercise*; [s 9(2), **Chap 9**]

   (c) the later purchaser needs to rely on PAA protection against revocation. Here a declaration is only needed if more than 12 months elapse between the execution of the power and its exercise [**PAA s 5(4)**].

Charitable etc trusts of land

8. Charitable, ecclesiastical and public trusts of land, whenever created, are all now trusts of land and have the benefit of the enlarged statutory powers of disposal. But they are not subject to the whole of the trusts of land regime (see text at 2.5) [s 2(5), **Chap 2**].

Concerns of purchaser with limitations on powers of consents

9. A purchaser is concerned with limitations on the absolute owner powers imposed by the instrument creating the trust (subject to (10) below) with requirements for consent if he has actual notice of them.

10. If the trust makes the exercise of trustees' functions subject to consents, then whatever the trust says, no more than two consents are needed to the exercise of *any* trustee function relating to the land, in order for a purchaser to be protected [s 10, Chap 7].

11. But although a minor's consent is not needed to protect a purchaser, that of the receiver of a mentally incapable person is [s 10(3), Chap 7].

Chart – Will giving Right of Residence

Comparison of procedures between strict settlement and trust for sale (old law) and trust of land (new law)

Probate to personal representatives

	TRUST FOR SALE OR TRUST OF LAND	SETTLED LAND only creatable pre-1997[1]	
	Assent to trustees can be: (1) trusts of will, or (2) independent trust.	Vesting assent to tenant for life	
Appoint new trustees	Implied vesting for unregistered land TA s 40. Separate appointment if assent created independent trust	Declaration of trustees	Appointment of trustees
Sale	Conveyance by trustees Two needed to overreach.	Conveyance by tenant for life, capital money to at least two trustees	
Trust/ settlement ceases inter vivos	**Conveyance to beneficiary Post-1996 + deed of discharge under TLATA s 16 But if pre-1997[2] BRINGS EQUITIES ON THE TITLE**	SLA s17 deed of discharge	
Trust/ settlement ceases on death	Probate Assent	Probate to general PRs Clean assent to beneficiary	

---

1 Assuming the commencement date of TLATA is 1 January 1997.
2 Assuming in both cases the commencement date of TLATA is 1 January 1997.

Assents – as affected and unaffected by the 1996 Act

Form and effect of an assent – AEA section 36(1)

Who can be the beneficiary under an assent?

– any person who may be entitled:

(a) by devise, bequest, devolution, appropriation *or otherwise*;
(b) whether beneficially or as trustee or personal representative.

What can be the subject of an assent?

– *any estate or interest in real estate* to which the testator or intestate was entitled ... and which devolved upon the personal representative.*

"or otherwise"
It is doubtful whether an executor is entitled to assent directly in favour of a purchaser from a beneficiary. *Emmet* suggests it is better to complete that transaction by a conveyance and not by an assent.

"any estate or interest in real estate"
The words include leaseholds but not apparently proceeds of sale under a trust for sale. This is unchanged by the 1996 Act section 17 which applies to sections 6(3) and 14, not generally.

Assents of personalty cannot be made under the statutory power; only under common law rules. There was little to be gained by assenting a share in the proceeds of sale. The main purpose of an assent is to pass, and prove the passing of, the legal estate. A purchaser can assume under AEA section 36(7), following an assent of a *legal estate*, that it was made to the correct person. He is then not concerned with the contents of the will. But those benefits do not follow an assent of an equitable interest. That remains the case since the commencement of TLATA. Despite the abolition of conversion, a beneficial interest is not a legal estate within AEA section 36(7) and an assent of such a beneficial interest will not protect a subsequent purchaser.

---

* The statutory power to assent therefore now extends to interests in land which, before TLATA s 3 abolished the doctrine of conversion, were only interests in proceeds of sale and therefore then outside the statutory power to assent. But assents of personalty still do have the benefit of AEA s 36(7). See text *"Assents of personalty"*.

Requirements of form (AEA s 36(4)) (unchanged under the 1996 Act)

(4) An assent to the vesting of a legal estate shall be:

    (a) in writing,
    (b) signed by the personal representative,
    (c) shall name the person in whose favour it is given,
    (d) shall operate to vest in that person the legal estate to which it relates; an assent not in writing or not in favour of a named person shall not be effectual to pass a legal estate.

"name the person in whose favour it is given"
Where the assent is in favour of "the Beneficiary", *Emmet* is happy if "the Beneficiary" is defined elsewhere in the assent as Joe Bloggs. But the safety first formula,"the Beneficiary the said Joe Bloggs", avoids requisitions.

Contents of assents

Assents should contain proper parcels. Describing the property only by referring to the will is not enough. If the deceased had neighbouring land, a plan and full description is needed to clarify the boundary, and granting and reserving suitable easements should not be forgotten – it often is! The assent should also contain an acknowledgment for production of the probate and any retained earlier deeds.

Registered land

Ordinary assent – use Form 56
Vesting assent for strict settlements – Form 57

Assent to trustees of a will

There are two alternative ways this may be drawn:

(a) On an **independent trust for sale (or now trust of land)** naming the persons having the power of appointing new trustees, if this is specified in the will.

    Consequences:
    (1) Some powers in the will (*e.g.* of a professional trustee to charge) may not apply unless drawn widely enough.
    (2) Because trustees now have absolute owner powers under the 1996 Act there is no need to enlarge powers of disposition.
    (3) But it is possible to limit those absolute owner powers and to vary the 1996 Act *e.g.* by negativing the duty to consult. Provisions like that should only appear in the assent to the extent that they echo the will.
    (4) When new trustees are appointed two appointments are necessary – one of new trustees of the assent, and one of new trustees of the will. A purchaser should look at only the appointment of new trustees *of the*

assent. The other appointment does not concern him, nor will it trigger implied vesting under TA section 40.

(5) Pre-1997[1] conveyances by trustees should be pursuant to the trust for sale *created by the assent,* not by the will; a post-1996[2] conveyance pursuant to the trust of land *in the assent.*

(6) The will is kept safely right off the title.

(b) Alternatively make the assent to the trustees **on the trusts of the will.**

Consequences:

(1) It brings the will on to the title. This will normally only be as far as the trust [for sale] (or trust of land) which the will contained(?) (But see "Which is better" below). Problems if the will did not contain a trust for sale – if the terms of the will constituted a strict settlement.

(2) The trust [for sale] in the will will have to be abstracted, and the purchaser needs to inspect it. To see if it is a trust of land the buyer needs to read further.

(3) Only one document is needed when new trustees are appointed.

(4) It automatically incorporates the powers given and restrictions imposed by the will into the assent. Does this give a purchaser notice of them? Probably not – see the 1996 Act section 16 and LPA section 27(1).

Which is better?

Of the two courses, before 1997[3] (a) was preferable, mainly because it avoided any recourse to the will. And in course (b) a purchaser who only looked at the trust for sale might not have been protected. In one case it was held that a subsequent beneficial limitation (the right to reside) was inconsistent with the trust for sale the document purported to contain, and so the land was settled. (*Dodsworth* v *Dodsworth* (1973) 228 EG 115).

Since 1996[4] the *Dodsworth* v *Dodsworth* danger has receded. Whatever the date of the assent it continues to be a danger where an inter vivos settlement was completed, or the testator of a will died, before 1997. In those circumstances course (a) remains the safer course. In other cases course (b) does not now run the risk of a post 1996 disposition creating a strict settlement). It still requires the purchaser to look at the will. That may still cause difficulty in practice, despite LPA section 27(1) and 1996 Act section 16.

Assent to beneficiaries

Where an assent is to two or more *beneficiaries,* they will necessarily be trustees. Before 1997[5] there would either be an express trust for sale, or failing

---

1 Assuming that the commencement date of TLATA is 1 January 1997.
2 With the same assumption about the commencement date.
3 Assuming the commencement date of TLATA is 1 January 1997.
4 This paragraph assumes 1 January 1997 as the commencement date of TLATA.
5 Assuming, throughout this paragraph the commencement date of TLATA is 1 January 1997.

that the statutory trust for sale would have arisen if the land was not settled. The position is mainly unchanged since 1996, but new express or implied trusts will always create trusts of land unless there is a pre-1997 SLA settlement.

Appointment of new trustees will of course be solely by appointing new trustees of the assent, and for unregistered land the implied vesting under TA 1925 section 40 will then operate.

Memorandum of assent on grant – protection of purchaser AEA section 36(5)
Who may require a memorandum?

Any person in whose favour an assent or conveyance of a legal estate is made by a personal representative. Endorsement is at the cost of the estate. AEA section 36(6)

Statement of no previous assent or conveyance – protection of purchaser

A personal representative may state in writing that he has not given or made an assent or conveyance in respect of a legal estate.

A conveyance by a personal representative of a legal estate to a purchaser accepted on the faith of that statement operates to transfer or create the legal estate expressly conveyed just as if no previous assent or conveyance had been made by the personal representative.

However:

(a) This is without prejudice to any previous disposition to another **purchaser** deriving title under the personal representative (whether mediately or immediately);
(b) The subsequent purchaser is not protected if there is a memorandum of a previous assent or conveyance on the grant.

So the devisee under an assent of unregistered land **must** ensure that the memorandum is endorsed. If he does not, he is vulnerable if there is a later conveyance by the personal representative containing a statement that there has been no previous assent or conveyance.

The purchaser from the personal representative does not run the same risk; he is protected by the words of the subsection, although it is good conveyancing practice to endorse a memorandum of a conveyance as well.

Morals
(1)   When drawing an assent of unregistered land ensure a memorandum is endorsed on the grant.

There is no need to include a recital in the assent that there was no previous assent or conveyance etc. In an *assent* it achieves nothing.

(2) (i) When acting for a purchaser of unregistered land from personal representatives it is good practice to ensure a memorandum is endorsed on the grant. But it is not essential.

(ii) **What is essential for a *purchaser* from personal representatives is**
   - to *obtain statement* that no previous assent or conveyance etc., and
   - to inspect original grant (to ensure no previous memorandum). *

Failure to obtain the statement leaves him vulnerable to an earlier overlooked disposal, even if there is no memorandum on the grant.

(3)   When acting for a subsequent buyer, insist that (1) and 2(ii) complied with on past transactions.
But pursuing requisitions about (2)(i) is a waste of time.

(4)   Memoranda are needless for registered land. When an assent is registered, the legal estate is vested in the beneficiary by the fact of registration.
No subsequent disposition by the personal representative can deprive him of it.

---

*Epitomes are often prepared by photocopying only the front sheet of the probate, and it is worth checking there is no memorandum on the back! Now that "examined" abstracts are frequently drawn up well in advance of completion, it may often be advisable to update the examination on or immediately before completion. Even though in practice, assuming he holds the original probate, the chances of the sellers' solicitor overlooking or disregarding the current disposal may, in the absence of fraud, be remote.

Protection of purchaser from devisee – AEA section 36(7)

(Unless there is a memorandum to the contrary endorsed on the probate or administration) an assent or conveyance by a personal representative of a legal estate shall in favour of a purchaser for money or money's worth be taken as *sufficient evidence* that the person in whose favour the assent or conveyance is given or made is the person entitled to have the legal estate conveyed to him and upon the proper trusts if any.

"Sufficient evidence". This does not mean the assent is conclusive that it is made in favour of the right person.

Re: Duce and Boots Cash Chemist (Southern) Limited Contract [1937] Ch 642
Abstract of title and a recital in the assent both showed the land was settled. It

should have been vested in the tenant for life but was nevertheless vested in the remaindermen.

Held – the purchaser was entitled to object to the title. Facts had come to his knowledge indicating that the assent was not made in favour of the right person.

Morals
(1) Don't abstract the will.
(2) Recitals in an assent are dangerous and normally should be avoided.
(3) If deceased was a surviving joint tenant, state he was solely and beneficially entitled to obtain the benefit of LP(JT)A 1964 (as amended by LP(MP)A 1994).

Assent by personal representatives in their own favour

Re: Kings Will Trust [1964] Ch 542

Held – the change of capacity from personal representative to trustee required to be in writing. No assent means the personal representatives continue to hold as personal representatives, even if they have concluded the administration of the estate.

The decision has been much criticised but nevertheless not overruled.

Consequences

(1)   On an appointment of new trustees the property only vests under TA section 40 if it is *already vested in the appointor as trustee.*

If there has been no previous assent then the appointment needs to be coupled with an assent to the new and continuing trustees. In that case however a purchaser will not need to see the appointment. He can rely on AEA section 36(7). Don't recite the appointment.

If there is a previous assent, then check its terms. If it created an *independent* trust for sale or trust of land , there will need to be two appointments, and a purchaser will only be concerned with the appointment under the trusts of the assent.

(2)   Once the assent has been made the property is held as trustees and not as personal representatives.
This means:

(a)   they can no longer assent, and
(b)   *any pre-1997[6] dealings* outside the exercise of their statutory powers such as sale, meant bringing the equities on the title.

---

6 Assuming the commencement date of TLATA is 1 January 1997.

For *post-1996*[7] *dealings* that is no longer the case if the new 1996 Act section 16 deed of discharge procedure is used.

Where on the other hand the land remained vested in the personal representatives as personal representatives, a purchaser could (and can) rely on an assent of a legal estate being in favour of the right person. (AEA section 36(7))

The snags in completing an assent to trustees have therefore now been removed. Those reasons for not assenting no longer hold good. But in investigating title of events and transactions which happened before 1997[8], a purchaser must still see that a conveyance to a beneficiary *by trustees* was justified by that beneficiary's equitable interest. Whether they are trustees for this purpose depends, if the trust was created by will, on whether there is an assent in their favour.

Bear in mind however that with no assent to the trustees, implied vesting under TA section 40 does not operate when new trustees are appointed.

---

7 Assuming the commencement date of TLATA is 1 January 1997.
8 Assuming the commencement date of TLATA is 1 January 1997.

Sale by Survivor of Co-owners

Conveyancing procedures where slightly modified, and where unchanged under the new law

Sale etc by surviving joint tenant

Unregistered land

A purchaser for value and in good faith from a surviving joint tenant of unregistered land is protected if:

(1) the original conveyance created a beneficial joint tenancy; and

(2) the conveyance states the survivor is solely and beneficially interested. (The alternative of *conveying* as beneficial owner has disappeared since LP(MP)A 1994 came into force in 1995); and

(3) there is no memorandum of severance on the original conveyance; and

(4) no receiving order or petition for one has been registered as a land charge.

LP(JT)A 1964 section 1(1)

Similar provisions apply to the personal representative of a surviving joint tenant. *An assent or conveyance by personal representatives of a surviving joint tenant should contain a statement that the deceased was solely and beneficially interested.*

Registered land

The 1964 Act does not apply to registered land. A sole proprietor has full powers of dealing if there is no restriction on the register. If there is a restriction on the register, *e.g.* under Rule 68 requiring capital money to be paid to at least two proprietors, a sole proprietor has the two options referred to below under the heading "Sale by surviving tenant in common".

The advantages of appointing a second trustee go beyond avoiding having to prove the beneficial interests. If the purchase money is paid to at least two trustees, a sale or other disposal will overreach the beneficial interests of occupiers under that trust.

City of London Building Society v *Flegg* [1988] AC 54

On the other hand, sales and mortgages by a sole owner will be subject to the overriding interests of occupiers.

Williams and Glyns Bank Ltd v *Boland* [1981] AC 487

Sale by surviving tenant(s) in common

The normal (and safer) practice is to avoid the equities, and sell as trustees (appointing a second trustee if necessary) to overreach the equitable interests.

Sometimes this practice is not followed when the dead tenant in common has bequeathed his beneficial interest to the survivor.

Where title is registered two courses are possible:
1. It is feasible for the survivor to sell. It will be necessary first to remove the restriction that receipts must be given by at least two [trustees]. The registry's practice is to require the application for removal to be accompanied by proof of the equitable title *e.g.* a statutory declaration that under the deceased's will the survivor is entitled solely and beneficially, that the survivor has not incumbered his own undivided share nor (as personal representative) received notice that the deceased had incumbered his share. (*Ruoff and Roper* 27-19). That is the course to take if there is time to complete the removal of the restriction before exchanging contracts on the sale.

2. There may not be time to do so. A buyer should be unwilling to pay money to one seller when an extant restriction requires the proceeds of sale to be paid to two. If time is short, it will usually be simpler to appoint a second trustee to comply with the restriction.

In unregistered land, sometimes death and probate are followed by an assent of the equitable interest to the survivor.

But what "proves" the equities is not the assent, but the will. An equitable assent does not entitle the purchaser to assume it was made to the right person – AEA section 36(7) only relates to assents of a legal estate. Even if he sees the will, a purchaser remains at risk if there have been further undisclosed dealings with the equitable interest - quite possible if by the deceased.

So for unregistered land it is easier and safer to insist on the appointment of a second trustee, even where all the equities appear to be held by the survivor of tenants in common. An equitable assent can only show the second trustee that the personal representatives have no claim on the property, and that he may therefore safely account to the survivor. Even then the equitable assent should not form part of the title deduced to a purchaser.

Outline Checklist

Trust for sale or trust of land
Strict settlement

Trust for sale
or trust of land

Settled land

For assent

(1)   Named beneficiary?
(2)   Acknowledgment for probate?
(3)   Notice of equity to
      override s 36(7)?
(4)   Memo on grant?
(5)   If PRs of surviving joint
      tenant, recite was solely
      and beneficially entitled

For vesting assent

(1)   Comply with SLA s 5(1)?
(2)   Acknowledgment for probate?
(3)   Notice of equity to
      override s 36(7)?
(4)   Memo on grant?
(5)   If PRs of surviving joint
      tenant, recite was solely
      and beneficially entitled

For appointment of new trustees

(1)   Is property vested in
      appointor as trustee?
(2)   If so implied vesting s 40
(3)   Did assent create independent
      trust?
(4)   If so separate appointment
      necessary.

For appointment of new trustees

(1)   Separate declaration of trustees?
(2)   Memo on vesting instrument?

For cessation inter vivos

(*i.e.* conveyance to beneficiary)
(1)   **If before 1997**[1], do equities show
      beneficiary entitled?
(2)   **If after 1996, TLATA s 16**
      deed of discharge?

For cessation inter vivos

(1)   SLA s 17 discharge?
(2)   Conveyance to beneficiary
      necessary?

For cessation on death

(1)   Probate?
(2)   Assent?
(3)   Memo on grant?

For cessation on death

(1)   Probate to general PRs
(2)   Clean assent?
(3)   Memo on grant?

---

1 Assuming, here and below, the commencement date of the Act is 1 January 1997.

Appointment of New Trustees

A reminder of the existing powers and mechanics as amended by the 1996 Act

Number

Normally limited to four (except charitable ecclesiastical or public trusts and some other rare cases). See TA section 34.

Powers of appointing

New trustees can be appointed:

(a) under an express power in the settlement, or
(b) under the statutory powers (TA s 36(1) and (6)), or
(c) by the court (TA s 41), or.
(d) by all the beneficiaries (indirectly, by determining the trust – Re Brockbank [1948] Ch 206 – or now by directing under the 1996 Act – see below).

Appointment at instance of the beneficiaries – the 1996 Act sections 19 and 20

See commentary in Chapter 11. Although these provisions enable beneficiaries to direct the appointment of new trustees, the appointment pursuant to the direction is nevertheless carried out under the existing powers in TA 1925 section 36 (see below). By implication (but not expressly) the terms of the direction do not concern a purchaser.

Statutory power of appointing new (i.e. replacement) trustees under TA section 36(1)

This is entirely unchanged by the 1996 Act. It arises where a trustee:

(a) remains out of UK for more than 12 months, or) The circumstance should
(b) refuses or is unfit to act, or) be recited for TA s 38
(c) is incapable of acting, or) protection of purchaser
(d) is dead, or)
(e) desires to be discharged, or)
(f) is an infant.)

Statutory power to appoint additional trustees under TA section 36(6)

This is simplified by the 1996 Act – it arises now where in any case there are not more than three trustees. The former "alternative" of a sole trustee other than a trust corporation has always been redundant (as it is included in the phrase above) and is now removed. Its removal also clarifies an individual can act with a trust corporation – see Receipts below.

Power to appoint is in:

(i)   person nominated for the purpose by the trust instrument, or
(ii) in default of the existence of (i), or if that person is not able or willing to act, the surviving or continuing trustee(s)
(iii) (under s 36(1) only) personal representative of the last surviving trustee.

Receipts

The 1996 Act substitutes "persons" for "individuals" in TA section 37(1)(c). That makes it clear a valid receipt can be given jointly by a trust corporation, two trust corporations, or a trust corporation and an individual(s). And that such a receipt will discharge the trustees. Previously the only options were receipts from (a) a trust corporation or (b) at least two individuals. It now matches the wording of LPA section 27(2).

Mechanics of appointing of new trustees

Where the trusts arose under a will

(1) Whether one or two appointments are needed depends on whether the assent to the trustees:

(a) was on the trusts if the will.
If so, one appointment only is needed, of the trusts of the will.

(b) or created an independent trust [for sale]
If so, two appointments are needed:
(i) one of the trusts of the will;
(ii) one of the trusts of the assent

(2) Endorse a memorandum of the appointment on the assent.

Where the trust was created by deed

(1) If there was a separate trust instrument and vesting deed two appointments are needed:

(a) one of the trusts of the the trust instrument;
(b) one of the trust [for sale] of the conveyance (vesting deed).

(2) If the trust was created by one deed, only one deed of appointment is needed.

(3) Endorse a memorandum of appointment on the trust instrument and (if any) vesting deed.

With twin appointments, appoint the same trustees. (TA s 35(1); LPA s 24(1))

Vesting land subject to the trust in new trustees

Unregistered land under TA section 40

If the appointment is by deed, the section automatically vests the legal estate of unregistered land in the new trustees. If the trust arose by will, section 40 only applies where the land already is vested in trustees *in that capacity* – you need an assent from personal representatives first. *Re King's Will Trusts* [1964] Ch 542. If there is no assent yet, draw it direct to the new and continuing trustees.

Registered land

There is no automatic vesting under TA section 40. In theory three alternative methods are available:

(1) Transfer in Form 19 to continuing and new trustees. "for the purpose of giving effect to the appointment of new trustees".

(2) Deed of appointment relating to unregistered and registered land executed off the register.
Form 19 as (1) but reads "for the purpose of giving effect to an appointment of new trustees pursuant to the provisions of a Deed of Appointment of even date and made between the same parties as are parties hereto".

(3) Produce deed of appointment to the Land Registry. The Registry discourage this course by:

(a) requiring deduction of title of right to appoint;
(b) (even more importantly!) there is no fee abatement.

Trusts of Land and Appointment of Trustees Act 1996

An Act to make new provision about trusts of land including provision phasing out the Settled Land Act 1925, abolishing the doctrine of conversion and otherwise amending the law about trusts for sale of land; to amend the law about the appointment and retirement of trustees of any trust; and for connected purposes.   [24th July 1996]

Be it enacted by the Queen's most Excellent Majesty, by and with the advice and consent of the Lords Spiritual and Temporal, and Commons, in this present Parliament assembled, and by the authority of the same, as follows:-

Part I

Trusts of land

Introductory

Meaning of "trust of land"
    1.–(1) In this Act–
      (a) "trust of land" means (subject to subsection (3)) any trust of property which consists of or includes land, and
      (b) "trustees of land" means trustees of a trust of land.
    (2) The reference in subsection (1)(a) to a trust–
      (a) is to any description of trust (whether express, implied, resulting or constructive), including a trust for sale and a bare trust, and
      (b) includes a trust created, or arising, before the commencement of this Act.
    (3) The reference to land in subsection (1)(a) does not include land which (despite section 2) is settled land or which is land to which the Universities and College Estates Act 1925 applies.
[See Text, 1.10]

Settlements and trusts for sale as trusts of land

Trusts in place of settlements
    2.–(1) No settlement created after the commencement of this Act is a settlement for the purposes of the Settled Land Act 1925; and no settlement shall be deemed to be made under that Act after that commencement.
    (2) Subsection (1) does not apply to a settlement created on the occasion of an alteration in any interest in, or of a person becoming entitled under, a settlement which–

(a) is in existence at the commencement of this Act, or

(b) derives from a settlement within paragraph (a) or this paragraph.

(3) But a settlement created as mentioned in subsection (2) is not a settlement for the purposes of the Settled Land Act 1925 if provision to the effect that it is not is made in the instrument, or any of the instruments, by which it is created.

(4) Where at any time after the commencement of this Act there is in the case of any settlement which is a settlement for the purposes of the Settled Land Act 1925 no relevant property which is, or is deemed to be, subject to the settlement, the settlement permanently ceases at that time to be a settlement for the purposes of that Act.

In this subsection "relevant property" means land and personal chattels to which section 67(1) of the Settled Land Act 1925 (heirlooms) applies.

(5) No land held on charitable, ecclesiastical or public trusts shall be or be deemed to be settled land after the commencement of this Act, even if it was· or was deemed to be settled land before that commencement.

(6) Schedule 1 has effect to make provision consequential on this section (including provision to impose a trust in circumstances in which, apart from this section, there would be a settlement for the purposes of the Settled Land Act 1925 (and there would not otherwise be a trust)).

[See Text, 2.1–2.5]

Abolition of doctrine of conversion

3.–(1) Where land is held by trustees subject to a trust for sale, the land is not to be regarded as personal property; and where personal property is subject to a trust for sale in order that the trustees may acquire land, the personal property is not to be regarded as land.

(2) Subsection (1) does not apply to a trust created by a will if the testator died before the commencement of this Act.

(3) Subject to that, subsection (1) applies to a trust whether it is created, or arises, before or after that commencement.

[See Text, Chap. 3]

Express trusts for sale as trusts of land

4.–(1) In the case of every trust for sale of land created by a disposition there is to be implied, despite any provision to the contrary made by the disposition, a power for the trustees to postpone sale of the land; and the trustees are not liable in any way for postponing sale of the land, in the exercise of their discretion, for an indefinite period.

(2) Subsection (1) applies to a trust whether it is created, or arises, before or after the commencement of this Act.

(3) Subsection (1) does not affect any liability incurred by trustees before that commencement.

[See Text, 4.1–4.6]

Implied trusts for sale as trusts of land

5.–(1) Schedule 2 has effect in relation to statutory provisions which impose a trust for sale of land in certain circumstances so that in those circumstances there is instead a trust of the land (without a duty to sell).

(2) Section 1 of the Settled Land Act 1925 does not apply to land held on any trust arising by virtue of that Schedule (so that any such land is subject to a trust of land).
[See Text, 4.7–4.10]

Functions of trustees of land

General powers of trustees

6.–(1) For the purpose of exercising their functions as trustees, the trustees of land have in relation to the land subject to the trust all the powers of an absolute owner.

(2) Where in the case of any land subject to a trust of land each of the beneficiaries interested in the land is a person of full age and capacity who is absolutely entitled to the land, the powers conferred on the trustees by subsection (1) include the power to convey the land to the beneficiaries even though they have not required the trustees to do so; and where land is conveyed by virtue of this subsection–

   (a) the beneficiaries shall do whatever is necessary to secure that it vests in them, and

   (b) if they fail to do so, the court may make an order requiring them to do so.

(3) The trustees of land have power to purchase a legal estate in any land in England or Wales.

(4) The power conferred by subsection (3) may be exercised by trustees to purchase land–

   (a) by way of investment,

   (b) for occupation by any beneficiary, or

   (c) for any other reason.

(5) In exercising the powers conferred by this section trustees shall have regard to the rights of the beneficiaries.

(6) The powers conferred by this section shall not be exercised in contravention of, or of any order made in pursuance of, any other enactment or any rule of law or equity.

(7) The reference in subsection (6) to an order includes an order of any court or of the Charity Commissioners.

(8) Where any enactment other than this section confers on trustees authority to act subject to any restriction, limitation or condition, trustees of land may not exercise the powers conferred by this section to do any act which they are prevented from doing under the other enactment by reason of the restriction, limitation or condition.
[See Text, 5.1–5.5]

Partition by trustees

7.–(1) The trustees of land may, where beneficiaries of full age are absolutely entitled in undivided shares to land subject to the trust, partition the land, or any part of it, and provide (by way of mortgage or otherwise) for the payment of any equality money.

(2) The trustees shall give effect to any such partition by conveying the

partitioned land in severalty (whether or not subject to any legal mortgage created for raising equality money), either absolutely or in trust, in accordance with the rights of those beneficiaries.

(3) Before exercising their powers under subsection (2) the trustees shall obtain the consent of each of those beneficiaries.

(4) Where a share in the land is affected by an incumbrance, the trustees may either give effect to it or provide for its discharge from the property allotted to that share as they think fit.

(5) If a share in the land is absolutely vested in a minor, subsections (1) to (4) apply as if he were of full age, except that the trustees may act on his behalf and retain land or other property representing his share in trust for him.
[See Text, 5.5]

Exclusion and restriction of powers

8.–(1) Sections 6 and 7 do not apply in the case of a trust of land created by a disposition in so far as provision to the effect that they do not apply is made by the disposition.

(2) If the disposition creating such a trust makes provision requiring any consent to be obtained to the exercise of any power conferred by section 6 or 7, the power may not be exercised without that consent.

(3) Subsection (1) does not apply in the case of charitable, ecclesiastical or public trusts.

(4) Subsections (1) and (2) have effect subject to any enactment which prohibits or restricts the effect of provision of the description mentioned in them.
[See Text, 5.6]

Delegation by trustees

9.–(1) The trustees of land may, by power of attorney, delegate to any beneficiary or beneficiaries of full age and beneficially entitled to an interest in possession in land subject to the trust any of their functions as trustees which relate to the land.

(2) Where trustees purport to delegate to a person by a power of attorney under subsection (1) functions relating to any land and another person in good faith deals with him in relation to the land, he shall be presumed in favour of that other person to have been a person to whom the functions could be delegated unless that other person has knowledge at the time of the transaction that he was not such a person.

And it shall be conclusively presumed in favour of any purchaser whose interest depends on the validity of that transaction that that other person dealt in good faith and did not have such knowledge if that other person makes a statutory declaration to that effect before or within three months after the completion of the purchase.

(3) A power of attorney under subsection (1) shall be given by all the trustees jointly and (unless expressed to be irrevocable and to be given by way of security) may be revoked by any one or more of them; and such a power is revoked by the appointment as a trustee of a person other than those by whom it is given (though not by any of those persons dying or otherwise ceasing to be a trustee).

(4) Where a beneficiary to whom functions are delegated by a power of attorney under subsection (1) ceases to be a person beneficially entitled to an interest in possession in land subject to the trust–

(a) if the functions are delegated to him alone, the power is revoked,

(b) if the functions are delegated to him and to other beneficiaries to be exercised by them jointly (but not separately), the power is revoked if each of the other beneficiaries ceases to be so entitled (but otherwise functions exercisable in accordance with the power are so exercisable by the remaining beneficiary or beneficiaries), and

(c) if the functions are delegated to him and to other beneficiaries to be exercised by them separately (or either separately or jointly), the power is revoked in so far as it relates to him.

(5) A delegation under subsection (1) may be for any period or indefinite.

(6) A power of attorney under subsection (1) cannot be an enduring power within the meaning of the Enduring Powers of Attorney Act 1985.

(7) Beneficiaries to whom functions have been delegated under subsection (1) are, in relation to the exercise of the functions, in the same position as trustees (with the same duties and liabilities); but such beneficiaries shall not be regarded as trustees for any other purposes (including, in particular, the purposes of any enactment permitting the delegation of functions by trustees or imposing requirements relating to the payment of capital money).

(8) Where any function has been delegated to a beneficiary or beneficiaries under subsection (1), the trustees are jointly and severally liable for any act or default of the beneficiary, or any of the beneficiaries, in the exercise of the function if, and only if, the trustees did not exercise reasonable care in deciding to delegate the function to the beneficiary or beneficiaries.

(9) Neither this section nor the repeal by this Act of section 29 of the Law of Property Act 1925 (which is superseded by this section) affects the operation after the commencement of this Act of any delegation effected before that commencement.

[See Text, Chap 6, 10.6]

Consents and consultation

Consents

10.–(1) If a disposition creating a trust of land requires the consent of more than two persons to the exercise by the trustees of any function relating to the land, the consent of any two of them to the exercise of the function is sufficient in favour of a purchaser.

(2) Subsection (1) does not apply to the exercise of a function by trustees of land held on charitable, ecclesiastical or public trusts.

(3) Where at any time a person whose consent is expressed by a disposition creating a trust of land to be required to the exercise by the trustees of any function relating to the land is not of full age–

(a) his consent is not, in favour of a purchaser, required to the exercise of the function, but

(b) the trustees shall obtain the consent of a parent who has parental

responsibility for him (within the meaning of the Children Act 1989) or of a guardian of his.
[See Text, 7.1–7.4]

Consultation with beneficiaries

11.–(1) The trustees of land shall in the exercise of any function relating to land subject to the trust–

(a) so far as practicable, consult the beneficiaries of full age and beneficially entitled to an interest in possession in the land, and

(b) so far as consistent with the general interest of the trust, give effect to the wishes of those beneficiaries, or (in case of dispute) of the majority (according to the value of their combined interests).

(2) Subsection (1) does not apply–

(a) in relation to a trust created by a disposition in so far as provision that it does not apply is made by the disposition,

(b) in relation to a trust created or arising under a will made before the commencement of this Act, or

(c) in relation to the exercise of the power mentioned in section 6(2).

(3) Subsection (1) does not apply to a trust created before the commencement of this Act by a disposition, or a trust created after that commencement by reference to such a trust, unless provision to the effect that it is to apply is made by a deed executed–

(a) in a case in which the trust was created by one person and he is of full capacity, by that person, or

(b) in a case in which the trust was created by more than one person, by such of the persons who created the trust as are alive and of full capacity.

(4) A deed executed for the purposes of subsection (3) is irrevocable.
[See Text, 7.5–7.8]

Right of beneficiaries to occupy trust land

The right to occupy

12.–(1) A beneficiary who is beneficially entitled to an interest in possession in land subject to a trust of land is entitled by reason of his interest to occupy the land at any time if at that time–

(a) the purposes of the trust include making the land available for his occupation (or for the occupation of beneficiaries of a class of which he is a member or of beneficiaries in general), or

(b) the land is held by the trustees so as to be so available.

(2) Subsection (1) does not confer on a beneficiary a right to occupy land if it is either unavailable or unsuitable for occupation by him.

(3) This section is subject to section 13.
[See Text, 8.1–8.4]

Exclusion and restriction of right to occupy

13.–(1) Where two or more beneficiaries are (or apart from this subsection would be) entitled under section 12 to occupy land, the trustees of land may exclude or restrict the entitlement of any one or more (but not all) of them.

(2) Trustees may not under subsection (1)–

   (a) unreasonably exclude any beneficiary's entitlement to occupy land, or

   (b) restrict any such entitlement to an unreasonable extent.

(3) The trustees of land may from time to time impose reasonable conditions on any beneficiary in relation to his occupation of land by reason of his entitlement under section 12.

(4) The matters to which trustees are to have regard in exercising the powers conferred by this section include–

   (a) the intentions of the person or persons (if any) who created the trust,

   (b) the purposes for which the land is held, and

   (c) the circumstances and wishes of each of the beneficiaries who is (or apart from any previous exercise by the trustees of those powers would be) entitled to occupy the land under section 12.

(5) The conditions which may be imposed on a beneficiary under subsection (3) include, in particular, conditions requiring him–

   (a) to pay any outgoings or expenses in respect of the land, or

   (b) to assume any other obligation in relation to the land or to any activity which is or is proposed to be conducted there.

(6) Where the entitlement of any beneficiary to occupy land under section 12 has been excluded or restricted, the conditions which may be imposed on any other beneficiary under subsection (3) include, in particular, conditions requiring him to–

   (a) make payments by way of compensation to the beneficiary whose entitlement has been excluded or restricted, or

   (b) forgo any payment or other benefit to which he would otherwise be entitled under the trust so as to benefit that beneficiary.

(7) The powers conferred on trustees by this section may not be exercised–

   (a) so as [to] prevent any person who is in occupation of land (whether or not by reason of an entitlement under section 12) from continuing to occupy the land, or

   (b) in a manner likely to result in any such person ceasing to occupy the land, unless he consents or the court has given approval.

(8) The matters to which the court is to have regard in determining whether to give approval under subsection (7) include the matters mentioned in subsection (4)(a) to (c).

[See Text, 8.5–8.8]

Powers of court

Applications for order

14.–(1) Any person who is a trustee of land or has an interest in property subject to a trust of land may make an application to the court for an order under this section.

(2) On an application for an order under this section the court may make any such order–

   (a) relating to the exercise by the trustees of any of their functions (including an order relieving them of any obligation to obtain the consent of, or to consult, any person in connection with the exercise of any of their functions), or

    (b) declaring the nature or extent of a person's interest in property subject to the trust,

as the court thinks fit.

(3) The court may not under this section make any order as to the appointment or removal of trustees.

(4) The powers conferred on the court by this section are exercisable on an application whether it is made before or after the commencement of this Act. [See Text, 9.1–9.2]

Matters relevant in determining applications

15.–(1) The matters to which the court is to have regard in determining an application for an order under section 14 include–

    (a) the intentions of the person or persons (if any) who created the trust,

    (b) the purposes for which the property subject to the trust is held,

    (c) the welfare of any minor who occupies or might reasonably be expected to occupy any land subject to the trust as his home, and

    (d) the interests of any secured creditor of any beneficiary.

(2) In the case of an application relating to the exercise in relation to any land of the powers conferred on the trustees by section 13, the matters to which the court is to have regard also include the circumstances and wishes of each of the beneficiaries who is (or apart from any previous exercise by the trustees of those powers would be) entitled to occupy the land under section 12.

(3) In the case of any other application, other than one relating to the exercise of the power mentioned in section 6(2), the matters to which the court is to have regard also include the circumstances and wishes of any beneficiaries of full age and entitled to an interest in possession in property subject to the trust or (in case of dispute) of the majority (according to the value of their combined interests).

(4) This section does not apply to an application if section 335A of the Insolvency Act 1986 (which is inserted by Schedule 3 and relates to applications by a trustee of a bankrupt) applies to it. [See Text, 9.3]

Purchaser protection

Protection of purchasers

16.–(1) A purchaser of land which is or has been subject to a trust need not be concerned to see that any requirement imposed on the trustees by section 6(5), 7(3) or 11(1) has been complied with.

(2) Where–

    (a) trustees of land who convey land which (immediately before it is conveyed) is subject to the trust contravene section 6(6) or (8), but

    (b) the purchaser of the land from the trustees has no actual notice of the contravention,

the contravention does not invalidate the conveyance.

(3) Where the powers of trustees of land are limited by virtue of section 8–

(a) the trustees shall take all reasonable steps to bring the limitation to the notice of any purchaser of the land from them, but

(b) the limitation does not invalidate any conveyance by the trustees to a purchaser who has no actual notice of the limitation.

(4) Where trustees of land convey land which (immediately before it is conveyed) is subject to the trust to persons believed by them to be beneficiaries absolutely entitled to the land under the trust and of full age and capacity–

(a) the trustees shall execute a deed declaring that they are discharged from the trust in relation to that land, and

(b) if they fail to do so, the court may make an order requiring them to do so.

(5) A purchaser of land to which a deed under subsection (4) relates is entitled to assume that, as from the date of the deed, the land is not subject to the trust unless he has actual notice that the trustees were mistaken in their belief that the land was conveyed to beneficiaries absolutely entitled to the land under the trust and of full age and capacity.

(6) Subsections (2) and (3) do not apply to land held on charitable, ecclesiastical or public trusts.

(7) This section does not apply to registered land.

[See Text, 10.3–10.5]

Supplementary

Application of provisions to trusts of proceeds of sale

17.–(1) Section 6(3) applies in relation to trustees of a trust of proceeds of sale of land as in relation to trustees of land.

(2) Section 14 applies in relation to a trust of proceeds of sale of land and trustees of such a trust as in relation to a trust of land and trustees of land.

(3) In this section "trust of proceeds of sale of land" means (subject to subsection (5)) any trust of property (other than a trust of land) which consists of or includes–

(a) any proceeds of a disposition of land held in trust (including settled land), or

(b) any property representing any such proceeds.

(4) The references in subsection (3) to a trust–

(a) are to any description of trust (whether express, implied, resulting or constructive), including a trust for sale and a bare trust, and

(b) include a trust created, or arising, before the commencement of this Act.

(5) A trust which (despite section 2) is a settlement for the purposes of the Settled Land Act 1925 cannot be a trust of proceeds of sale of land.

(6) In subsection (3)–

(a) "disposition" includes any disposition made, or coming into operation, before the commencement of this Act, and

(b) the reference to settled land includes personal chattels to which section 67(1) of the Settled Land Act 1925 (heirlooms) applies.

[See Text, 5.4, 9.5]

Application of Part to personal representatives

18.–(1) The provisions of this Part relating to trustees, other than sections 10, 11 and 14, apply to personal representatives, but with appropriate modifications and without prejudice to the functions of personal representatives for the purposes of administration.

(2) The appropriate modifications include–

    (a) the substitution of references to persons interested in the due administration of the estate for references to beneficiaries, and

    (b) the substitution of references to the will for references to the disposition creating the trust.

(3) Section 3(1) does not apply to personal representatives if the death occurs before the commencement of this Act.

Part II

Appointment and retirement of trustees

Appointment and retirement of trustee at instance of beneficiaries

19.–(1) This section applies in the case of a trust where–

    (a) there is no person nominated for the purpose of appointing new trustees by the instrument, if any, creating the trust, and

    (b) the beneficiaries under the trust are of full age and capacity and (taken together) are absolutely entitled to the property subject to the trust.

(2) The beneficiaries may give a direction or directions of either or both of the following descriptions–

    (a) a written direction to a trustee or trustees to retire from the trust, and

    (b) a written direction to the trustees or trustee for the time being (or, if there are none, to the personal representative of the last person who was a trustee) to appoint by writing to be a trustee or trustees the person or persons specified in the direction.

(3) Where–

    (a) a trustee has been given a direction under subsection (2)(a),

    (b) reasonable arrangements have been made for the protection of any rights of his in connection with the trust,

    (c) after he has retired there will be either a trust corporation or at least two persons to act as trustees to perform the trust, and

    (d) either another person is to be appointed to be a new trustee on his retirement (whether in compliance with a direction under subsection (2)(b) or otherwise) or the continuing trustees by deed consent to his retirement,

he shall make a deed declaring his retirement and shall be deemed to have retired and be discharged from the trust.

(4) Where a trustee retires under subsection (3) he and the continuing trustees (together with any new trustee) shall (subject to any arrangements for the protection of his rights) do anything necessary to vest the trust property in the continuing trustees (or the continuing and new trustees).

(5) This section has effect subject to the restrictions imposed by the Trustee Act 1925 on the number of trustees.
[See Text, 11.2–11.7]

Appointment of substitute for incapable trustee
20.–(1) This section applies where–
- (a) a trustee is incapable by reason of mental disorder of exercising his functions as trustee,
- (b) there is no person who is both entitled and willing and able to appoint a trustee in place of him under section 36(1) of the Trustee Act 1925, and
- (c) the beneficiaries under the trust are of full age and capacity and (taken together) are absolutely entitled to the property subject to the trust.

(2) The beneficiaries may give to–
- (a) a receiver of the trustee,
- (b) an attorney acting for him under the authority of a power of attorney created by an instrument which is registered under section 6 of the Enduring Powers of Attorney Act 1985, or
- (c) a person authorised for the purpose by the authority having jurisdiction under Part VII of the Mental Health Act 1983,

a written direction to appoint by writing the person or persons specified in the direction to be a trustee or trustees in place of the incapable trustee.
[See Text, 11.8]

Supplementary
21.–(1) For the purposes of section 19 or 20 a direction is given by beneficiaries if–
- (a) a single direction is jointly given by all of them, or
- (b) (subject to subsection (2)) a direction is given by each of them (whether solely or jointly with one or more, but not all, of the others),

and none of them by writing withdraws the direction given by him before it has been complied with.

(2) Where more than one direction is given each must specify for appointment or retirement the same person or persons.

(3) Subsection (7) of section 36 of the Trustee Act 1925 (powers of trustees appointed under that section) applies to a trustee appointed under section 19 or 20 as if he were appointed under that section.

(4) A direction under section 19 or 20 must not specify a person or persons for appointment if the appointment of that person or those persons would be in contravention of section 35(1) of the Trustee Act 1925 or section 24(1) of the Law of Property Act 1925 (requirements as to identity of trustees).

(5) Sections 19 and 20 do not apply in relation to a trust created by a disposition in so far as provision that they do not apply is made by the disposition.

(6) Sections 19 and 20 do not apply in relation to a trust created before the commencement of this Act by a disposition in so far as provision to the effect that they do not apply is made by a deed executed–
- (a) in a case in which the trust was created by one person and he is of full capacity, by that person, or

   (b) in a case in which the trust was created by more than one person, by such of the persons who created the trust as are alive and of full capacity.

(7) A deed executed for the purposes of subsection (6) is irrevocable.

(8) Where a deed is executed for the purposes of subsection (6)–

   (a) it does not affect anything done before its execution to comply with a direction under section 19 or 20, but

   (b) a direction under section 19 or 20 which has been given but not complied with before its execution shall cease to have effect.

[See Text, 11.9–11.11]

Part III

Supplementary

Meaning of "beneficiary"

   22.–(1) In this Act "beneficiary", in relation to a trust, means any person who under the trust has an interest in property subject to the trust (including a person who has such an interest as a trustee or a personal representative).

   (2) In this Act references to a beneficiary who is beneficially entitled do not include a beneficiary who has an interest in property subject to the trust only by reason of being a trustee or personal representative.

   (3) For the purposes of this Act a person who is a beneficiary only by reason of being an annuitant is not to be regarded as entitled to an interest in possession in land subject to the trust.

[See Text, 1.11]

Other interpretation provisions

   23.–(1) In this Act "purchaser" has the same meaning as in Part I of the Law of Property Act 1925.

   (2) Subject to that, where an expression used in this Act is given a meaning by the Law of Property Act 1925 it has the same meaning as in that Act unless the context otherwise requires.

   (3) In this Act "the court" means–

   (a) the High Court, or

   (b) a county court.

[See Text, 1.12–1.13]

Application to Crown

   24.–(1) Subject to subsection (2), this Act binds the Crown.

   (2) This Act (except so far as it relates to undivided shares and joint ownership) does not affect or alter the descent, devolution or nature of the estates and interests of or in–

   (a) land for the time being vested in Her Majesty in right of the Crown or of the Duchy of Lancaster, or

   (b) land for the time being belonging to the Duchy of Cornwall and held in right or respect of the Duchy.

[See Text, 1.7]

Amendments, repeals etc.

25.–(1) The enactments mentioned in Schedule 3 have effect subject to the amendments specified in that Schedule (which are minor or consequential on other provisions of this Act).

(2) The enactments mentioned in Schedule 4 are repealed to the extent specified in the third column of that Schedule.

(3) Neither section 2(5) nor the repeal by this Act of section 29 of the Settled Land Act 1925 applies in relation to the deed of settlement set out in the Schedule to the Chequers Estate Act 1917 or the trust instrument set out in the Schedule to the Chevening Estate Act 1959.

(4) The amendments and repeals made by this Act do not affect any entailed interest created before the commencement of this Act.

(5) The amendments and repeals made by this Act in consequence of section 3–

(a) do not affect a trust created by a will if the testator died before the commencement of this Act, and

(b) do not affect personal representatives of a person who died before that commencement;

and the repeal of section 22 of the Partnership Act 1890 does not apply in any circumstances involving the personal representatives of a partner who died before that commencement.

Power to make consequential provision

26.–(1) The Lord Chancellor may by order made by statutory instrument make any such supplementary, transitional or incidental provision as appears to him to be appropriate for any of the purposes of this Act or in consequence of any of the provisions of this Act.

(2) An order under subsection (1) may, in particular, include provision modifying any enactment contained in a public general or local Act which is passed before, or in the same Session as, this Act.

(3) A statutory instrument made in the exercise of the power conferred by this section is subject to annulment in pursuance of a resolution of either House of Parliament.

[See Text, 1.7]

Short title, commencement and extent

27.–(1) This Act may be cited as the Trusts of Land and Appointment of Trustees Act 1996.

(2) This Act comes into force on such day as the Lord Chancellor appoints by order made by statutory instrument.

(3) Subject to subsection (4), the provisions of this Act extend only to England and Wales.

(4) The repeal in section 30(2) of the Agriculture Act 1970 extends only to Northern Ireland.

[See Text, 1.5–1.7]

Schedule 1

Provisions consequential on section 2

Minors

Section 2

1.–(1) Where after the commencement of this Act a person purports to convey a legal estate in land to a minor, or two or more minors, alone, the conveyance–

    (a) is not effective to pass the legal estate, but

    (b) operates as a declaration that the land is held in trust for the minor or minors (or if he purports to convey it to the minor or minors in trust for any persons, for those persons).

(2) Where after the commencement of this Act a person purports to convey a legal estate in land to–

    (a) a minor or two or more minors, and

    (b) another person who is, or other persons who are, of full age,

the conveyance operates to vest the land in the other person or persons in trust for the minor or minors and the other person or persons (or if he purports to convey it to them in trust for any persons, for those persons).

(3) Where immediately before the commencement of this Act a conveyance is operating (by virtue of section 27 of the Settled Land Act 1925) as an agreement to execute a settlement in favour of a minor or minors–

    (a) the agreement ceases to have effect on the commencement of this Act, and

    (b) the conveyance subsequently operates instead as a declaration that the land is held in trust for the minor or minors.

2. Where after the commencement of this Act a legal estate in land would, by reason of intestacy or in any other circumstances not dealt with in paragraph 1, vest in a person who is a minor if he were a person of full age, the land is held in trust for the minor.

Family charges

3. Where, by virtue of an instrument coming into operation after the commencement of this Act, land becomes charged voluntarily (or in consideration of marriage) or by way of family arrangement, whether immediately or after an interval, with the payment of–

    (a) a rentcharge for the life of a person or a shorter period, or

    (b) capital, annual or periodical sums for the benefit of a person,

the instrument operates as a declaration that the land is held in trust for giving effect to the charge.

Charitable, ecclesiastical and public trusts

4.–(1) This paragraph applies in the case of land held on charitable, ecclesiastical or public trusts (other than land to which the Universities and College Estates Act 1925 applies).

(2) Where there is a conveyance of such land–
  (a) if neither section 37(1) nor section 39(1) of the Charities Act 1993 applies to the conveyance, it shall state that the land is held on such trusts, and
  (b) if neither section 37(2) nor section 39(2) of that Act has been complied with in relation to the conveyance and a purchaser has notice that the land is held on such trusts, he must see that any consents or orders necessary to authorise the transaction have been obtained.

(3) Where any trustees or the majority of any set of trustees have power to transfer or create any legal estate in the land, the estate shall be transferred or created by them in the names and on behalf of the persons in whom it is vested.

Entailed interests

5.–(1) Where a person purports by an instrument coming into operation after the commencement of this Act to grant to another person an entailed interest in real or personal property, the instrument–
  (a) is not effective to grant an entailed interest, but
  (b) operates instead as a declaration that the property is held in trust absolutely for the person to whom an entailed interest in the property was purportedly granted.

(2) Where a person purports by an instrument coming into operation after the commencement of this Act to declare himself a tenant in tail of real or personal property, the instrument is not effective to create an entailed interest.

Property held on settlement ceasing to exist

6. Where a settlement ceases to be a settlement for the purposes of the Settled Land Act 1925 because no relevant property (within the meaning of section 2(4)) is, or is deemed to be, subject to the settlement, any property which is or later becomes subject to the settlement is held in trust for the persons interested under the settlement.
[See Text, 2.6]

Schedule 2

Amendments of statutory provisions imposing trust for sale

Mortgaged property held by trustees after redemption barred

Section 5
1.–(1) Section 31 of the Law of Property Act 1925 (implied trust for sale of mortgaged property where right of redemption is barred) is amended as follows.
  (2) In subsection (1), for the words "on trust for sale." substitute "in trust–
    (a) to apply the income from the property in the same manner as interest paid on the mortgage debt would have been applicable; and

(b) if the property is sold, to apply the net proceeds of sale, after payment of costs and expenses, in the same manner as repayment of the mortgage debt would have been applicable."

(3) In subsection (2), for the words from the beginning to "this subsection" substitute–

"(2) Subsection (1) of this section".

(4) Omit subsection (3).

(5) For subsection (4) substitute–

"(4) Where–

(a) the mortgage money is capital money for the purposes of the Settled Land Act 1925;

(b) land other than any forming the whole or part of the property mentioned in subsection (1) of this section is, or is deemed to be, subject to the settlement; and

(c) the tenant for life or statutory owner requires the trustees to execute with respect to land forming the whole or part of that property a vesting deed such as would have been required in relation to the land if it had been acquired on a purchase with capital money,

the trustees shall execute such a vesting deed."

(6) In accordance with the amendments made by sub-paragraphs (2) to (5), in the sidenote of section 31 for the words "Trust for sale" substitute "Trust".

(7) The amendments made by this paragraph–

(a) apply whether the right of redemption is discharged before or after the commencement of this Act, but

(b) are without prejudice to any dealings or arrangements made before the commencement of this Act.

Land purchased by trustees of personal property etc.

2.–(1) Section 32 of the Law of Property Act 1925 (implied trust for sale of land acquired by trustees of personal property or of land held on trust for sale) is omitted.

(2) The repeal made by this paragraph applies in relation to land purchased after the commencement of this Act whether the trust or will in pursuance of which it is purchased comes into operation before or after the commencement of this Act.

Dispositions to tenants in common

3.–(1) Section 34 of the Law of Property Act 1925 is amended as follows.

(2) In subsection (2) (conveyance of land in undivided shares to operate as conveyance to grantees on trust for sale), for the words from "upon the statutory trusts" to "those shares" substitute "in trust for the persons interested in the land".

(3) In subsection (3) (devise etc. of land in undivided shares to operate as devise etc. to trustees of will etc. on trust for sale)–

(a) omit the words from "the trustees (if any)" to "then to" and the words "in each case", and

(b) for the words "upon the statutory trusts hereinafter mentioned" substitute "in trust for the persons interested in the land".

(4) After that subsection insert–

"(3A) In subsections (2) and (3) of this section references to the persons interested in the land include persons interested as trustees or personal representatives (as well as persons beneficially interested)."

(5) Omit subsection (4) (settlement of undivided shares in land to operate only as settlement of share of profits of sale and rents and profits).

(6) The amendments made by this paragraph apply whether the disposition is made, or comes into operation, before or after the commencement of this Act.

Joint tenancies

4.–(1) Section 36 of the Law of Property Act 1925 is amended as follows.

(2) In subsection (1) (implied trust for sale applicable to land held for persons as joint tenants), for the words "on trust for sale" substitute "in trust".

(3) In subsection (2) (severance of beneficial joint tenancy)–

(a) in the proviso, for the words "under the trust for sale affecting the land the net proceeds of sale, and the net rents and profits until sale, shall be held upon the trusts" substitute "the land shall be held in trust on terms", and

(b) in the final sentence, for the words "on trust for sale" substitute "in trust".

(4) The amendments made by this paragraph apply whether the legal estate is limited, or becomes held in trust, before or after the commencement of this Act.

Intestacy

5.–(1) Section 33 of the Administration of Estates Act 1925 (implied trust for sale on intestacy) is amended as follows.

(2) For subsection (1) substitute–

"(1) On the death of a person intestate as to any real or personal estate, that estate shall be held in trust by his personal representatives with the power to sell it."

(3) In subsection (2), for the words from the beginning to "pay all" substitute–

"(2) The personal representatives shall pay out of–

(a) the ready money of the deceased (so far as not disposed of by his will, if any); and

(b) any net money arising from disposing of any other part of his estate (after payment of costs),

all".

(4) In subsection (4), for the words from "including" to "retained" substitute "and any part of the estate of the deceased which remains".

(5) The amendments made by this paragraph apply whether the death occurs before or after the commencement of this Act.

Reverter of sites

6.–(1) Section 1 of the Reverter of Sites Act 1987 (right of reverter replaced by trust for sale) is amended as follows.

(2) In subsection (2)–

    (a) after "a trust" insert "for the persons who (but for this Act) would from time to time be entitled to the ownership of the land by virtue of its reverter with a power, without consulting them,", and

    (b) for the words "upon trust" onwards substitute "in trust for those persons; but they shall not be entitled by reason of their interest to occupy the land."

(3) In subsection (3), for the words "trustees for sale" substitute "trustees".

(4) In subsection (4), for the words "on trust for sale" substitute "in trust".

(5) In accordance with the amendments made by this paragraph, in the sidenote, for "trust for sale" substitute "trust".

(6) The amendments made by this paragraph apply whether the trust arises before or after the commencement of this Act.

Trusts deemed to arise in 1926

7. Where at the commencement of this Act any land is held on trust for sale, or on the statutory trusts, by virtue of Schedule 1 to the Law of Property Act 1925 (transitional provisions), it shall after that commencement be held in trust for the persons interested in the land; and references in that Schedule to trusts for sale or trustees for sale or to the statutory trusts shall be construed accordingly. [See Text, 4.9, 4.11]

Schedule 3

Minor and consequential amendments

The Law of Property Act 1922 (c.16)

Section 25(1)

1. In paragraph 17(3) and (4) of Schedule 15 to the Law of Property Act 1922, for the words "held on trust for sale" substitute "subject to a trust of land".

The Settled Land Act 1925 (c.18)

2.–(1) The Settled Land Act 1925 is amended as follows.

(2) In section 1(1)(ii)(c), after the word "fee" insert "(other than a fee which is a fee simple absolute by virtue of section 7 of the Law of Property Act 1925)".

(3) In section 3, for the words "not held upon trust for sale which has been subject to a settlement" substitute "which has been subject to a settlement which is a settlement for the purposes of this Act".

(4) In section 7(5), for the words "trustee for sale" substitute "trustee of land".

(5) In section 12(1), for the words "trustee for sale" substitute "trustee of land".

(6) In section 17–

(a) in subsection (1)–

(i) for the words "trust for sale", in the first three places, substitute "trust of land", and

(ii) for the words "held on trust for sale" substitute "subject to a trust of land",

(b) in subsection (2)(c), for the words "a conveyance on trust for sale" substitute "land", and

(c) in subsection (3), for the words "any trust for sale" substitute "a trust of land".

(7) In section 18(2)(b), for the words "trustee for sale" substitute "trustee of land".

(8) In section 20(1)(viii), for the words "an immediate binding trust for sale" substitute "a trust of land".

(9) In section 30(1)–

(a) in paragraph (iii), for the words "power of or upon trust for sale of" substitute "a power or duty to sell", and

(b) in paragraph (iv)–

(i) for the words "future power of sale, or under a future trust for sale of" substitute "a future power or duty to sell", and

(ii) for the words "or trust" substitute "or duty".

(10) In section 33(1), for the words "any power of sale, or trust for sale" substitute "a power or duty to sell".

(11) In section 36–

(a) for the words–

(i) "upon the statutory trusts" in subsection (2), and

(ii) "on the statutory trusts" in subsection (3),

substitute "in trust for the persons interested in the land",

(b) in subsection (4), for the words "trust for sale" substitute "trust of land",

(c) for subsection (6) substitute–

"(6) In subsections (2) and (3) of this section references to the persons interested in the land include persons interested as trustees or personal representatives (as well as persons beneficially interested).", and

(d) in accordance with the amendments made by paragraphs (a) to (c), in the sidenote, for the words "trust for sale of the land" substitute "trust of land".

(12) In section 110(5), for the words "trustee for sale" substitute "trustee of land".

(13) In section 117(1)–

(a) in paragraph (ix), for the words "not being" substitute ", but does not (except in the phrase "trust of land") include", and

(b) in paragraph (xxx), for the words " "trustees for sale" and "power to postpone a sale" have the same meanings" substitute "has the same meaning".

The Trustee Act 1925 (c.19)

3.–(1) The Trustee Act 1925 is amended as follows.

(2) In section 12–

(a) in subsection (1), for the words "a trust for sale or a power of sale of property is vested in a trustee" substitute "a trustee has a duty or power to sell property", and

(b) in subsection (2), for the word "trust", in both places, substitute "duty".

(3) In section 14(2), for paragraph (a) substitute–

"(a) proceeds of sale or other capital money arising under a trust of land;".

(4) In section 19–

(a) in subsection (1), for the words "against loss or damage by fire any building or other insurable property" substitute "any personal property against loss or damage", and

(b) in subsection (2), for the words "building or" substitute "personal".

(5) In section 20(3)(c), for the words "property held upon trust for sale" substitute "land subject to a trust of land or personal property held on trust for sale".

(6) In section 24–

(a) for the words "the proceeds of sale of land directed to be sold, or in any other" substitute "any",

(b) for the words "trust for sale" substitute "trust",

(c) for the words "trustees for sale" substitute "trustees", and

(d) for the words "trust or" substitute "duty or".

(7) In section 27(1), for the words "or of a disposition on trust for sale" substitute ", trustees of land, trustees for sale of personal property".

(8) In section 32, for subsection (2) substitute–

"(2) This section does not apply to capital money arising under the Settled Land Act 1925."

(9) In section 34(2), for the words "on trust for sale of land" substitute "creating trusts of land".

(10) In section 35–

(a) for subsection (1) substitute–

"(1) Appointments of new trustees of land and of new trustees of any trust of the proceeds of sale of the land shall, subject to any order of the court, be effected by separate instruments, but in such manner as to secure that the same persons become trustees of land and trustees of the trust of the proceeds of sale.",

(b) for subsection (3) substitute–

"(3) Where new trustees of land are appointed, a memorandum of the persons who are for the time being the trustees of the land shall be endorsed on or annexed to the conveyance by which the land was vested in trustees of land; and that conveyance shall be produced to the persons who are for the time being the trustees of the land by the person in possession of it in order for that to be done when the trustees require its production.", and

(c) in accordance with the amendments made by paragraphs (a) and (b), in the sidenote, for the words "dispositions on trust for sale of land" substitute "and trustees of land".

(11) In section 36(6), for the words before paragraph (a) substitute–
"(6) Where, in the case of any trust, there are not more than three trustees–".

(12) In section 37(1)(c), for the word "individuals" substitute "persons".

(13) In section 39(1), for the word "individuals" substitute "persons".

(14) In section 40(2), for the words "the statutory power" substitute "section 39 of this Act or section 19 of the Trusts of Land and Appointment of Trustees Act 1996".

[See Text, 11.12]

The Law of Property Act 1925 (c.20)

4.–(1) The Law of Property Act 1925 is amended as follows.

(2) In section 2–
(a) in subsection (1), in paragraph (ii)–
(i) for the words "trustees for sale" substitute "trustees of land", and
(ii) for the words "the statutory requirements respecting the payment of capital money arising under a disposition upon trust for sale" substitute "the requirements of section 27 of this Act respecting the payment of capital money arising on such a conveyance",
(b) after that subsection insert–
"(1A) An equitable interest in land subject to a trust of land which remains in, or is to revert to, the settlor shall (subject to any contrary intention) be overreached by the conveyance if it would be so overreached were it an interest under the trust.", and
(c) in subsection (2)–
(i) for the words "a trust for sale" substitute "a trust of land",
(ii) for the words "under the trust for sale or the powers conferred on the trustees for sale" substitute "by the trustees", and
(iii) for the words "to the trust for sale" substitute "to the trust".

(3) In section 3(1)(c), for the words "Where the legal estate affected is neither settled land nor vested in trustees for sale" substitute "In any other case".

(4) In section 16–
(a) in subsection (2), for the words "pursuant to a trust for sale" substitute "by trustees of land", and
(b) in subsection (6), for the words "trustee for sale" substitute "trustee of land".

(5) In section 18–
(a) in subsection (1)–
(i) after the word "settled" insert "or held subject to a trust of land", and
(ii) for the words "trustee for sale" substitute "trustee of land", and
(b) in subsection (2)(b), for the words "of the land or of the proceeds of sale" substitute "or trust".

(6) In section 22(2)–
    (a) for the words "held on trust for sale" substitute "subject to a trust of land", and
    (b) for the words "under the trust for sale or under the powers vested in the trustees for sale" substitute "by the trustees",
and, in accordance with the amendments made by paragraphs (a) and (b), in the sidenote of section 22, for the words "on trust for sale" substitute "in trust".
(7) For section 24 substitute–

"Trusts of land

Appointment of trustees of land
    24.–(1) The persons having power to appoint new trustees of land shall be bound to appoint the same persons (if any) who are for the time being trustees of any trust of the proceeds of sale of the land.
    (2) A purchaser shall not be concerned to see that subsection (1) of this section has been complied with.
    (3) This section applies whether the trust of land and the trust of proceeds of sale are created, or arise, before or after the commencement of this Act."
    (8) In section 27–
    (a) for subsection (1) substitute–
        "(1) A purchaser of a legal estate from trustees of land shall not be concerned with the trusts affecting the land, the net income of the land or the proceeds of sale of the land whether or not those trusts are declared by the same instrument as that by which the trust of land is created.", and
    (b) in subsection (2)–
        (i) for the words "trust for sale" substitute "trust",
        (ii) for the words "the settlement of the net proceeds" substitute "any trust affecting the net proceeds of sale of the land if it is sold", and
        (iii) for the words "trustees for sale" substitute "trustees".
    (9) In section 33–
    (a) for the words "trustees for sale" substitute "trustees of land", and
    (b) for the words "on trust for sale" substitute "land in trust".
    (10) In section 39(4), for the words "trusts for sale" substitute "trusts".
    (11) In section 42–
    (a) in subsection (1)(a), for the words "trust for sale" substitute "trust of land", and
    (b) in subsection (2)–
        (i) in paragraph (a), for the words "a conveyance on trust for sale" substitute "land", and
        (ii) in paragraph (b), for the words "on trust for sale" substitute "in trust".
    (12) In section 66(2), for the words "trustee for sale" substitute "trustee of land".
    (13) In section 102(1)–
    (a) for the words "share in the proceeds of sale of the land and in the rents

and profits thereof until sale" substitute "interest under the trust to which the land is subject", and

(b) for the words "trustees for sale" substitute "trustees".

(14) In section 131, after the words "but for this section" insert "(and paragraph 5 of Schedule 1 to the Trusts of Land and Appointment of Trustees Act 1996)".

(15) In section 137–

(a) in subsection (2)(ii), for the words "the proceeds of sale of land" onwards substitute "land subject to a trust of land, or the proceeds of the sale of such land, the persons to be served with notice shall be the trustees.", and

(b) in subsection (5), for the words "held on trust for sale" substitute "subject to a trust of land".

(16) In section 153(6)(ii), for the words "in trust for sale" substitute "as a trustee of land".

The Land Registration Act 1925 (c.21)

5.–(1) The Land Registration Act 1925 is amended as follows.

(2) In section 3(xv)(a)–

(a) for the words "held on trust for sale" substitute "subject to a trust of land", and

(b) for the words "trustees for sale" substitute "trustees".

(3) In section 4, for the words "trustee for sale" substitute "trustee of land".

(4) In section 8(1), for the words "trustee for sale" substitute "trustee of land".

(5) In section 49–

(a) in subsection (1)(d)–

(i) for the words "the proceeds of sale of land held on trust for sale" substitute "land subject to a trust of land", and

(ii) for the words "disposition on trust for sale or of the" substitute "trust or",

(b) in subsection (2), for the words "trust for sale" substitute "trust of land",

(c) in the proviso to that subsection, for the words "a disposition on trust for sale or" substitute "land, or trustees of", and

(d) in subsection (3), for the words "on trust for sale" substitute "subject to a trust of land".

(6) In section 78(4), at the end insert "registered at the commencement of this Act".

(7) In section 83, in paragraph (b) of the proviso to subsection (11), for the words "held on trust for sale" substitute "subject to a trust of land".

(8) In section 94–

(a) for subsection (1) substitute–

"(1) Where registered land is subject to a trust of land, the land shall be registered in the names of the trustees.",

(b) in subsection (3), for the words "trust for sale, the trustees for sale" substitute "trust of land, the trustees",

(c) after that subsection insert–

"(4) There shall also be entered on the register such restrictions as may be prescribed, or may be expedient, for the protection of the rights of the persons beneficially interested in the land.

(5) Where a deed has been executed under section 16(4) of the Trusts of Land and Appointment of Trustees Act 1996 by trustees of land the registrar is entitled to assume that, as from the date of the deed, the land to which the deed relates is not subject to the trust unless he has actual notice that the trustees were mistaken in their belief that the land was conveyed to beneficiaries absolutely entitled to the land under the trust and of full age and capacity.", and

(d) in accordance with the amendments made by paragraphs (a) to (c), in the sidenote, for the words "on trust for sale" substitute "in trust".

(9) In section 95, for the words "on trust for sale" substitute "subject to a trust of land".

(10) In paragraph (b) of the proviso to section 103(1)–

(a) for the words "on trust for sale" substitute "subject to a trust of land", and

(b) for the words "the execution of the trust for sale" substitute "a sale of the land by the trustees".

(11) In section 111(1), for the words "trustees for sale" substitute "trustees of land".

[See Text, 10.5]

The Administration of Estates Act 1925 (c.23)

6.–(1) The Administration of Estates Act 1925 is amended as follows.

(2) In section 39(1)–

(a) in paragraph (i), at the beginning insert "as respects the personal estate,",

(b) for paragraph (ii) substitute–

"(ii) as respects the real estate, all the functions conferred on them by Part I of the Trusts of Land and Appointment of Trustees Act 1996;", and

(c) in paragraph (iii), for the words "conferred by statute on trustees for sale, and" substitute "necessary".

(3) In section 41(6), for the words "trusts for sale" substitute "trusts".

(4) In section 51(3)–

(a) after the word "married" insert "and without issue",

(b) before the word "settlement", in both places, insert "trust or", and

(c) for the words "an entailed interest" substitute "a life interest".

(5) In section 55(1), after paragraph (vi) insert–

"(via) "Land" has the same meaning as in the Law of Property Act 1925;".

The Green Belt (London and Home Counties) Act 1938 (c.xciii)

7. In section 19(1) of the Green Belt (London and Home Counties) Act 1938–
   (a) for the words "trustee for sale within the meaning of the Law of Property Act 1925" substitute "trustee of land", and
   (b) for the words "of a trustee for sale" substitute "of a trustee of land".

The Settled Land and Trustee Acts (Court's General Powers) Act 1943 (c.25)

8. In section 1 of the Settled Land and Trustee Acts (Court's General Powers) Act 1943–
   (a) in subsection (1)–
      (i) for the words "trustees for sale of land" substitute "trustees of land", and
      (ii) for the words "land held on trust for sale" substitute "land subject to a trust of land", and
   (b) in subsections (2) and (3), for the words "trust for sale" substitute "trust of land".

The Historic Buildings and Ancient Monuments Act 1953 (c.49)

9. In sections 8(3), 8A(3) and 8B(3) of the Historic Buildings and Ancient Monuments Act 1953, for the words from "held on" to "thereof" substitute "subject to a trust of land, are conferred by law on the trustees of land in relation to the land and to the proceeds of its sale".

The Leasehold Reform Act 1967 (c.88)

10. In the Leasehold Reform Act 1967–
   (a) in section 6(1), for the words "the statutory trusts arising by virtue of sections 34 to 36" substitute "a trust arising under section 34 or section 36",
   (b) in section 24(1)(a), for the words "held on trust for sale" substitute "subject to a trust of land", and
   (c) in paragraph 7 of Schedule 2–
      (i) in sub-paragraph (1), for the words "a disposition on trust for sale" substitute "trust of land", and
      (ii) in sub-paragraph (3), for the words "held on trust for sale" substitute "subject to a trust of land".

The Agriculture Act 1970 (c.40)

11. In section 33(2) of the Agriculture Act 1970–
   (a) for the words "held under a trust for sale" substitute "subject to a trust of land", and
   (b) for the words "the trustees for sale" substitute "the trustees of land".

The Land Charges Act 1972 (c.61)

12.–(1) The Land Charges Act 1972 is amended as follows.
(2) In section 2(4)(iii)(b), for the words "trust for sale" substitute "trust of land".
(3) In section 6, after subsection (1) insert–
  "(1A) No writ or order affecting an interest under a trust of land may be registered under subsection (1) above."

The Land Compensation Act 1973 (c.26)

13. In subsection (2) of section 10 of the Land Compensation Act 1973, for the words "held on trust for sale" substitute "subject to a trust of land" and, in accordance with that amendment, in the sidenote of that section, for the words "trusts for sale" substitute "trusts of land".

The Local Land Charges Act 1975 (c.76)

14. In section 11(2) of the Local Land Charges Act 1975, for the words "held on trust for sale" substitute "subject to a trust of land".

The Rentcharges Act 1977 (c.30)

15.–(1) The Rentcharges Act 1977 is amended as follows.
(2) In section 2(3), for paragraphs (a) and (b) substitute–
  "(a) in the case of which paragraph 3 of Schedule 1 to the Trusts of Land and Appointment of Trustees Act 1996 (trust in case of family charge) applies to the land on which the rent is charged;
  (b) in the case of which paragraph (a) above would have effect but for the fact that the land on which the rent is charged is settled land or subject to a trust of land;".
(3) In section 10(2)(b), for the words "trust for sale" substitute "trust of land".

The Interpretation Act 1978 (c.30)

16. In Schedule 1 to the Interpretation Act 1978, after the definition of "The Treasury" insert–
" "Trust of land" and "trustees of land", in relation to England and Wales, have the same meanings as in the Trusts of Land and Appointment of Trustees Act 1996."

The Ancient Monuments and Archaeological Areas Act 1979 (c.46)

17. In the Ancient Monuments and Archaeological Areas Act 1979–
  (a) in section 12(3), for the words "trust for sale" substitute "trust of land", and

(b) in section 18(4), for paragraph (b) substitute–
  "(b) as trustees of land;".

The Limitation Act 1980 (c.58)

18. In paragraph 9 of Schedule 1 to the Limitation Act 1980, for the words "held on trust for sale" substitute "subject to a trust of land".

The Highways Act 1980 (c.66)

19. In section 87(4)(b) of the Highways Act 1980, for the words from "and section 28" to "apply" substitute "applies".

The Wildlife and Countryside Act 1981 (c.69)

20. In section 30(4)(c) of the Wildlife and Countryside Act 1981, for the words "trusts for sale" substitute "trusts of land".

The Health and Social Services and Social Security Adjudications Act 1983 (c.41)

21. In section 22 of the Health and Social Services and Social Security Adjudications Act 1983–
  (a) in subsection (5)–
        (i) for the words "a joint tenant in the proceeds of sale of land held upon trust for sale" substitute "an equitable joint tenant in land", and
        (ii) for the words "those proceeds" substitute "the land",
  (b) in subsection (6)–
        (i) for the words "a joint tenant in the proceeds of sale of land held upon trust for sale" substitute "an equitable joint tenant in land",
        (ii) for the words "proceeds is" substitute "land is", and
        (iii) for the words "interests in the proceeds" substitute "interests in the land", and
  (c) in subsection (8), for the words "an interest in the proceeds of sale of land" substitute "the interest of an equitable joint tenant in land".

The Telecommunications Act 1984 (c.12)

22. In paragraph 4(10) of Schedule 2 to the Telecommunications Act 1984, for the words "trusts for sale" substitute "trusts of land".

The Insolvency Act 1986 (c.45)

23. At the beginning of Chapter V of Part IX of the Insolvency Act 1986 insert–

"Rights under trusts of land

Rights under trusts of land

335A.–(1) Any application by a trustee of a bankrupt's estate under section 14 of the Trusts of Land and Appointment of Trustees Act 1996 (powers of court in relation to trusts of land) for an order under that section for the sale of land shall be made to the court having jurisdiction in relation to the bankruptcy.

(2) On such an application the court shall make such order as it thinks just and reasonable having regard to–

    (a) the interests of the bankrupt's creditors;

    (b) where the application is made in respect of land which includes a dwelling house which is or has been the home of the bankrupt or the bankrupt's spouse or former spouse–

        (i) the conduct of the spouse or former spouse, so far as contributing to the bankruptcy,

        (ii) the needs and financial resources of the spouse or former spouse, and

        (iii) the needs of any children; and

    (c) all the circumstances of the case other than the needs of the bankrupt.

(3) Where such an application is made after the end of the period of one year beginning with the first vesting under Chapter IV of this Part of the bankrupt's estate in a trustee, the court shall assume, unless the circumstances of the case are exceptional, that the interests of the bankrupt's creditors outweigh all other considerations.

(4) The powers conferred on the court by this section are exercisable on an application whether it is made before or after the commencement of this section."
[See Text, 9.4]

The Patronage (Benefices) Measure 1986 (No.3)

24. In section 33 of the Patronage (Benefices) Measure 1986–

    (a) in subsection (1), for the words from "held by any trustee" to "capable of sale" substitute "subject to a trust of land", and

    (b) in subsection (2), for the words "section 26(1) and (2) of the Law of Property Act 1925 (consents to the execution of a trust for sale)" substitute "section 10 of the Trusts of Land and Appointment of Trustees Act 1996 (consents)".

The Family Law Reform Act 1987 (c.42)

25. In section 19(2) of the Family Law Reform Act 1987, for the words "which is used to create" substitute "purporting to create".

The Charities Act 1993 (c.10)

26. In section 23 of the Charities Act 1993–

    (a) in subsection (1)(b), for the words "trust for sale" substitute "trust",

    (b) in subsection (5), for the words "trustee for sale" substitute "trustee",

    (c) in subsection (7), for the words "trustees for sale" substitute "trustees", and

    (d) in subsection (9), for the words "trust for sale" substitute "trust".

Leasehold Reform, Housing and Urban Development Act 1993 (c.28)

27.–(1) The Leasehold Reform, Housing and Urban Development Act 1993 is amended as follows.

  (2) In Schedule 2–

    (a) in paragraph 5(1) and (2), for the words "held on trust for sale" substitute "subject to a trust of land" (and, accordingly, in the heading immediately preceding paragraph 5 for the words "on trust for sale" substitute "in trust"),

    (b) in paragraph 6, for the words "as mentioned in paragraph 5(2)(b) above" substitute "by the landlord on the termination of a new lease granted under Chapter II or section 93(4) (whether the payment is made in pursuance of an order under section 61 or in pursuance of an agreement made in conformity with paragraph 5 of Schedule 14 without an application having been made under that section)", and

    (c) in paragraphs 7(2)(b) and 8(3)(b) and (4)(c), for "5(2)(b)" substitute "6".

  (3) In Schedule 14–

    (a) in paragraph 7(1), for the words "disposition on trust for sale" substitute "trust of land", and

    (b) in paragraph 9(a), for the words "held on trust for sale" substitute "subject to a trust of land".

Schedule 4

Repeals

Section 25(2)

Chapter	Short title	Extent of repeal
3 & 4 Will.4 c. 74.	The Fines and Recoveries Act 1833.	In section 1, the words ", and any undivided share thereof", in both places.
7 Will.4 & 1 Vict. c. 26	The Wills Act 1837.	In section 1, the words "and to any undivided share thereof,". Section 32.
53 & 54 Vict. c. 39.	The Partnership Act 1890.	Section 22.
12 & 13 Geo.5 c. 16.	The Law of Property Act 1922.	In section 188– in subsection (1), the words "but not an undivided share in

Chapter	Short title	Extent of repeal
		land;" and the words "but not an undivided share thereof", and subsection (30).
15 & 16 Geo.5 c. 18.	The Settled Land Act 1925.	Section 27. Section 29.

15 & 16 Geo.5 c. 19.	The Trustee Act 1925.	In section 10(2)–
		    in the first paragraph, the words "by trustees or" and the words "the trustees, or", and
		    in the second paragraph, the words from the beginning to "mortgage; and".
		In section 19(1), the words "building or", in the second place.
		In section 68–
		    in subsection (6), the words ", but not an undivided share in land" and the words ", but not an undivided share thereof", and
		    in subsection (19), the word "binding", the words ", and with or without power at discretion to postpone the sale" and the definition of "trustees for sale".

15 & 16 Geo.5 c. 20.	The Law of Property Act 1925.	In section 3–
		    subsections (1)(b) and (2), and
		    in subsection (5), the words "trustees for sale or other".
		In section 7(3), the second paragraph.
		In section 18–
		    in subsection (1), the words from ", and personal estate" to "payable", in the

Chapter	Short title	Extent of repeal
		second place, and the words "or is capable of being", and
		in subsection (2), the words "of the settlement or the trustees for sale", in both places.
		Section 19.
		Section 23 (and the heading immediately preceding it).
		Sections 25 and 26.
		Sections 28 to 30.
		Section 31(3).
		Section 32.
		In section 34–
		in subsection (3), the words from "the trustees (if any)" to "then to" and the words "in each case", and
		subsection (4).
		Section 35.
		Section 42(6).
		In section 60, paragraphs (b) and (c) of the proviso to subsection (4).
		In section 130, subsections (1) to (3) and (6) (and the words "Creation of" in the sidenote).
		Section 201(3).
		In section 205(1)–
		in paragraph (ix), the words "but not an undivided share in land;" and the words "but not an undivided share thereof",
		in paragraph (x), the words "or in the proceeds of sale thereof", and
		in paragraph (xxix), the word "binding", the words ", and with or

Chapter	Short title	Extent of repeal

15 & 16 Geo.5 c. 21.	The Land Registration Act 1925.	without a power at discretion to postpone the sale" and the words "and "power" onwards.
		In section 3–
		  in paragraph (viii), the words "but not an undivided share in land;",
		  in paragraph (xi), the words "or in the proceeds of sale thereof",
		  in paragraph (xiv), the words ", but not an undivided share thereof", and paragraphs (xxviii) and (xxix).

15 & 16 Geo.5 c. 23.	The Administration of Estates Act 1925.	In section 3(1)(ii), the words "money to arise under a trust for sale of land, nor".
		In section 39(1)(i), the words from ", and such power" to "legal mortgage".
		In section 51–
		  in subsection (3), the word "settled", and
		  subsection (4).
		In section 55(1)–
		  in paragraph (vii), the words "or in the proceeds of sale thereof",
		  in paragraph (xxiv), the word " "land" ", and paragraph (xxvii).

15 & 16 Geo.5 c. 24.	The Universities and College Estates Act 1925.	In section 43(iv), the words ", but not an undivided share in land".
16 & 17 Geo.5 c. 11.	The Law of Property (Amendment) Act 1926.	In the Schedule, the entries relating to section 3 of the Settled Land Act 1925 and sections 26, 28 and 35 of the Law of Property Act 1925.

Chapter	Short title	Extent of repeal
17 & 18 Geo.5 c. 36.	The Landlord and Tenant Act 1927.	In section 13– in subsection (1), the words from "(either" to "Property Act, 1925)", in subsection (2), the words ", trustee for sale, or personal representative", and in subsection (3), the words ", and "settled land"" onwards.
22 & 23 Geo.5 c. 27.	The Law of Property (Entailed Interests) Act 1932.	Section 1.
2 & 3 Geo.6 c. 72.	The Landlord and Tenant (War Damage) Act 1939.	Section 3(c).
9 & 10 Geo.6 c. 73.	The Hill Farming Act 1946.	Section 11(2).
12 & 13 Geo.6 c. 74.	The Coast Protection Act 1949.	In section 11(2)(a)– the words ", by that section as applied by section twenty-eight of the Law of Property Act, 1925, in relation to trusts for sale,", and the words ", by that section as applied as aforesaid,".
2 & 3 Eliz.2 c. 56.	The Landlord and Tenant Act 1954.	In the Second Schedule, in paragraph 6– the words ", by that section as applied by section twenty-eight of the Law of Property Act, 1925, in relation to trusts for sale,", and the words ", by that section as applied as aforesaid,".
7 & 8 Eliz.2 c. 72.	The Mental Health Act 1959.	In Schedule 7, in Part I, the entries relating to sections 26 and 28 of the Law of Property Act 1925.
1964 No. 2.	The Incumbents and Churchwardens (Trusts) Measure 1964.	In section 1, in the definition of "land", the words "nor an undivided share in land".

Chapter	Short title	Extent of repeal
1967 c. 10.	The Forestry Act 1967.	In Schedule 2, paragraph 1(4).
1967 c. 88.	The Leasehold Reform Act 1967.	In section 6(5)– the words ", or by that section as applied by section 28 of the Law of Property Act 1925 in relation to trusts for sale,", the words "or by that section as applied as aforesaid", and the words "or by trustees for sale". In Schedule 2, in paragraph 9(1)– the words ", or by that section as applied by section 28 of the Law of Property Act 1925 in relation to trusts for sale, and the words "or by that section as applied as aforesaid".
1969 c.10.	The Mines and Quarries (Tips) Act 1969.	In section 32(2)(a) and (b), the words ", by that section as applied by section 28 of the Law of Property Act 1925 in relation to trusts for sale".
1970 c. 40.	The Agriculture Act 1970.	In section 30– in subsection (1), the words "(including those provisions as extended to trusts for sale by section 28 of the Law of Property Act 1925)", and in subsection (2), the words "the words from "(including those provisions" to "Law of Property Act 1925)" and".

Chapter	Short title	Extent of repeal
1972 c. 61.	The Land Charges Act 1972.	In section 17(1), the definition of "trust for sale".
1976 c. 31.	The Legitimacy Act 1976.	Section 10(4).
1976 c. 36.	The Adoption Act 1976.	Section 46(5).
1977 c. 42.	The Rent Act 1977.	In Schedule 2, in Part I, in paragraph 2(b), the words "or, if it is held on trust for sale, the proceeds of its sale are".
1980 c. 58.	The Limitation Act 1980.	In section 18– in subsection (1), the words ", including interests in the proceeds of the sale of land held upon trust for sale,", and in subsections (3) and (4), the words "(including a trust for sale)" and the words "or in the proceeds of sale". In section 38(1)– in the definition of "land", the words ", including an interest in the proceeds of the sale of land held upon trust for sale,", and the definition of "trust for sale". In Schedule 1, in Part I, in paragraph 9– the words "or in the proceeds of sale", the words "or the proceeds", and the words "or the proceeds of sale".
1981 c. 54.	The Supreme Court Act 1981.	In section 128, in the definition of "real estate", in paragraph (b), the words "money to arise under a trust for sale of land, nor".

Chapter	Short title	Extent of repeal
1983 c. 41.	The Health and Social Services and Social Security Adjudications Act 1983.	Section 22(3).
1984 c. 28.	The County Courts Act 1984.	In Schedule 2, in Part II, in paragraph 2– in sub-paragraph (1), the entry relating to section 30 of the Law of Property Act 1925, sub-paragraph (2), and in sub-paragraph (3), "30(2),".
1984 c. 51.	The Inheritance Tax Act 1984.	In section 237(3), the words "and undivided shares in land held on trust for sale, whether statutory or not,".
1986 c. 5.	The Agricultural Holdings Act 1986.	In section 89(1), the words "or the Law of Property Act 1925".
1986 c. 45.	The Insolvency Act 1986.	In section 336– subsection (3), and in subsection (4), the words "or (3)" and the words "or section 30 of the Act of 1925".
1988 c. 50.	The Housing Act 1988.	In Schedule 1, in Part III, in paragraph 18(1)(b), the words "or, if it is held on trust for sale, the proceeds of its sale are".
1989 c. 34.	The Law of Property (Miscellaneous Provisions) Act 1989.	In sections 1(6) and 2(6), the words "or in or over the proceeds of sale of land".
1990 c. 8.	The Town and Country Planning Act 1990.	In section 328– in subsection (1)(a), the words "and by that section as applied by section 28 of the Law of Property Act 1925 in relation to trusts for sale", and in subsection (2)(a), the words "and by that section as so applied".

Chapter	Short title	Extent of repeal
1991 c. 31.	The Finance Act 1991.	Section 110(5)(b).
1993 c. 10.	The Charities Act 1993.	Section 37(6). Section 39(5).

1993 c. 28.	The Leasehold Reform, Housing and Urban Development Act 1993.	In section 93A(4)–
		    the words ", or by that section as applied by section 28 of the Law of Property Act 1925 in relation to trusts for sale",
		    the words ", or by that section as so applied,", and
		    the words "or by trustees for sale".
		In Schedule 2, paragraph 5(2)(b) and the word "and" immediately preceding it.

1994 c. 36.	The Law of Property (Miscellaneous Provisions) Act 1994.	In section 16–
		    subsection (2), and
		    in subsection (3), the words "; and subsection (2)" onwards.

1995 c. 8.	The Agricultural Tenancies Act 1995.	In section 33–
		    in subsections (1) and (2), the words from "(either" to "Property Act 1925)", and
		    in subsection (4), the definition of "settled land" and the word "and" immediately preceding it.

1996 c. 53.	The Housing Grants, Construction and Regeneration Act 1996.	Section 55(4)(b). Section 73(3)(b). In section 98(2)(a), the words "or to the proceeds of sale of the dwelling".

Law of Property Act 1925

Sections 23-36 as amended

Dispositions on trust for sale [now trusts of land]

23. Duration of trusts for sale

[*Repealed by TLATA. Redundant because of the new wide definition of "trusts of land".*]

[Appointment of trustees of land

24.(1) The persons having power to appoint new trustees of land shall be bound to appoint the same persons (if any) who are for the time being trustees of any trust of the proceeds of sale of the land.

(2) A purchaser shall not be concerned to see that subsection (1) of this section has been complied with.

(3) This section applies whether the trust of land and the trust of proceeds of sale are created, or arise, before or after the commencement of this Act.][1]

25. Power to postpone sale

[*Repealed by TLATA Sched 4. Replaced by section 4 and (indirectly) by section 5.*]

26. Consents to the execution of a trust for sale

[*Repealed and replaced by TLATA s 10 and Sched 4.*]

27. Purchaser not to be concerned with the trusts of the proceeds of sale which are to be paid to two or more trustees or to a trust corporation

[(1) A purchaser of a legal estate from trustees of land shall not be concerned with the trusts affecting the land, the net income of the land or the proceeds of sale of the land whether or not those trusts are declared by the same instrument as that by which the trust of land is created.][2]

---

1 substituted by TLATA, s 25(1), Sched 3, para 4(7).
2 substituted by *ibid*, para 4(8)(a).

(2) Notwithstanding anything to the contrary in the instrument (if any) creating a [trust][3] of land or in [any trust affecting the net proceeds of sale of the land if it is sold][3], the proceeds of sale or other capital money shall not be paid to or applied by the direction of fewer than two persons as [trustees][3], except where the trustee is a trust corporation, but this subsection does not affect the right of a sole personal representative as such to give valid receipts for, or direct the application of, proceeds of sale or other capital money, nor, except where capital money arises on the transaction, render it necessary to have more than one trustee.

28. Powers of management etc conferred on trustees for sale

[*Repealed and replaced by TLATA sections 6, 7 and 8.*]

29. Delegation and powers of management by trustees for sale

[*Repealed and replaced by TLATA section 9.*]

30. Powers of court where trustees for sale refuse to exercise powers

[*Repealed and replaced by TLATA section 14.*]

31. Trust of mortgaged property where right of redemption is barred

(1) Where any property, vested in trustees by way of security, becomes, by virtue of the statutes of limitation, or of an order for foreclosure or otherwise, discharged from the right of redemption, it shall be held by them [in trust –

(a) to apply the income from the property in the same manner as interest paid on the mortgage debt would have been applicable; and

(b) if the property is sold, to apply the net proceeds of sale, after payment of costs and expenses, in the same manner as repayment of the mortgage debt would have been applicable.][4]

(2) [Subsection (1) of this section][5] operates without prejudice to any rule of law relating to the apportionment of capital and income between tenant for life and remaindermen.

(3) [*Omitted by TLATA, Schedule 2, para 1(4).*]

[(4) Where –

(a) the mortgage money is capital money for the purposes of the Settled Land Act 1925;

---

3 substituted by *ibid*, para 4(8)(b).
4 substituted by TLATA, s 5, Sched 2, para 1(2).
5 substituted by *ibid*, para 1(3).

(b) land other than any forming the whole or part of the property mentioned in subsection (1) of this section is, or is deemed to be, subject to the settlement; and

(c) the tenant for life or statutory owner requires the trustees to execute with respect to land forming the whole or part of that property a vesting deed such as would have been required in relation to the land if it had been acquired on a purchase with capital money,

the trustees shall execute such a vesting deed.][6]

(5) This section applies whether the right of redemption was discharged before or after the first day of January, nineteen hundred and twelve, but has effect without prejudice to any dealings or arrangements made before that date.

[*Note: The amendments to this section made by TLATA:*

(a) *apply whether the right of redemption is discharged before or after the commencement of TLATA;*

(b) *are without prejudice to any dealings or arrangement made before the commencement of TLATA.*]

32. Implied trust for sale in personalty settlements

[*Omitted. Replaced indirectly by sections 1 and 6(3).*]

33. Application of Part I to personal representatives

The provisions of this Part of this Act relating to [trustees of land][7] apply to personal representatives holding [land in trust][8]

Undivided shares and joint ownership

34. Effect of future dispositions to tenants in common

(1) An undivided share in land shall not be capable of being created except as provided by the Settled Land Act 1925 or as hereinafter mentioned.

(2) Where, after the commencement of this Act, land is expressed to be conveyed to any persons in undivided shares and those persons are of full age, the conveyance shall (notwithstanding anything to the contrary in this Act)

---

6 substituted by *ibid*, para 1(5).
7 substituted by TLATA, s 25(1), Sched 3, para 4(9)(a).
8 substituted by *ibid*, para 4(9)(b).

operate as if the land had been expressed to be conveyed to the grantees, or, if there are more than four grantees, to the four first named in the conveyance, as joint tenants [in trust for the persons interested in the land].⁹

Provided that, where the conveyance is made by way of mortgage the land shall vest in the grantees or such four of them as aforesaid for a term of years absolute (as provided by this Act) as joint tenants subject to cesser on redemption in like manner as if the mortgage money had belonged to them on a joint account, but without prejudice to the beneficial interests in the mortgage money and interest.

(3) A devise bequest or testamentary appointment, coming into operation after the commencement of this Act, of land to two or more persons in undivided shares shall operate as a devise bequest or appointment of the land to the personal representatives of the testator and in each case (but without prejudice to the rights and powers of the personal representatives for purposes of administration) and [in trust for the persons interested in the land].¹⁰

[(3(A)) In subsections (2) and (3) of this section references to the persons interested in the land include persons interested as trustees or personal representatives (as well as persons beneficially interested).]¹¹

[(4) *Omitted by TLATA, section 5, Sched 2, para 3(5).*]

[*Note: The amendments to section 34 made by TLATA apply whether the disposition is made, or comes into operation, before or after the commencement of TLATA.*]

35. *Meaning of the statutory trusts*

[*Repealed by TLATA, section 25(2), Sched 4.*]

36. *Joint tenancies*

(1) Where a legal estate (not being settled land) is beneficially limited to or held in trust for any persons as joint tenants, the same shall be held [in trust]¹² in like manner as if the persons beneficially entitled were tenants in common, but not so as to sever their joint tenancy in equity.

(2) No severance of a joint tenancy of a legal estate, so as to create a tenancy in common in land, shall be permissible, whether by operation of law or otherwise, but this subsection does not affect the right of a joint tenant to

---

9 substituted by TLATA, s 5, Sched 2, para 3(2).
10 substituted by *ibid*, para 3(3)(b).
11 inserted by *ibid*, para 3(4).
12 substituted by *ibid*, para 4(2).

release his interest to the other joint tenants, or the right to sever a joint tenancy in an equitable interest whether or not the legal estate is vested in the joint tenants:

Provided that, where a legal estate (not being settle land) is vested in joint tenants beneficially, any any tenant desires to sever the joint tenancy in equity, he shall give to the other joint tenants a notice in writing of such desire or do such other acts or things as would, in the case of personal estate, have been effectual to sever the tenancy in equity, and thereupon [the land shall be held in trust on terms][13] which would have been requisite for giving effect to the beneficial interests if there had been an actual severance.

Nothing in this Act affects the right of a survivor of joint tenants, who is safely and beneficially interested, to deal with his legal estate as if it were not held [in trust].[14]

(3) Without prejudice to the right of a joint tenant to release his interests to the other joint tenants no severance of a mortgage term or trust estate, so as to create a tenancy in common, shall be permissible.

[*Note: The amendments to section 36 by TLATA apply whether the land is limited, or becomes held in trust, before or after the commencement of TLATA.*]

---

13 substituted by *ibid*, para 4(3)(a).
14 substituted by *ibid*, para 4(3)(b).

Trustee Act 1925

Sections 34-40 as amended

Part III
Appointment and Discharge of Trustees

34. Limitation of the number of trustees

(1) Where, at the commencement of this Act, there are more than four trustees of a settlement of land, or more than four trustees holding land on trust for sale, no new trustees shall (except where as a result of the appointment the number is reduced to four or less) be capable of being appointed until the number is reduced to less than four, and thereafter the number shall not be increased beyond four.

(2) In the case of settlements and dispositions[creating trusts of land]¹ made or coming into operation after the commencement of this Act—

(a) the number of trustees thereof shall not in any case exceed four, and where more than four persons are named as such trustees, the four first named (who are able and willing to act) shall alone be the trustees, and the other persons named shall not be trustees unless appointed on the occurrence of a vacancy;
(b) the number of the trustees shall not be increased beyond four.

(3) This section only applies to settlements and dispositions of land, and the restrictions imposed on the number of trustees do not apply—

(a) in the case of land vested in trustees for charitable, ecclesiastical, or public purposes; or
(b) where the net proceeds of the sale of the land are held for like purposes; or
(c) to the trustees of a term of years absolute limited by a settlement on trusts for raising money, or of a like term created under the statutory remedies relating to annual sums charged on land.

35. Appointments of trustees of settlements and [and trustees of land]²

[(1) Appointments of new trustees of land and of new trustees of any trust of the proceeds of sale of the land shall, subject to any order of the court, be

---

1 substituted by TLATA, s 25(1), Sched 3, para 3(9).
2 substituted by *ibid*, para 3(10)(c).

effected by separate instruments, but in such manner as to secure that the same persons become trustees of land and trustees of the trust of the proceeds of sale.]³

(2) Where new trustees of a settlement are appointed, a memorandum of the names and addresses of the persons who are for the time being the trustees thereof for the purposes of the Settled Land Act 1925, shall be endorsed on or annexed to the last or only principal vesting instrument by or on behalf of the trustees of the settlement, and such vesting instrument shall, for that purpose, be produced by the person having the possession thereof of the trustees of the settlement when so required.

[(3) Where new trustees of land are appointed, a memorandum of the persons who are for the time being the trustees of the land shall be endorsed on or annexed to the conveyance by which the land was vested in trustees of land; and that conveyance shall be produced to the persons who are for the time being the trustees of the land by the person in possession of it in order for that to be done when the trustees require its production.]⁴

(4) This section applies only to settlements and dispositions of land.

36. Power of appointing new or additional trustees

(1) Where a trustee, either original or substituted, and whether appointed by a court or otherwise, is dead, or remains out of the United Kingdom for more than twelve months, or desires to be discharged from all or any of the trusts or powers reposed in or conferred on him, or refuses or is unfit to act therein, or is incapable of acting therein, or is an infant, then, subject to the restrictions imposed by this Act on the number of trustees,—

(a) the person or persons nominated for the purpose of appointing new trustees by the instrument, if any, creating the trust; or
(b) if there is no such person, or no such person able and willing to act, then the surviving or continuing trustees or trustee for the time being, or the personal representatives of the last surviving or continuing trustee;

may, by writing, appoint one or more other persons (whether or not being the persons exercising the power) to be a trustee or trustees in the place of the trustee so deceased remaining out of the United Kingdom, desiring to be discharged, refusing, or being unfit or being incapable, or being an infant, as aforesaid.

(2) Where a trustee has been removed under a power contained in the instrument creating the trust, a new trustee or new trustees may be appointed in

---

3 substituted by *ibid*, para 3(10)(a).
4 substituted by *ibid*, para 3(10)(b).

the place of the trustee who is removed, as if he were dead, or, in the case of a corporation, as if the corporation desired to be discharged from the trust, and the provisions of this section shall apply accordingly, but subject to the restrictions imposed by this Act on the number of trustees.

(3) Where a corporation being a trustee is or has been dissolved, either before or after the commencement of this act, then, for the purposes of this section and of any enactment replaced thereby, the corporation shall be deemed to be and to have been from the date of the dissolution incapable of acting in the trusts or powers reposed in or conferred on the corporation.

(4) The power of appointment given by subsection (1) of this section or any similar previous enactment to the personal representatives of a last surviving or continuing trustee shall be and shall be deemed always to have been exercisable by the executors for the time being (whether original or by representation) of such surviving or continuing trustee who have proved the will of their testator or by the administrators for the time being of such trustee without the concurrence of any executor who has renounced or has not proved.

(5) But a sole or last surviving executor intending to renounce, or all the executors where they all intend to renounce, shall have and shall be deemed always to have had power, at any time before renouncing probate, to exercise the power of appointment given by this section, or by any similar previous enactment, if willing to act for that purpose and without thereby accepting the office of executor.

[(6) Where, in the case of any trust, there are not more than three trustees][5]

    (a) the person or persons nominated for the purpose of appointing new trustees by the instrument, if any, creating the trust; or
    (b) if there is no such person, or no such person able and willing to act, then the trustee or trustees for the time being;

may, by writing appoint another person or other persons to be an additional trustee or additional trustees, but it shall not be obligatory to appoint any additional trustee, unless the instrument, if any, creating the trust, or any statutory enactment provides to the contrary, nor shall the number of trustees be increased beyond four by virtue of any such appointment.

(7) Every new trustee appointed under this section as well before as after all the trust property becomes by law, or by assurance, or otherwise, vested in him, shall have the same powers, authorities, and discretions, and may in all respects act as if he had been originally appointed a trustee by the instrument, if any, creating the trust.

---

5 substituted by *ibid*, para 3(11).

(8) The provisions of this section relating to a trustee who is dead include the case of a person nominated trustee in a will but dying before the testator, and those relative to a continuing trustee include a refusing or retiring trustee, if willing to act in the execution of the provisions of this section.

[(9) Where a trustee is incapable, by reason of mental disorder within the meaning of [the Mental Health Act 1983],[6] of exercising his functions as trustee and is also entitled in possession to some beneficial interest in the trust property, no appointment of a new trustee in his place shall be made by virtue of paragraph (b) of subsection (1) of this section unless leave to make the appointment has been given by the authority having jurisdiction under [Part VII of the Mental Health Act 1983][7].][8]

37. Supplemental provisions as to appointment of trustees

(1) On the appointment of a trustee for the whole or any part of trust property—

  (a) the number of trustees may, subject to the restrictions imposed by this Act on the number of trustees, be increased; and

  (b) a separate set of trustees, not exceeding four, may be appointed for any part of the trust property held on trusts distinct from those relating to any other part or parts of the trust property, notwithstanding that no new trustees or trustee are or is to be appointed for other parts of the trust property, and any existing trustee may be appointed or remain one of such separate set of trustees, or, if only one trustee was originally appointed, then, save as hereinafter provided, one separate trustee may be so appointed; and

  (c) it shall not be obligatory, save as hereinafter provided, to appoint more than one new trustee where only one trustee was originally appointed, or to fill up the original number of trustees where more than two trustees were originally appointed, but, except where only one trustee was originally appointed, and a sole trustee when appointed will be able to give valid receipts for all capital money, a trustee shall not be discharged from his trust unless there will be either a trust corporation or at least two [persons][9] to act as trustees to perform the trust; and

  (d) any assurance or thing requisite for vesting the trust property, or any part thereof, in a sole trustee, or jointly in the persons who are the trustees, shall be executed or done.

(2) Nothing in this Act shall authorise the appointment of a sole trustee, not being a trust corporation, where the trustee, when appointed, would not be able to give valid receipts for all capital money arising under the trust.

---

6 substituted by Mental Health Act 1983, s 148, Sched 4, para 4.
7 substituted by *ibid*.
8 substituted by Mental Health Act 1959, s 149(1), Sched 7, Pt I.
9 substituted by TLATA, s 25(1), Sched 3, para 3(12).

38. Evidence as to a vacancy in a trust

(1) A statement, contained in any instrument coming into operation after the commencement of this Act by which a new trustee is appointed for any purpose connected with land, to the effect that a trustee has remained out of the United Kingdom for more than twelve months or refuses or is unfit to act, or is incapable of acting, or that he is not entitled to a beneficial interest in the trust property in possession, shall, in favour of a purchaser of a legal estate, be conclusive evidence of the matter stated.

(2) In favour of such purchaser any appointment of a new trustee depending on that statement, and any vesting declaration, express or implied, consequent on the appointment, shall be valid.

39. Retirement of trustee without a new appointment

(1) Where a trustee is desirous of being discharged from the trust, and after his discharge there will be either a trust corporation or at least two [persons]¹⁰ to act as trustees to perform the trust, then, if such trustee as aforesaid by deed declares that he is desirous of being discharged from the trust, and if his co-trustees and such other person, if any, as is empowered to appoint trustees, by deed consent to the discharge of the trustee, and to the vesting in the co-trustees alone of the trust property, the trustee desirous of being discharged shall be deemed to have retired from the trust, and shall, by the deed, be discharged therefrom under this Act, without any new trustee being appointed in his place.

(2) Any assurance or thing requisite for vesting the trust property in the continuing trustees alone shall be executed or done.

40. Vesting of trust property in new or continuing trustees

(1) Where by a deed a new trustee is appointed to perform any trust, then—

(a) if the deed contains a declaration by the appointor to the effect that any estate or interest in any land subject to the trust, or in any chattel so subject, or right to recover or receive any debt or other thing in action so subject, shall vest in the persons who by virtue of the deed become or are the trustees for performing the trust, the deed shall operate, without any conveyance or assignment, to vest in those persons as joint tenants and for the purposes of the trust the estate interest or right to which the declaration relates; and
(b) if the deed is made after the commencement of this Act and does not contain such a declaration, the deed shall, subject to any express provision to the contrary therein contained, operate as if it had contained such a declaration by the appointor extending to all the estates interests and rights with respect to which a declaration could have been made.

---

10 substituted by *ibid*, para 3(13).

(2) Where by a deed a retiring trustee is discharged under [section 39 of this Act or section 19 of the Trusts of Land and Appointment of Trustees Act 1996][11] without a new trustee being appointed, then—

(a) if the deed contains such a declaration as aforesaid by the retiring and continuing trustees, and by the other person, if any, empowered to appoint trustees, the deed shall, without any conveyance or assignment, operate to vest in the continuing trustees alone, as joint tenants, and for the purposes of the trust, the estate, interest, or right to which the declaration relates; and

(b) if the deed is made after the commencement of this Act and does not contain such a declaration, the deed shall, subject to any express provision to the contrary therein contained, operate as if it had contained such a declaration by such persons as aforesaid extending to all the estates, interests and rights with respect to which a declaration could have been made.

(3) An express vesting declaration, whether made before or after the commencement of this Act, shall, notwithstanding that the estate, interest or right to be vested is not expressly referred to, and provided that the other statutory requirements were or are complied with, operate and be deemed always to have operated (but without prejudice to any express provision to the contrary contained in the deed of appointment or discharge) to vest in the persons respectively referred to in subsections (1) and (2) of this section, as the case may require, such estates, interests and rights as are capable of being and ought to be vested in those persons.

(4) This section does not extend—

(a) to land conveyed by way of mortgage for securing money subject to the trust, except land conveyed on trust for securing debentures or debenture stock;

(b) to land held under a lease which contains any covenant, condition or agreement against assignment or disposing of the land without licence or consent, unless, prior to the execution of the deed containing expressly or impliedly the vesting declaration, the requisite licence or consent has been obtained, or unless, by virtue of any statute or rule of law, the vesting declaration, express or implied, would not operate as a breach of covenant or give ruse to a forfeiture;

(c) to any share, stock, annuity or property which is only transferable in books kept by a company or other body, or in manner directed by or under an Act of Parliament.

In this subsection "lease" includes an underlease and an agreement for a lease or underlease.

---

11 substituted by *ibid*, para 3(14).

(5) For purposes of registration of the deed in any registry, the person or persons making the declaration expressly or impliedly, shall be deemed the conveying party or parties, and the conveyance shall be deemed to be made by him or them under a power conferred by this Act.

(6) This section applies to deeds of appointment or discharge executed on or after the first day of January, eighteen hundred and eighty-two.

Precedents

Precedent 1
Gift of successive interests in land by will after TLATA is in force

Precedent 2
Gift of land by will to co-owners after TLATA is in force

Precedent 3
Transfer to beneficial joint tenants or tenants in common

Precedent 4
Declaration of trust for tenants in common after TLATA has come into force

Precedent 5
ASSENT by personal representatives vesting property in themselves as trustees
where the testator has died after TLATA has come into force

Precedent 6
Deed of discharge under TLATA section 16

Precedent 7
Power of attorney under TLATA section 9

Precedent 1

Gift of successive interests in land by will after TLATA is in force[1]

0.1 I give my property[2] known as (*description*) ("the Property")[3] to my Trustees in trust[4] for (*life tenant*) ("the Life Tenant") for life and subject to the Life Tenant's interest for such of (*remaindermen*) as are living at the vesting date and if more than one in equal shares absolutely.

0.2 References in the previous and following subclause to the vesting date are to the date of termination of the Life Tenant's interest whether by death[5] or otherwise.

0.3 If [any of] (*remaindermen*) die[s] before me or before the vesting date leaving children who survive me and the vesting date and reach [18] such children shall take absolutely (if more than one in equal shares) the same share of the Property which his or her parent would have taken if he or she had survived me and the vesting date.

0.4 If none of (*remaindermen*) or their children live to be absolutely entitled to the Property or a share in it then .....(*gift over*).

[0.5 The powers given to my Trustees in relation to the Property by sections 6 and 7 of the Trusts of Land and Appointment of Trustees Act 1996[6] or otherwise are subject to the following exclusions:[7]

---

1 Before TLATA came into force, drafting successive interests involved either imposing an immediate binding trust for sale, or in default the successive interests would operate as a SLA strict settlement. Now, after TLATA is in force, it is not necessary to impose a trust for sale and the trusts will operate in any event as a trust of land - strict settlements can no longer be created. See text Chapters 2 and 4.

2 If the testator has adjoining land or neighbouring land it will probably be appropriate to make provision for the grant and reservation of easements. It will also be more necessary to define the extent of the land comprised in this gift.

3 It is assumed in this precedent that the life interest is limited to the land and buildings and does not extend to contents. Except for especially valuable contents, or certain contents which have a special family interest ("heirlooms"), the nature of most chattels means it is not usually practicable to preserve them indefinitely or consequently to subject them to a life interest, and they are more suitably dealt with by absolute gift.

4 There is no need to insert a trust for sale, either to avoid creating a SLA strict settlement or to trigger the statutory powers of trustees for sale of land. The trustees will have the powers of trustees of land to the extent they are not negatived or restricted by the will. See text 5.2 to 5.7.

5 This book is not intended to be a commentary on taxation consequences. But unless the life tenant is the testator's surviving spouse (when there is no charge on the death of the testator), life interests will of course result in a charge to Inheritance Tax on the deaths both of the testator and the life tenant, if the estate is above the IT threshold.

6 There is no need to enlarge the powers of the trustees in relation to the land in view of TLATA ss 6 and 7. See text 5.2. *But if the testator wishes the trustees to have a wide power of investment other than in land, then, until corresponding amendments are in force to the Trustee Investments Act regime it will be necessary to include here or elsewhere in the will a*

(a)   My Trustees have no power to purchase any leasehold land which at the time of completing the purchase has an unexpired residue of less than [forty] years.

(b)   My Trustees have no power to sell lease or otherwise dispose of the Property or any part of it or any interest in or right over it [or to exercise the power of advancement in Clause *** following] unless, whether or not capital money is payable, there are at least two persons or a trust corporation acting as my Trustees.]⁸

[0.6   During the life of the Life Tenant my Trustees have no power to carry out any of the following functions without [his/her] written consent:⁹
(a)   the grant or disposal of any freehold or leasehold estate or interest in the Property or any part of it;
(b)   the purchase of any land out of proceeds of sale of the Property.]

[0.7   (a)   I declare that it is my wish and intention¹⁰ that my Trustees delegate¹¹ to the Life Tenant such of their functions in relation to the Property as they consider appropriate to give the Life Tenant adequate powers of management [and that unless in their discretion they consider there are good reasons not to do so that they delegate powers equivalent to those which a tenant for life would have had in relation to settled land under the Settled Land Act 1925]¹².]

(b)   Nothing in this clause is to impose an absolute duty on my Trustees to delegate if in their discretion they decide not to do so nor is it to prevent my Trustees from revoking any delegation made by them if in their discretion they decide to do so.

---

widened power of investment. Here are two optional examples of provisions limiting the wide statutory powers under TLATA.

7   By TLATA s 8(1) the absolute owner and other powers granted by ss 6 and 7 do not apply in so far as provision to that effect is made by the disposition creating the trust. See text 5.6.

8   A provision in this form would be inconsistent with delegation of these powers to the life tenant.

9   Under TLATA s 8(2) the will may require consent to be obtained to the exercise of any power conferred by ss 6 or 7. In favour of a purchaser however, where the consent of more than two persons is required by the disposition creating the trust, the consent of any two is sufficient (TLATA s 10(1)). See text 5.6, and 7.2 to 7.3.

10   Under TLATA s 15(1) the court, in determining an application for an order under s 14, is to have regard to the matters there specified which include the intentions of the person who created the trust. See text 9.3.

11   The trustees have power under s 9(1) to delegate any of their functions to a beneficiary of full age entitled to an interest in possession. See text Chapter 6.

12   The words in square brackets are provided for those who wish the trust of land to replicate as far as possible the features of a SLA strict settlement. See Precedent 7. Unless the interests of the life tenant are to predominate however, some will consider that this goes too far and that decisions for the sale of the property for example should be made by persons (ie the trustees) able to balance less subjectively the possibly conflicting interests of the life tenant and the persons entitled in remainder. See text 2.1 para 7. This wide delegation would be inconsistent with clause 0.5(b).

[0.8 Section 11(1) of the Trusts of Land and Appointment of Trustees Act 1996 (which requires trustees to consult certain beneficiaries and give effect to their wishes) shall not apply.][13]

0.9 (a) I declare that the purposes of the trust include making the Property available for the occupation of the Life Tenant[14].

(b) For the guidance of my Trustees in imposing conditions of occupation on the Life Tenant under section 13(3) of the Trusts of Land and Appointment of Trustees Act 1996 I declare that it is my wish and intention[15] that the Life Tenant is to be responsible for paying outgoings (other than insurance)[16] in respect of the Property and, if the circumstances of the Life Tenant (including access to loans from my estate or elsewhere)[17] make that reasonably practicable, for keeping it in good repair and condition or for paying the cost of doing so.

(c) My Trustees shall pay the cost of insuring the Property out of[18] ....(*stipulate fund*)

OR

0.9 The purposes of the trust do not include making the Property available for the occupation of the Life Tenant[19].

---

13 For further discussion see text 7.5 to 7.7.
14 TLATA s 12(1) gives to a beneficiary beneficially entitled to an interest in possession the right to occupy the land at any time if at that time:
(a) the purposes of the trust include making the land available for his occupation .... or
(b) the land is held by the trustees so as to be so available.
See text Chapter 8.
15 Under TLATA s 13(4) the matters to which trustees are to have regard when imposing conditions of occupation under s 13(3) include
(a) the intentions if any of the person or persons who created the trust, and
(b) the purposes for which the land is held, and
(c) the circumstances of each of the beneficiaries who is (or apart from any previous exercise by the trustees of those powers would be) entitled to occupy the land under s 12.
16 It is suggested that it is preferable to leave the responsibility to insure with the trustees who are more directly concerned with preserving the interests of the persons entitled in remainder. (Although a delegatee also has the responsibility of a trustee - see s 9(7) and text 6.10.)
17 Unless the financial circumstances of the life tenant are known with certainty it would seem better to leave obligations of the life tenant flexible for the trustees to decide according to circumstances at the time. If however it is possible that the life tenant will not be able to pay for necessary repairs it will be prudent for the testator to provide a fund elsewhere in the will for this purpose. Where the estate funds repairs it will usually be more tax efficient to do so by way of loan to the life tenant, although unless the life tenant's residuary estate passes to the same destination as that of the testator, it will alter the distribution as between the respective residuary beneficiaries.
18 It will be necessary for the testator to provide a fund to pay the premiums and see notes 16 and 17 above.
19 See note 14 above.

0.10 (a)   If the Property or any part of it is sold, then in addition to their other powers my Trustees have power to pay or apply capital to or apply it for the benefit of the Life Tenant.

(b)   My Trustees may exercise such power from time to time and in such way as they think fit in their absolute discretion.

NOTE

Other clauses, unchanged from pre TLATA drafting, which may be appropriate are:

(1)   Making the gift free of any mortgage existing at the testator's death; and

(2)   If the property is income producing, negativing apportionment on the deaths of the testator and life tenant.

Precedent 2

Gift of land by will to co-owners after TLATA is in force[20]

I give my property known as (*description*)[21] to X and Y jointly but if either die before me then I give it to the survivor absolutely.

OR

(a)   I give my property known as (*description*)[22]("the Property") to X and Y in [equal] shares.

(b)   If either X or Y die before me leaving children who survive me and reach [18]such children shall take (if more than one in equal shares) absolutely the same share of the Property which his or her parent would have taken if he or she had survived me.

(c)   If either X or Y die before me leaving no children who survive me and reach [18] then I give the Property to the survivor of X and Y absolutely.

---

20 There is nothing in this precedent which would not be equally effective before TLATA comes into force.
    Before the commencement date however the gifts would create a statutory trust for sale and the co-owners would have the powers of trustees for sale under LPA s 28. They would have to prove and rely on their beneficial interests to have full powers of dealing with the property. After the commencement date the gift creates a trust of land, and unless the powers have been negatived or restricted, the co-owners statutorily have the powers of an absolute owner in relation to the property under TLATA s 6.
21 If the testator has adjoining land or neighbouring land it will probably be appropriate to make provision for the grant and reservation of easements.
22 If the testator has adjoining land or neighbouring land it will probably be appropriate to make provision for the grant and reservation of easements.

Precedent 3

Transfer to beneficial joint tenants or tenants in common[23]

HM LAND REGISTRY
LAND REGISTRATION ACTS 1925 to 1986

County and district or London Borough
Title Number
Property
DATE

1. In consideration of .... pounds (£........) receipt of which is acknowledged I (*registered proprietor*) of (*address*) transfer [with full title guarantee] to X of (*address*) and Y of (*address*) ("the Buyers") the land comprised in the above title ("the Property").

2. The Buyers declare that they hold the Property jointly[24] both legally and beneficially and that the survivor of them can give a valid receipt for capital money arising on a disposition of the land

OR

2. The Buyers declare that they hold the Property beneficially in equal shares[25] and that the survivor of them cannot give a valid receipt for capital money arising on a disposition of the land.
    OR
    The Buyers declare that they hold the Property beneficially in the following shares[26] .... and that the survivor of them cannot give a valid receipt for capital money arising on a disposition of the land.

---

23 The form follows closely Form 19(JP), only departing from it in order to define the beneficial interests of the buyers. See text 4.12.

As in the previous precedent, there is nothing here which would not be equally effective before TLATA comes into force.

Before the commencement date however the transfer creates a statutory trust for sale and the co-owners would have the powers of trustees for sale under LPA s 28. In theory they would have to rely on their beneficial interests to have full powers of dealing with the property, although in practice registration gives them full powers of dealing with the property subject to any restriction on the register. See text 5.1 para (d). After the commencement date the transfer creates a trust of land, and unless the powers have been negatived or restricted, the co-owners statutorily have the powers of an absolute owner in relation to the property under TLATA s 6.

24 "Jointly" signifies a joint tenancy and is reinforced by the implicit reference to survivorship. It is used in preference to the traditional phrase to avoid confusing lay clients by referring to "tenants".

25 The reference to shares signifies a tenancy in common. Some draftsmen may prefer the traditional phrase, but it is omitted here to to avoid confusing lay clients by referring to "tenants".

26 See note 24 above.

OR

The Buyers declare that they hold the Property upon the trusts declared in a Declaration of Trust dated .... made by the Buyers and apply to the Chief Land Registrar for entry of the following restrictions on the register:

(a) No disposition by a sole proprietor of the land (not being a trust corporation) under which capital money arises is to be registered except under an order of the Registrar or of the court.

(b) *(as appropriate eg requiring consents for the registration of disposals if that is a term of the underlying trusts)*

3. *(Certificate of value if appropriate)*

Precedent 4

Declaration of trust for tenants in common after TLATA has come into force[27]

The [Buyers] agree that they hold the Property [on trust for themselves][28] beneficially [as tenants in common][29] [in equal shares] *or* [as tenants in common][30] [in the following shares..........]

---

27 This clause would probably be effective before TLATA comes into force.
    Before the commencement date it was frequent practice to create an express trust for sale. Where this was not done, beneficial co-ownership of land would have created a statutory trust for sale. In defining the beneficial interests it was therefore usual to refer to the proceeds of sale and the income until sale. After the commencement date this is not necessary. The interests of the co-owners are in a trust of land and are directly in the land.
    It is nevertheless still possible to create an express trust for sale. It creates a duty to sell which may, in that case, still predominate in some circumstances over the now inviolable power to postpone sale. See text 4.6. For most straightforward co-ownership that will however not be appropriate.
    Before the commencement date the co-owners would have the powers of trustees for sale under LPA s 28. In unregistered land it was better practice to enlarge the powers of trustees although they could if necessary show their beneficial interests to prove they had full powers of dealing with the property. In the case of registered land, an enlargement could be included but in practice registration gave them full powers of dealing with the property subject to any restriction on the register. See text 5.1 para (d). After the commencement date there is a trust of land, and unless the powers have been negatived or restricted, the co-owners statutorily have the powers of an absolute owner in relation to the property under TLATA s 6.
28 These words in square brackets are optional. If they are included there will be an express trust of land. If they are excluded there will be a statutorily implied trust of land.
29 The reference to tenancy in common is not necessary as it is implicit from the reference to shares.
30 See note 29.

Precedent 5

ASSENT by personal representatives vesting property in themselves as trustees where the testator has died after TLATA has come into force

THIS ASSENT dated .... is made by X of (address) and Y of (address) ("the Trustees").

Whereas:

(1) Z late of .... ("the Testator") was at the date of [his/her] death recited below seised of the property described in the Schedule [Part 1] ("the Property") in fee simple in possession subject as referred to below but otherwise free from incumbrances.

(2) The Testator died on .... and [his/her] will was proved by the Trustees on .... in the .... [District] Probate Registry.

NOW THIS DEED WITNESSES as follows:

1. We the Trustees assent to the vesting in ourselves [the said X and Y][31] of the Property in fee simple [Together with the benefit of and Subject to the matters contained or referred to in [Part 1 of] the Schedule] [and Except and Reserved as set out in Part 2 of the Schedule][32]:
    [upon trust for sale][33]
    OR
    [upon the trust for sale contained in the will of the Testator]
    OR
    [upon trust][34]
    OR
    [upon the trusts contained in the will of the Testator]

2   We acknowledge the right of our successors in title to the Property to production and delivery of copies of the probate of the will of the Testator.

---

31 See text Appendix 2 - Requirements of form. It puts the matter beyond argument, if it is almost certainly over-cautious, to mention again by name the persons who are the objects of the assent, even where they are, as here, previously named and defined.

32 If the testator had adjoining land or neighbouring land it will probably be appropriate to grant and reserve of easements.

33 If the will imposed a trust for sale, the assent should be on trust for sale too. As to the difference between an assent creating an independent trust for sale, as in this clause, and incorporating the trust for sale in the will (as in the following alternative) see text Appendix 2 - Assent to trustees of a will.

34 If the will imposed no trust for sale, the assent should not refer to one. As to the difference between an assent creating an independent trust of land, as in this clause, and incorporating the trust of land in the will (as in the following alternative) see text Appendix 2 - Assent to trustees of a will.

3.   *(If the will requires the consent of any person to the exercise of a function by the Trustees, or if it negatives or restricts any of the TLATA ss 6 and 7 absolute owner powers, then unless the assent is expressly on the trusts of the will, repeat or refer to those provisions here)*

IN WITNESS etc

THE SCHEDULE
[Part 1]
(Description of the Property and of any matters of which it has the benefit or is subject)

[Part 2
Details of any new rights granted with or excepted and reserved from the Property]

SIGNED by X as a deed in the presence of:

SIGNED by Y as a deed in the presence of:

NOTE
A memorandum of the assent should be endorsed on the probate. See Appendix 2.

Precedent 6

Deed of discharge under TLATA section 16[35]

THIS DEED OF DISCHARGE dated   is made by X of (*address*) and Y of (*address*) ("the Trustees")

Whereas:

(1)   By an [Assent] dated .... and made between .... the land shortly described in the Schedule ("the Property") was vested in [the Trustees] upon the trusts there referred to ("the Trusts").

[(2)   Immediately before the Conveyance recited below the Property was vested in the Trustees on the Trusts.]

(3)   By a Conveyance dated .... and made between the Trustees (1) and Z ("the Beneficiary") (2) the Trustees conveyed the Property to the Beneficiary as the person believed by them to be the beneficiary absolutely entitled to the Property under the Trusts and of full age and capacity[36].

NOW THIS DEED WITNESSES as follows:

The Trustees in pursuance of section 16 of the Trusts of Land and Appointment of Trustees Act 1996 declare they are discharged from the Trusts in relation to the Property.

IN WITNESS etc

THE SCHEDULE
(*Short description of the Property*)

Signed by X as a deed in the presence of:

Signed by Y as a deed in the presence of:

---

35 Under TLATA s 16(4), where trustees convey land which (immediately before it is conveyed) is subject to the trust to persons believed by them to be beneficiaries absolutely entitled to the land under the trust and of full age and capacity they are bound to execute a deed declaring they are discharged from the trust in relation to that land. See text 10.4.

36 The purpose of the deed of discharge is to give protection to subsequent purchasers under TLATA s 16(5). *There is nothing to be gained by reciting the circumstances considered to cause the beneficiary to be absolutely entitled, and there is something to be lost - it might give the purchaser notice of some factor which would deprive him of the protection of s 16(5). (For transactions after the commencement of TLATA, the same goes for recitals in the Conveyance to the beneficiary too.)* But it is of course good practice to keep a note of the circumstances in the records of the trust which will be retained by the trustees and not produced to a purchaser.

Precedent 7

Power of attorney under the TLATA 1996 section 9

THIS POWER OF ATTORNEY dated   is made between X of [*address*] and Y of [*address*] ("the Trustees") and Z of [*address*] ("the Attorney[s]").

SUPPLEMENTAL to the [settlement ("the Settlement")] [trust of land ("the Trust")] [and to the other documents and events] specified in the Schedule.

WHEREAS

(1)   The Trustees are the present trustees of the [Settlement] [Trust].

(2)   The property subject to the [Settlement] [Trust] includes [*describe the land*] ("the Land").

(3)   The Trustees wish to delegate to the Attorney[s] certain of their functions as trustees under the [Settlement] [Trust] which relate to the Land.

NOW THIS DEED WITNESSES as follows:

(1)   In this Deed the expression "the Trustees" has the same meaning as in the [Settlement] [Trust].

(2)   The Trustees in exercise of the power conferred on them by section 9 of the Trusts of Land and Appointment of Trustees Act 1996 and of every and any other power enabling them hereby delegate to the Attorney[s] [jointly [and severally]] [for the period of [*state period*] from the date of this Deed] [for an indefinite period until revoked by the Trustees] (but subject to the provisions of the said section 9)

Either

the following functions as trustees which relate to the Land:

[*set out functions*]

or

all such of their functions as trustees which relate to the Land as may be necessary to put the Attorney[s] in the position of or in a position as near as may be to that occupied by the tenant for life of a settlement within the meaning of the Settled Land Act 1925 immediately before the commencement of the Trusts of Land and Appointment of Trustees Act 1996 [on the assumption that the terms of such settlement made no modification to the statutory position] [but modified as follows: [*set out modifications*]].

or

all of their functions as trustees which relate to the Land [except giving a receipt for capital monies].

(3) The Trustees in exercise of the powers and to the extent of the delegation referred to in clause (2) above hereby appoint the Attorney[s] in the name of the Trustees and on their behalf or otherwise to execute and do all deeds, documents, acts and things which may be required to be executed or done in the execution or exercise of the above functions as fully and effectively as the Trustees would have exercised or done the same.

THE SCHEDULE

Date	Document of Event	Parties

IN WITNESS, etc.

SIGNED AS A DEED OF DELIVERED BY X
IN THE PRESENCE OF:

SIGNED AS A DEED AND DELIVERED BY Y
IN THE PRESENCE OF:

SIGNED AS A DEED AND DELIVERED BY Z
IN THE PRESENCE OF:

Index

[References are to the commentary, not to the text of the Act.]

Absolute owner,
disposition giving widened powers of,
51, 52
restrictive interpretation of, 52
trustees of land having statutory powers
of, 54-56, 70, 139, 141, 146
Annuitant,
beneficiary entitled to interest in
possession, not, 11-12, 84
Appointment of trustees,
awkward cases, in, 127
beneficiaries' right to direct, 126-129,
131-132
consequences of provisions, 136
construction of provisions, 124-126
corporate trustee, dissolution of, 127
direction to trustee, 126, 127, 132
discharge of existing trustees by, 128-129,
134-135
duty to, 130
existing law, amendment to, 134, 135
existing powers and mechanisms,
160-162
full age and capacity, beneficiaries of, 125
last trustee not having personal
representative, where, 127
mentally incapacitated trustee, in place
of, 131
new, 125
new provisions, 123, 124
no person nominated for, 124-126
opted-out trusts, 132-134
oral trust, of, 124
pre-Act trusts, 133-134
summary of provisions, 144-145
"two individuals" trap, 134-135
Trustee Act 1925 provisions, 168-174
Assents,
beneficiary under, 150
contents of, 151
equitable interests, do not protect a
purchaser, 150, 158
form, requirements of, 150
memorandum of, 153
personal representative, by in their own
favour, 155

Assents—*cont.*
personalty, 150, 158
precedent for, 221
purchaser, protection of, 153, 154
registered land, for, 151
subject of, 150
trustees not of will, to, 152
trustees of will, to, 151
Attorney. *See* **Power of Attorney**

Beneficiaries,
absolutely entitled, 12, 123-126
beneficially entitled, 11
co-operation by, 60
consultation with,
changes of law, 84, 85
consequences of provisions, 88
conveyance, before, 85
opting-in existing trusts, 86-88
opting out, 85, 86
requirement of, 142
statutory provisions, 83, 84
transitional effect, 85, 86
conveyance to, by way of appropriation,
58-60
conveyance to, by trustees,
brought trusts on title, 111, 155
now requires deed of discharge,
111-113, 155
protection for purchaser by deed of
discharge, 112
definition, 9-13, 89-90
duty to consult, 57
duty to have regard to interests of, 56,
57, 63
entitlement to land, 59, 60
interest in possession, entitled to, 11
interest in property subject to trust,
having, 10
meaning, 9, 89-90, 101
occupation, rights of,
availability of land, 91
beneficiary, meaning, 89-90
beneficiary as trustee for another, 93
conditions for, 90-91
consequences of provisions, 96

Beneficiaries—*cont.*
  occupation, rights of—*cont.*
    delegation of powers, interaction,
      73-74, 95
    entitlement, 92-93
    exclusion from,
      conditions and compensation,
        94-95
      discretionary powers, 92
      limitations, 93, 94
      simultaneous claims, 91-93
      unanimity by trustees, 92
    other rights, exercise with, 95
    purposes of trust, 90-92
    statutory provision, 89
    summary of, 142
  partition of land among, 58, 61-62
  pension trusts, of, 12-13, 90, 92
  powers of attorney. *See* **Power of
    Attorney**
  powers similar to tenant for life, having,
    69, 70
  rights, additions to, 3
  rights to direct appointment or retirement
    of trustees. *See* **Appointment of
    trustees** and **Retirement of trustees**
  trustees, appointment and removal of,
    powers in relation to. *See*
    Appointment of trustees and
    Retirement of trustees
  trustees having regard to rights of, 56,
    57, 103-104, 106

Capital money,
  receipts, no power under s 9 to delegate
    right to receive and give, 74, 75
  trustees named, payment to restriction
    requiring, 53
  trustees, payment to at least two, 53,
    104, 115, 146, 157, 158
Charitable trust,
  conveyance of land held on, 29, 30
  notion of, 14
  purchasers, protection for, 109
  summary of provisions, 147
  trust of land, as, 27, 141
  trustees, powers of, 65, 66
Co-owners, *and see* **Trust of land,
    concurrent interests**
  joint tenants, legal estate beneficially
    limited to or held in trust for, 47
  LPA provisions, 165-167
  survivor, sale by, 157, 158
  tenants in common, beneficiaries as, 47

Consents,
  consequences of provisions, 88
  court, applications to, 83, 97-98
  exercise of trustees' powers, requirement
    of, 64
  functions relating to land, to, 82
  limit on number needed, 81-82
  limitations on powers, concerns of
    purchaser, 148
  mentally disordered persons, on behalf
    of, 83
  minors, of, 82, 83
  new provisions, 81, 82
  partition, to, 62
  purchasers, protecting, 82
  trust for sale regime, under, 81
Consultation,
  changes from old law, 84-85
  duty of trustees, 83-84
  existing trusts, and, 86-88
  transitional effect, 85-86
Conversion, doctrine of,
  abolition, 3, 32-37, 140
    conflict of laws, 37
    consequential amendments and
      repeals, 34
    construction, effect on, 35
    documents, drafting and construing,
      35, 36
    "land" in statutory definitions, 34
    Law Commission recommendations,
      33
    reasons for, 32, 33
    retroaction, wills before
      commencement of Act, 33, 34
    statutes, construing, 35
    statutory provision, 33
    tax legislation, consequential
      adjustments to, 36, 37
  consequences of provisions, 37
  effect of, 32
  reality, lack of, 33
Court,
  application to, 97
  definition, 13
  powers of, 97-102
    case law, treatment of, 99
    consequences of provisions, 102
    extension of, 142, 143
    factors taken into account, 98-99, 139
    old scheme, under, 97
    personal representative and, 101
    purposes of trust, giving effect to, 97
    scope of provisions, 97-98

Court—*cont.*
  powers of—*cont.*
    transitional provision, 98
    trust for sale, compared to, 97-98
    trust of proceeds of sale, in relation to,
      101
    trustee in bankruptcy, application by, 100

Deed of discharge. *See* **Trust of land, deed
    of discharge**
Delegation by trustees of land. *See* **Trustee
    of land, delegation by**
Disposition,
  trust created by, 15
Drafting implication,
  ss 4-5, of, 48-50
  ss 6-8, of, 66-67
  Trusts of Land and Appointment of
    Trustees Act generally, of, 140

Ecclesiastical trust,
  conveyance of land held on, 29, 30
  notion of, 14
  purchasers, protection for, 109
  summary of provisions, 147
  trust of land, as, 27, 141
Enduring power, attorney under, 131
Enduring power, protection of purchaser,
    118-119
Entailed interests,
  attempt to create, effect of, 30, 138
Equitable interests,
  proceeds of sale, exclusion of interests in,
    34

Family charge,
  instruments imposing, operation of, 29
Function,
  land, relating to, 14, 15
  notion of, 14

Inheritance tax,
  doctrine of conversion, effect of
    abolition, 36, 37
Intentions of settlor. *See* **Settlor, intentions of**

Land,
  definition, amended, in statutes, 34, 36
  partition,
    consent to, 62
    equality money, 62
    power to, 58, 61, 62
  statutory definitions, in, 34, 36
  trustees' power to purchase, 57, 58

Land—*cont.*
  trusts of. *See* **Trust of land**
  undivided shares in, 34
Law Commission,
  draft Bill, 5
  Reports, 5
Lien, trustee's, 129
Life tenant. *See* **Tenant for life**

Mentally disordered persons,
  consents on behalf of, 83
Minors,
  consents of, 82, 83
  dispositions to, 28, 29
Mortgagee,
  protection when dealing with trustees, 106

Occupation,
  beneficiaries' rights of, 89-95, *and see*
      Beneficiaries, occupation, rights of
Overreaching,
  concept of, 32-33
  protection for purchasers, 103, 104-105
  settlor, influence of on delegation, 72
  Trustee Act 1925 s 25, under, 70

Parliamentary materials,
  use in interpretation of statutes, 17-19
Partition. *See* **Trustee of land, power to
    partition**
Pension trusts,
  beneficiaries of, 12, 13
Personal representative,
  assent in own favour by, 155
  last trustee not having, 127
  no duty to consult beneficiaries, 85
  powers of court do not apply, 101
Power of attorney,
  alternative mechanisms, 70
  attorney. *See* **section 9 attorney**
  delegatee. *See* **section 9 attorney**
  delegation by means of, 76
  enduring, under Enduring Powers of
    Attorney Act, 70, 118, 119, 131
  invalidity or revocation of, 120, 121
  limitations on use by trustees, 117
  outside 1996 Act, 117-119
  powers capable of delegation, 73
  revocation,
    appointment of new trustee, by, 76, 77
    attorney ceasing to be eligible, on, 77
    joint and separate attorney, effect on,
      71
    voluntary, 76

Power of attorney—*cont.*
    section 9 attorney,
        appointment of, 72, 73
        beneficial entitlement to interest, 71
        beneficiary as, 71
        capacity, 71
        capital money, not authorised to
            receive, 74-75
        ceasing to be eligible, 77
        default, liability of trustee for, 78, 79
        duties and liabilities of, 78
        full age, of, 71
        later purchasers and persons dealing
            with, protection for, 79, 80, 119-
            121
        meaning, 71
        possession, in, 72
        purchasers, protection of, 79, 80,
            119-121
        subdelegation, limitation of, 74
Powers of court. *See* **Court, powers of**
Powers of trustees. *See* **Trustee of land,**
        powers of
Power to postpone sale,
    inviolability of, 40-41
Proceeds of sale,
    trust of, powers of court, 101
Public trust,
    conveyance of land held on, 29, 30
    notion of, 14
    purchasers, protection for, 109
    summary of provisions, 147
    trust of land, as, 27, 141
Purchaser,
    breach of trust, protection from, 82
    definition, 13, 82, 120
    good faith of, 13, 115, 126
    limitations brought to notice of, 108, 116
    limitations on powers of consents,
        concerns with, 148
    meaning, 13, 82, 120
    protection for,
        actual notice, reference to, 108, 109
        attorney, purchase from. *See* **Power of**
            attorney
        charitable, ecclesiastical or public
            trusts, land held on, 109
        consequences of provisions, 122
        consent for partition, following failure
            to obtain, 106
        consult beneficiaries, following failure
            to, 106
        conveyance to beneficiaries, following
            deed of discharge, 111-114

Purchaser—*cont.*
    protection for—*cont.*
        deed of discharge on termination of
            trust, 111-114
        delegatee, purchase from. *See* **Power**
            of attorney
        de*vise*e, from, 154
        enlargement of trustees' powers, on,
            108
        equitable interests and powers,
            conveyances overreaching, 105
        exercise of delegated powers, relying
            on, 117-121
        existing provisions, 103-105
        invalidity and need to overreach, 110
        invalidity caused by contraventions of
            provisions, as to, 107
        limitations, under TLATA s 8, against,
            107, 108
        memorandum following assent, need
            for, 153
        mortgagees dealing with trustees, 106
        new provisions, 104
        no previous assent or conveyance,
            statement of, 153, 154
        notice of limitations, removes
            protection against, 107-109
        registered land, 114, 115
        restrictions, registration of, 115-117
        rights and duties not required to be
            checked, 106
        rights of beneficiaries, following
            failure to have regard to, 106
        trustees for sale, purchase from, 104
        trustees of land, purchase from,
            103-110
        unregistered land, purchase of,
            106-110
Purposes of holding the land,
    relevance of, 98-99, 102

Receiver of incapable trustee, 131
Resettlement,
    mechanism for, 24, 138
    new settlement, whether strict settlement,
        23, 24
    reversionary entail, barring, 23, 24
    strict settlements, of, 23-24, 143, 144
    trust of land, conversion of strict
        settlement to, 24
Retirement of trustees,
    beneficiaries' rights to direct, 126-129,
        131-132
    consequences of provisions, 136

Retirement of trustees—*cont.*
  construction of provisions, 124-126
  consult beneficiaries, following failure to,
    106
  conveyance to beneficiaries, following
    deed of discharge, 111-114
  direction to trustee, 126, 127, 132
  discharge, and 128-129, 134-135
  duty of, 128, 128
  existing law, amendment to, 134, 135
  indemnity, 129
  lien, 129
  mentally incapable trustee, 131-132
  new provisions, 123, 124
  opted-out trusts, 132-134
  pre-Act trusts, 133-134
  pre-conditions, 128
  protection of rights, reasonable
    arrangements for, 129
  summary of provisions, 144, 145
  "two individuals" trap, 134-135
  vesting of property on, 129
Retroaction,
  conversion, abolition of doctrine of, 3,
    140
  deed of discharge, 113-114
  generally, 17
  powers to postpone sale, 41
Reverter of sites,
  sale of land, 45, 46

Settlements,
  Settled Land Act. *See* **Strict settlements**
  strict. *See* **Strict settlements**
Settlor,
  intentions of, relevance of, 98-99, 102
  more than one, 16
Stamp duty,
  doctrine of conversion, effect of
    abolition, 36, 37
Statutes,
  consequential amendments and repeals, 4
  interpretation, use of Parliamentary
    materials, 17-19
Strict settlements,
  abolition, case for, 20-22
  acquisition of property after settlement
    ceasing to be, 28
  alteration of, as resettlement, 23
  cessation where no land or heirlooms
    subject to, 25-27
  cessation where no relevant property
    subject, 24-27
  conflict of interests, 21
  consequences of provisions in s 2, 31

Strict settlements—*cont.*
  death of life tenant, ending on, 24
  deed of discharge. 25
  default, creation by, 21
  definition, 20
  delegation of powers to replicate, 69-70
  enhanced, 21
  entails under. *See* **Entailed interests**
  exchange of settled land, 26, 27
  existing, continuation of, 22
  extinction of, 20
  land and heirlooms, sale of all, 25-27,
    144
  meaning, 20
  mimicking by delegating trustees' powers,
    69, 70, 80, 143
  new, prohibition on, 138
  part of settled land exchanged for land,
    where, 26
  part of settled land sold, effect of, 25, 26
  phasing out, 2, 20, 22-30, 138
  prohibited. *See* **phasing out** *above*
  replication. *See* **mimicking** *above*
  resettlement of, 143, 144
  resettlement, effect of, 23, 24
  sale of settled land, 25
  trustees, capital money paid to, 53
  trusts of land in place of, 22
  whole of settled land exchanged for land,
    where, 27
  whole of settled land sold, 25
Successive interests. *See* **Trust of land,**
    successive interests

Tenant for life,
  conveyance to trustees of settlement by,
    24
  death of, 24
  delegation of powers to, 3, 69-80, 139,
    143
  power to deal with land under strict
    settlement, 22
Transfers to co-owners
  precedent for, 218
Trust,
  bare, 8, 9
  created by reference, 87-88
  disposition, created by, 15, 133
  land of, *See* **Trust of land**
  more than one person, created by, 16, 88,
    134
  sale for. *See* **Trust for sale**
Trust for sale,
  absence, effect of, 46, 137
  consents. *See* **Consents**

Trust for sale—*cont.*
    continued existence of express trusts for
        sale, 40
    dispositions on, LPA provisions as
        amended, 163-165
    drafting, 48-50
    express,
        continuing use of, 40, 138
        duty to sell, prima facie relevance of,
            43
        inappropriate, 138
        trust of land, included in, 7, 8
        unnecessary, 137, 138
    outline checklist, 159
    power to postpone sale,
        drafting, 50
        duty to sell, balance between, 42-44
        immunity, 44
        inviolability of, 40, 41
        retroaction, 41
    replacement as central concept, 2, 40
    statutory, abolition, 2, 40, 44-46
    trust of land, as, 9
    trust of land without duty to sell,
        substitution for statutory trusts,
            44, 45
    trustee of as trustee of land, 132
    trustees, capital money paid to, 53
Trust of land,
    additional, 40
    charitable, ecclesiastical and public trusts
        as, 27, 141
    concurrent interests,
        application of regime to, 46, 47
        beneficiaries, conveyance to in
            undivided shares, 47
        joint tenants, legal estate beneficially
            limited to or held in trust for, 47
        sale by survivor of co-owners, 157,
            158
        tenants in common. *See* **undivided
            shares** *below*
        trustees, conveyance of land on trust
            for beneficiaries to, 47
        undivided shares, conveyance to
            beneficiaries in, 47
    consents. *See* **Consents**
    court, powers of. *See* **Court**
    creation,
        by reference, 87-88
        manner of, 8
        time of, 8
    deed of discharge,
        conveyance of unregistered land to
            beneficiary, necessary on, 111, 144

Trust of land—*cont.*
    deed of discharge—*cont.*
        duty to execute, 111, 113
        equitable interests on title, and, 111,
            112
        new procedure for, 111
        precedent for, 223
        purchaser, protecting, 111, 144
        requirement of, 111, 147
        retroaction, 113, 114
        statutory provisions, 112, 113
    definition, 7, 8, 104, 105
    dispositions on, LPA provisions, 163-165
    drafting,
        areas for consideration, 139, 140
        key provisions and consequences on,
            137-140
        power to postpone sale, 50
        trust for sale, 48-50
    enlarged definition, relevance of, 39
    express and statutorily implied,
        characteristics shared by, 38
        concurrent interests, application to,
            46, 47
        duty to sell and power to postpone,
            balance between, 42-44
        identical, whether, 42
        successive interests, application to, 47
    mixed, 9
    outline checklist, 159
    power to postpone sale,
        drafting, 50
        duty to sell, balance between, 42-44
        immunity, 44
        inviolability of, 40, 41
        retroaction, 41
    resettlement converted to, 24
    restrictions on register, 115-117
    retroaction, 141
    sale and retention, balance between, 141
    sites, reverter of, 45
    statutory powers or duties, negativing or
        restricting, 44
    statutory trust for sale, substitution for,
        44, 45
    statutory,
        express, reclassification as, 39
        trusts for sale, abolition, 40
    strict settlement regime, features of, 22
    successive interests, application of regime
        to, 47
    trust for sale as, 9
    trust for sale, replacing, 2
    trustee of as trustee for sale, 132

Trust of land—*cont.*
 type of trust being, 8, 9
Trustee Act 1925, Part III, as amended,
  168-174
Trustee in bankruptcy,
 court, application to, 100
Trustee of land,
 appointment. *See* **Appointment of
  trustees**
 beneficiaries,
  consultation with. *See* **Beneficiaries,
   consultation with**
  conveying to. *See* **Beneficiaries,
   conveying to**
  duty to consult, 56, 57
  having regard to rights of, 56, 57, 63
 capital money paid to. *See* **Capital money**
 corporate, dissolution of, 127
 delegation by,
  authorisation of, 70
  beneficiaries, powers given to, 69, 70
  consequences of provisions, 80
  conveyancing implications, 75
  default of attorney, liability for, 78, 79
  disposals under, 147
  functions, of, 70
  later purchasers and persons dealing
   with attorney, protection for, 79,
   80, 106-108, 117-121
  means of, 76
  mimicking strict settlement, 69-70, 80,
   139, 143
  powers of attorney. *See* **Power of
   attorney**
  powers subject to, 73-75
  purchaser, protection of, 79, 80,
   106-108, 117-121
  receipts for capital money, inability of
   attorney to receive and give, 74, 75
  replicating strict settlement. *See*
   mimicking strict settlement *above*
  rights to occupy, and, 73
  settlor, influence of, 72, 73
  statutory provision, 76
  subdelegation, limitation of, 74
  tenant for life, to, 143
  transitional provisions, 80
 direction to, by beneficiaries, 126-127
 discharge, Trustee Act 1925 provisions,
  168-174
 incapable, receiver of, 131
 incapable, replacement of, 131-132
 lien, 129
 limitations, bringing to notice of
  purchaser, 108

Trustee of land—*cont.*
 powers of,
  absolute owner, of, 51, 52, 54-56, 70,
   139
  beneficiaries, rights of, having regard
   to, 56, 57, 63
  charitable trusts, 65, 66
  compulsory, not, 62
  consent before exercise of,
   requirement of, 64
  consent of two enough in favour of a
   purchase, 81-83
  consequences of provisions, 68
  consult beneficiaries, duty to,
   relationship with, 57
  delegation to life tenant. *See* **Trustee
   of land, delegation by**
  disposition, exclusion and restriction
   by, 62-64
  drafting implications, 66
  enlargement of, 52
  excluding, 62-64
  function as trustees, for purposes of
   exercising, 55
  investigating, 146
  investment, of, 56
  land,
   purchase of, 57, 58
   relating to, 56
  LPA s 28, limitations of, 51-52
  life tenant, delegation to, 3
  limitations, 51-54
  negativing or restricting, 62-64, 139
  new provision, 54
  old regime, under, 51-54
  other enactments, references to, 65, 66
  partition, to, 58, 61, 62
  registered land, wide powers in
   practice, 53-54
  restricting, 62-64
  retroaction, 67
  rights of beneficiaries, having regard
   to, 56, 57, 63
  statutory, enlarging or restricting, 66
  tenant for life, delegation to, 3
  total exclusion of, 63, 64
 retirement. *See* **Retirement of trustees**
 rights and duties, additions to, 3
 sale, former duty of, 103
 vesting in, delaying, 112
Trusts of Land and Appointment of Trustees
  Act 1996,
 commencement, 5
 consequences of provisions,
  consolidation of, 137-140

Trusts of Land and Appointment of Trustees
        Act 1996—*cont.*
    extent of, 5
    general content of, 2-4
    general provisions, 6
    general scheme of, 4
    interpretation, 7
    interrelation of parts of, 3
    introduction to, 1
    key provisions in, 137-148
    modification, power of, 6
    objectives, 2-4
    Parliamentary discussion of, 18, 19

Trusts of Land and Appointment of Trustees
        Act 1996—*cont.*
    retroactive effect, 17
    text of, 163-199

Will,
    gift creating successive interests,
            precedent for, 213
    gift of concurrent interests in land,
            precedent for, 217
    right of residence, giving, comparison of
            procedures, 149